ULTRA-DISTANCE CYCLING

ULTRA-DISTANCE CYCLING

CYCLING

AN EXPERT GUIDE TO
ENDURANCE CYCLING

Simon Jobson and **Dominic Irvine**

BLOOMSBURY

LONDON · OXFORD · NEW YORK · NEW DELHI · SYDNEY

Bloomsbury Sport
An imprint of Bloomsbury Publishing Plc

50 Bedford Square,   1385 Broadway
London   New York
WC1B 3DP   NY 10018
UK   USA

www.bloomsbury.com

BLOOMSBURY and the Diana logo are trademarks of Bloomsbury Publishing Plc

First published in 2017
© Simon Jobson and Dominic Irvine
Photos/Illustrations © details on page 272

Simon Jobson and Dominic Irvine have asserted their right under the Copyright,
Designs and Patents Act, 1988, to be identified as the Authors of this work.

British Library Cataloguing-in-Publication Data
A catalogue record for this book is available from the British Library.

ISBN: Paperback: 9781472919878
ePub: 9781472919892
ePDF: 9781472919885

2 4 6 8 10 9 7 5 3 1

Typeset in Minion and Din by Louise Millar
Printed and bound in China by Toppan Leefung Printing

Bloomsbury Publishing Plc makes every effort to ensure that the papers used in the manufacture
of our books are natural, recyclable products made from wood grown in well-managed forests.
Our manufacturing processes conform to the environmental regulations of the country of origin.

To find out more about our authors and books visit www.bloomsbury.com.
Here you will find extracts, author interviews, details of forthcoming
events and the option to sign up for our newsletters.

CONTENTS

9   FOREWORD

11   PREFACE

15   INTRODUCTION

33   CHAPTER 1: **RIDING TECHNIQUE**

57   CHAPTER 2: **IN BALANCE: LIFE, WORK AND CYCLING**

69   CHAPTER 3: **DIET AND HYDRATION**

101 CHAPTER 4: **EQUIPMENT**

133 CHAPTER 5: **FITNESS**

169 CHAPTER 6: **APPROACH: DEVELOPING AN ULTRA-DISTANCE MINDSET**

201 CHAPTER 7: **SPONSORSHIP AND PR**

217 CHAPTER 8: **TEAMWORK**

251 CHAPTER 9: **PUTTING IT ALL TOGETHER**

262 GLOSSARY

265 AUTHOR BIOGRAPHIES

266 ACKNOWLEDGEMENTS

267 INDEX

272 PHOTO ACKNOWLEDGEMENTS

To Helene and Chlöe, my rock and my inspiration – Dominic
For Lizzie, my best friend and future wife – Simon

FOREWORD

At Team Dimension Data for Qhubeka our mission goes beyond winning bike races to creating a legacy that has inexorably changed people's lives for the good. Qhubeka is an Nguni word that means 'to carry on', 'to progress', 'to move forward'. The charity rewards work done by people in Africa with the gift of a bike. As a child, you will remember the freedom made possible by being able to ride a bike. We are using the power of an elite cycle racing team to change the world as well as to win races. Simon Jobson and Dominic Irvine reflect this altruistic approach in writing this book. Having invested five years of time and energy attempting and succeeding in breaking a 49-year-old ultra-distance cycling record that had defeated several Olympians, they have then taken the time to distil the lessons learnt and share them with the cycling community in order for others to succeed at their own ultra-distance goal.

To break a cycling record at the age of 47 meant Dominic Irvine had to challenge the accepted wisdom of the day in order to achieve what many thought impossible. As his coach, Simon Jobson left no stone unturned in his quest to help Dominic and his tandem riding partner Charlie Mitchell reach the level of performance needed to set a new cycling record. Helping ordinary people achieve extraordinary results is a core philosophy of my team's approach to cycling. It has led to several historical achievements including Daniel Teklehaimanot becoming the first Eritrean, and indeed African, to wear the polka-dot jersey on the Tour de France. This is a stepping stone in our ambition to put an African rider on the podium in the Tour de France.

For me, success in cycling is the culmination of having the right process, the right tools and the right people. It requires athletes and indeed all members of the team to think in terms of a whole system. The chapter headings in this book provide a neat summary of all the areas involved. It's not enough to be fit enough. You also need to create a compelling vision, generate a sense of team, develop a high-performance culture with those involved and know how to translate this into value for others to secure their support and investment. It doesn't matter whether you are about to compete in your first ultra-distance race or organise a team for a world tour, the principles that underpin both are the same. This book ably covers the key points.

But perhaps the greatest skill is the ability to translate complexity into usable, practical information. In this, Simon Jobson and Dominic Irvine have excelled themselves. They have, to paraphrase Einstein (as the authors do), made things as simple as possible but no simpler. So whether you are embarking upon your first century ride or first 1,000km ride, this book is essential reading. It's something I shall be encouraging the members of our team to read.

Douglas Ryder
Team Principal, Dimension Data for Qhubeka

PREFACE

Having failed twice, the authors' thirst for knowledge in order to break the United Kingdom 'End-to-End' tandem record was insatiable. The record had stood for 49 years at 50 hours, 14 minutes and 25 seconds to cover the 1,365km from Land's End to John o'Groats. Prior to their third attempt, happy circumstance brought together coach Simon Jobson and athletes Dominic Irvine and Charlie Mitchell. Combining knowledge and experience, and tapping into a network of other experts, Dominic and Charlie, along with their support team, made one final attempt on the record. Many hours had been spent training and many more poring over research papers, articles and blogs in order to establish the things two ordinary amateur athletes and their support team needed to do to beat an extraordinary record. This record had withstood assaults by Olympians and others.

On 7 May, 2015, at 3.41 a.m., Dominic and Charlie rolled over the finishing line in a time of 45 hours, 11 minutes to set a new record, improving the existing one by over five hours. The knowledge and experience gained from breaking the record, added to the many lessons learned from participating in other ultra-distance events, were substantial, taking much time and effort. Unfortunately, no single guide was available that made sense of what it takes to ride a long way, fast.

When consulted about how to find the treasure of a general who had been defeated, the Oracle of Delphi's advice was 'leave no stone unturned'. The mountain of knowledge is a rocky place, and while many stones to unearth insights to help the reader ride ultra-distance have been excavated, there are a great many others left to explore.

Ultra-distance is a team game and this book is no exception. Those experts who helped Dominic and Charlie break the record have also assisted with content. Rather than rewrite their wisdom, sections written in their own words have been included. The authors have also reached out to other coaches and athletes for their insights. This book seeks to assimilate the many lessons learned into a single volume to save the reader the pain of having to trawl through vast amounts of content to find the nuggets of knowledge that really will make a difference. As a result, it is the hope that this book will help you to ride a long way, fast!

Record breakers:
Dominic Irvine and
Charlie Mitchell

INTRODUCTION

Cycling over the sun-drenched hills of the Dolomites, anticipating the night ride ahead, is the quintessential experience of ultra-distance cycling. It's so much more than just riding a bike.

WHAT IS ULTRA-DISTANCE CYCLING?

Ultra-distance cycling competitions or events are generally defined as endurance performances of at least six hours in duration and 160km. They may be as long as several thousand kilometres and may last many days in duration. Riders can be self-supported, needing to find food and fluid and (if necessary) shelter along the way. Others need a support team, whose job it is to carry supplies and spare equipment to keep the rider going throughout the event. *Non-stop* in relation to ultra-distance does not mean riding the bike without stopping: there are times you will need to change kit, repair the bike, go to the toilet or get some food. If you do need to sleep it will be for minutes rather than hours – although in many races you will probably not sleep at all. Time off the bike is as short as possible in order to maintain momentum.

Your choice of event will depend on your preferred type of ride. Do you like lots of hills or do you prefer the flat? For example, the Race Across America (RAAM) climbs an average of 11m per km. In contrast, Ultracycling Dolomitica climbs 26.6m for every km. How long do you want to be riding: 24, 36, 48 hours or longer? In the Race Across the Alps (RATA) you could be finished in under 24 hours, whereas in the Race Across Europe you'd still be riding for another seven days at the very least. Do you wish to do it supported or unsupported? London–Edinburgh–London (LEL) serves hot meals at the control points, whereas The Japanese Odyssey requires you to shop for whatever you want, whenever you want. Would you prefer to race as part of a team or on your own? Most events will give you a choice. Do you prefer large-scale events with the infrastructure to match, or is low-key your thing?

One of the most popular formats of ultra-distance events is the 'Race around…'. You can 'Race Around' Austria, Germany, Switzerland or Ireland, for example. You can race across continents in, for example, the Race Across America or the Race Across Europe. Then there are a whole host of races that do loops of difficult terrain, such as Ultracycling Dolomitica in the Dolomites or the Race Across the Alps in, of course, the Alps. Each year, more and more events are created.

Whatever your choice of event, make sure it is one with significant appeal. You're going to spend a long time training in order to take part, so it had better be something that you really want to do. The following examples will give you a flavour of what is available. Two are competitive (RAAM and Ultracycling Dolomitica), and two are not (The Japanese Odyssey and LEL). Two are large, organised events (LEL and RAAM), whereas The Japanese Odyssey and Ultracycling Dolomitica are small, low-key events.

>> In the UK riders are likely to experience everything from warm sunshine to fog and heavy rain. >>

LONDON–EDINBURGH–LONDON (LEL), UK

The LEL travels to and from the capital cities of England and Scotland. The 1,433km route starts in the Essex town of Loughton, about 20km north of the centre of London, and travels up the east side of England before drifting to the north-west and then on through Southern Scotland to Edinburgh. The return route retraces the outward leg. Most of the route is on small roads. Of the 11,128m of climbing, most occurs in the north of England and Scotland. When compared to many other ultra-distance events, the amount of climbing is modest for the distance ridden.

The prevailing wind in the UK is from the south west. In theory, this means riders should not suffer from a headwind. However, the UK is renowned for very changeable weather and riders are likely to experience everything from warm sunshine to fog and heavy rain, sometimes within the same day.

Riders have up to five days to complete the route. It is a non-competitive event, so there are no winning times. The faster riders will finish in around two-and-a-half days. Established in 1989, it takes place every four years, two years after Paris–Brest–Paris, probably the most famous *Audax/Brevet* (a non-competitive long-distance cycling event that must be completed within a given time period). It attracts hundreds of riders from around the world. Because it is not a race, there is a real mix of riders and riding styles. Some ride carrying plenty of spare kit to cover most eventualities; others go as minimalist as possible. A few ride single-speed or fixed-gear bikes.

There are 20 control points (including the start and finish) in towns along the way and in places such as schools and other institutions. At these 'controls' hot food is provided and, for those in need of sleep, mattresses are laid out in rows in large halls. At the busiest control points riders have to book a slot on a mattress in order to rest. Some kit can be sent ahead to two control points. While helpful, there is no guarantee that what you have sent ahead is what you will need at the time that you arrive. The controls are staffed by volunteers, many of whom are experienced cyclists, so have a great deal of empathy for the riders coming through. As a result, the event has a reputation for being very friendly and caring. It is a great introduction to ultra-distance cycling.

ULTRACYCLING DOLOMITICA, ITALY

Billing itself as the hardest race in the world, this relatively short ultra-distance race, at 600km, manages to squeeze in a staggering 16,000m of ascent in a loop through and over the Dolomites. The climbing is relentless; riders travel over 16 passes including the Campolongo, which includes a short section with a gradient in excess of 33 per cent. The race is open to solo and teams of supported riders, as well as unsupported riders. While other races may claim to be harder, there is no doubt that this is a demanding event. In 2015, only one unsupported rider managed to finish, the rest falling victim to the cold temperatures, rain and early snowfall at the top of some of the passes. In contrast, in the valleys the temperature can easily exceed 30°C.

The route is on delightfully small single-track roads that wind their way over the mountains. From a distance it's as if someone has draped a strand of spaghetti on the side of the hill. The scenery is epic, with steep-sided craggy mountains, remote villages and high mountain pastures. While stunning during the day, these same roads become very challenging to descend at speed at night.

There are several control points throughout the race and a GPS tracker fitted to each bike to provide evidence of compliance with the route. Unsupported riders can send a bag of supplies and kit ahead to a couple of the control points, but the distances in-between mean either a heavily-laden bike or a swift trip to a shop to stock up on supplies.

The fastest supported riders complete the distance in 25–30 hours, and the unsupported riders in 36 hours. The inaugural race in 2014 comprised just a handful of riders, but its popularity increases every year. Nevertheless, it remains a low-key event; it's quite possible to ride for hours without seeing another competitor. Participation in this event, unsupported, without prior experience of alpine climbs or ultra-distance riding, would be unwise.

RACE ACROSS AMERICA (RAAM), USA

According to the RAAM website, this is 'The World's Toughest Bicycle Race', a claim that is justified by the 4,800km distance and the 53,300m of ascent. Unlike most other events, participation is dependent on completing a qualifying event. The race starts in Oceanside in California and travels east to Annapolis, the capital of the state of Maryland. The terrain includes everything from mountains to vast plains, from forests to deserts. The fastest riders will sleep on average fewer than two hours a night for the eight or nine days it will take them to complete the route. In 2014, Christoph Strasser averaged 16.42mph to win. This average speed included all stops for sleep, toilet breaks and changing kit. It is staggeringly fast.

The stories from competitors in this race tell of epic battles with sleep deprivation, headwinds, soft tissue injury, pain and sickness. Unsurprisingly, given the intense mental and physical ordeal, only about 50 per cent of those who start make it through to the finish.

It's not easy for the support crews either. They have to deal with their own fatigue, while also supporting a rider who'll be making increasingly little sense and may be somewhat irrational in their expectations of the team. Given that this race has been around since 1982, there must be some appeal. As is so often the case with ultra-distance rides, it's only afterwards that the sense of achievement is sufficiently addictive to drive people to do it again and again.

THE JAPANESE ODYSSEY, JAPAN

This is a non-competitive endurance ride across central Japan, established in 2015. The time limit for completion is 14 days and the route takes in 11 mountain passes between the cities of Tokyo in the North and Osaka in the South. It is at the other extreme of ultra-distance events in that you can *only* complete it unsupported. You have to find your own supplies on the way and posting supplies ahead is forbidden. A satellite tracker is used to display your position and prove completion of the route.

The route takes in some very small single carriageway roads that wind their way over beautiful mountains. Riders can, however, choose whatever route they wish, as long as they

≫ Events are merely the placeholders in the calendar that provide a motivation to train for the rest of the year. ≫

pass through a few checkpoints along the way.

The Japanese Odyssey is minimalist in almost all dimensions. There are 10 ground rules that participants are expected to follow. These 174 words are less than the information on where RAAM participants are expected to park at registration. The RAAM rulebook runs to in excess of 14,000 words, necessarily given the complexity of the event, the number of people involved and the significance of the race.

THE ULTRA-DISTANCE AESTHETE

These are simply the literal descriptions of what ultra-distance cycling is. This introduction does not give any insight into what makes ultra-distance cycling a sport many find themselves drawn towards. In the authors' experience, it is so much more than the event itself. Events are merely the placeholders in the calendar that provide a motivation to train for the rest of the year. And it is the training where much pleasure is to be had. Being able to head out early in the morning for a 350km training ride that takes in kilometres of roads you may never have ridden before, through towns you have not yet visited,

is a wonderful thing. To paraphrase T.S. Eliot, it is the journey, not the arrival, that matters. It is the joy of discovering more of the world around where you live.

The weather adds to the memories. An overnight ride along the bridleways of the South Downs in the South of the UK can reward with stunning views of church steeples and the tops of tall trees poking through the mist lining the valley floors, the ridges bathed in the thin light of a spring morning. Riding through the silence of snow falling, when all the world is tucked up inside and you have the roads and tracks to yourself, can feel very special.

At night, animal life is much more visible. At dusk, watching a beautiful owl silently work up and down a field, hunting for prey, can make for a magical distraction, as can watching a Condor ride the thermals in the high Andes.

Some training sessions are short and fearsome in nature, requiring absolute focus and huge commitment to complete. In the moment, these are deeply uncomfortable. However, thinking about how such sessions will make a future event so much easier helps keep you going.

Then there are the events themselves. Most are organised by people who know the area well. As a result, the routes planned often take in the best an area has to offer; roads and tracks that, if you were planning your own route, you may well have ignored or excluded. Because you are able to ride distances most find incomprehensible, you get to see a significant amount of an area in a very short space of time. You become more than simply an athlete; you also become an aesthete, attuned to the beauty of the world around you. It's a sport that lends itself to intense moments. These can be incredibly fulfilling and even spiritual in nature. While rides can last hours, sometimes a moment can last forever, and hours of riding seem to vanish in a second. Many of the experiences seem impossible to describe to others, be it battling extreme weather over a remote mountain col, or the exquisite beauty of an unexpected view early in the morning. While they may be ineffable, they remain memories for life.

Ultra-distance cycle racing is a demanding sport. Other competitors know this and the attitude to racing seems much more congenial and supportive. Fellow competitors and their support teams are very likely to check that you're OK if they find you stopped on the side of the road. There seems to be a respect for the fact that an incident in an ultra-distance race has far greater consequences than, for example, a 100–115km sportive where you are never more than 40–50km from the start or finish.

From all of these experiences riders learn more about themselves. You'll find out how well you cope under pressure when you're tired, hungry, or in the middle of the night when you're trying to fix your broken bike. Spending a lot of time on your own provides significant opportunities for introspection about what you're doing and

why, both on the bike and in life in general. The sense of achievement when you complete a very challenging ride is palpable. The euphoria lasts for days, weeks, months, even years.

You will, however, have to get used to people telling you they 'don't have time to fit the training in', as if somehow your life is part-time and easy. Expect your close friends and family to treat your extreme riding behaviour as 'just what you do'. An epic ride, taking in hundreds of kilometres, will gradually cease to inspire awe, and instead be greeted with, 'Can you put the bins out once you've put your bike away?'

The list of tasks that needed doing before you set out will still be awaiting completion on your return. If you make the extraordinary seem ordinary, then that is how it will quickly be perceived. Expect people to fail to understand that, just because you're riding a bike doesn't mean you can't think about other things, such as that knotty work problem you've been mulling over for a while.

There is good evidence to suggest that the process of de-focusing by doing something else can help significantly with creativity and innovation. As you get more experienced and your ability to pace yourself improves, expect others to no longer wish to ride with you. Your overall pace on long rides will be too high and, second, your ability to maintain a constant effort up and downhill will contrast with the average weekend rider who attacks the hills and then collapses over the bars on the way down. All of these negatives are a small price to pay for having transformed yourself from an ordinary cyclist into an extraordinary ultra-distance endurance athlete. The sensations, experiences, memories, insights and aesthetic pleasure that come from riding your bike a long way, fast, provide rich memories that will sustain you through whatever else life brings your way.

>> The world of
cycling is rich
in opinion, but
a little less
so in research
underpinning
these
viewpoints. >>

SIMPLE BUT NO SIMPLER

The quote, 'Everything should be as simple as possible but not simpler', is often attributed to Einstein, and has heavily influenced the approach of this book. There are some topics, such as the discussion on training zones, that necessitate lengthier explanation than, for example, the right choice of top tube bag in which to carry your food. The latter justifies a short paragraph and no more, while the former necessitates a significant part of a chapter. The assumption has also been made that the very fact you have bought this book means you're an experienced cyclist. Some of the topics in the book you may already have mastered; in which case, ignore them and read those sections of more use. It also means this is not the book to read if you're unsure whether to buy a hybrid, mountain bike or road bike.

The world of cycling is rich in opinion, but a little less so in research underpinning those viewpoints. Where the evidence is clear, conflicting, uncertain or missing, this is noted. You may wish to scan those areas with which you're already familiar just in case you have fallen for an opinion that has no basis in fact.

While the basic principles of cycling have remained constant, ongoing research and developments in technology are having a profound impact on the way in which riders can prepare and participate in ultra-distance events. Power meters, unheard of 30 years ago and within reach of only professional cyclists just 10 years ago, are now available to all enthusiastic amateurs. They have transformed cycle training.

While cyclists of old had to carry route cards and maps to help them navigate, the advent of the bike-mounted GPS and phone apps has enabled complex routes to be ridden with ease by simply following an arrow on a screen. The broad principles that underpin both technologies have remained constant over time – how do you get the best training bang for your buck of effort? And how will you know where to go? And so, because the specific tools that are used make any text outdated before it is even published, this book will not focus on which power meter is better than another, but on the principles behind training with power.

It will not discuss the merits of different frame materials or how the different types of carbon fibres that are used in frame construction can affect handling and comfort; instead, it talks about what is critical in your bike set-up to survive riding for, on occasion, days at a time. Your budget will dictate how best to achieve the outcome sought.

In researching this book, the authors have combined knowledge gleaned from conversations with ultra-distance cyclists, coaches and scientists with their own riding experience in order to provide an insight into the 'lived experience' of the ideas discussed. The necessity of completing training sessions that stress different energy systems is discussed, as well as that horrible sensation when the training is simply not going to plan. Should you abandon the session, or keep going at a lower intensity? This is the lived experience of training that exists in the context of a busy life involving work, training, family, friends and all the many issues that all riders have to deal with on a day-to-day basis.

MARGINAL GAINS

Made popular by British Cycling, the concept of marginal gains came from the idea that if you identified everything that makes a positive difference to cycling performance, and improved each element by 1 per cent, the overall impact would be a significant increase in performance. Within the cloud of all possible gains, some are more significant than others, and similarly, each rider's development areas will be different to others. What might be an area of marginal gain for one rider could be a substantive area of development for another. For example, while being able to hold an aerodynamic position will help you go faster, it's a waste of time if you're unable to ride the race distance in that position. Similarly, reducing body fat to a single digit percentage will undoubtedly make you lighter, but if you haven't sorted out how to eat properly in order to fuel your body for the duration of your long rides, you won't last the distance.

Becoming a better ultra-distance cyclist is at its heart both complex and simple. Most aspects of performance are inter-related. For example,

your mental state is influenced by the extent to which you are depleted of energy, which in turn affects your ability to make good decisions. Each marginal gain should be considered in relation to the other factors that impact, or are impacted by, the change you intend to make.

At the same time, it is also simple. Improving your performance can be achieved by something as simple as swapping an endurance ride for a shorter, high-intensity session. When broken down into lots of small steps the accumulated impact can be phenomenal. Unless you're a professional cyclist, the chances are there are some big pieces of the jigsaw worth getting right first, such as fitness, nutrition, comfort and the right mental approach.

IT'S MORE THAN JUST RIDING THE BIKE

While the most attention is usually given to fitness and equipment, becoming a successful ultra-distance cyclist involves so much more. The assumption is made that you are a busy person with a full-time job and, among work and family commitments, you're squeezing in some cycling and have an ambition to go further and faster. The trouble is, there are only so many hours in the day. The challenge lies in carving out time to train without destroying your personal or working life.

When you *have* managed to find some time to ride, the next thing to establish is how to get the best value from that time. While ultra-distance cycling is in itself a solitary activity, in practical terms it can often involve a substantial team of people. If you're riding with a support team, you'll need to persuade them to give up some of their annual leave to support you while you take on an ultra-distance challenge. Then there are those who support you in getting to the start line, such as a coach, nutritionist, and physiotherapist. The challenge is how to get the best from all of these people.

>>While ultra-distance cycling at its heart is just riding a bike for a long time, there are many factors that contribute to this ability.>>

Ultra-distance cycling is an expensive sport and, as you become more successful, seeking assistance from others in covering the costs requires an understanding of how sponsorship and public relations works. Fitness alone will not get you to the finish line; the right mental approach is needed to cope with fatigue, bad weather and when things go wrong. Cycling for a long time requires knowledge of what to eat and drink to maintain the effort. Getting to the finish line won't happen unless you can remain comfortable on your bike and have with you the right equipment to cope with whatever conditions you're likely to experience in your chosen event. Behind all your efforts in this area are your family and friends. Without their support and cooperation, you won't get far.

While ultra-distance cycling, at its heart, is just riding a bike for a long time, the factors that contribute to this ability are many. While this book is divided into a series of chapters that tackle specific areas of performance, the lived experience is such that they all impact one another. For example, being over-trained will mean you tire more quickly. When tired, decision-making starts to deteriorate. This in turn can impact your discipline to eat and drink according to your ride plan, which in turn reduces your ability to perform, as well as affecting your ability to process information. Being fatigued also reduces the efficiency and effectiveness of the energy made available from the food you've eaten. If the food you need is stored somewhere difficult to access on the bike, the impact of fatigue will lead you to take the easy option, which may mean not eating the right thing. Your choice of equipment will have been limited by your budget, which is determined, in part, by your ability to raise money in sponsorship. Your success in generating sponsorship will have depended on carving out enough time to fulfil your sponsors' objectives. It becomes a downward spiral, impacting how you set up your bike, the way you train, your mental preparation, your choice of food, and the resources you have. Each impacts, and is impacted by, the others. In short, it is complex.

Becoming a successful ultra-distance cyclist means taking a holistic approach to your

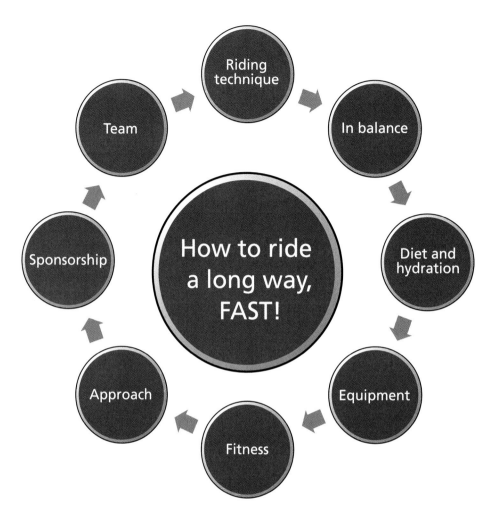

Figure 1: R.I.D.E.F.A.S.T:
The structure of this book

performance. Raising your game in one dimension on its own is not enough. It's about developing all the dimensions at the same time in order to produce an improvement in performance. This is the joy of ultra-distance cycling; it's like a game of chess. You need to be thinking several moves ahead the whole time, and have an awareness of how the broader context is likely to impact what you do. Thus, a successful ultra-distance cyclist is not necessarily the best in terms of physical prowess; instead, their strength lies in their ability to bring together a range of skills in many different areas, blending them together to create a winning performance. The ability to ride a bike well is just the tip of the iceberg. As you will see in this book, it is what lies beneath the water, which most people do not think about, that really makes the difference.

The content of the book is broken down into eight main chapters, concluding with a summary in Chapter 9. Each can be read as a standalone section when required.

THE STRUCTURE OF THIS BOOK

CHAPTER ONE: RIDING TECHNIQUE

This covers the technical aspects of bike riding, including cadence, bike fit, standing versus seated riding, climbing, maintaining momentum, descending, and the racing line.

CHAPTER TWO: IN BALANCE: LIFE, WORK AND CYCLING

This addresses the challenge of balancing the competing pressures of work, home/family and training. It includes developing guiding principles to help make decisions easier, and some suggestions on how to fit training into a busy work and home life.

CHAPTER THREE: DIET AND HYDRATION

The focus here is on what you need to eat and drink during training, racing and when recovering, as well as practical suggestions on packing and packaging food for consumption during an event or race.

CHAPTER FOUR: EQUIPMENT

Bearing in mind the rapid rate of development in cycling products, this chapter explores the principles that underpin equipment choice in order to be sufficiently comfortable to ride a long way in all conditions.

CHAPTER FIVE: FITNESS

This chapter is about how to arrive at the start of an event or race in top form, having achieved the best level of fitness within the constraints of the time available.

CHAPTER SIX: APPROACH: DEVELOPING AN ULTRA-DISTANCE MINDSET

Ultra-distance cycling is as much about your mindset as it is your fitness. In this chapter, topics such as mental toughness and coping strategies are explored.

CHAPTER SEVEN: SPONSORSHIP AND PR

Ultra-distance riding can be expensive. Securing sponsorship to defray the costs can help. This chapter examines some of the things you need to do to get support from sponsors, including generating great public relations content.

CHAPTER EIGHT: TEAMWORK

While on the face of it, ultra-distance cycling is a solitary activity, in reality it involves extensive support from a diverse range of people. Getting the best from them is the focus of this chapter.

CHAPTER NINE: PUTTING IT ALL TOGETHER

While examining each issue in isolation helps gain a better understanding of what you should be doing, often the experience of riding presents a set of symptoms that need to be interpreted to work out the underlying cause. This chapter illustrates how.

It is anticipated that the reader will dip in and out of the book, trying out the ideas and suggestions made, and then coming back to experiment a bit more. However you choose to use this text, enjoy the path to ultra-distance cycling.

CHAPTER 1:
RIDING TECHNIQUE

If you're going to ride tens of thousands of kilometres a year in training and racing, you'd better get your technique right!

ATHLETE'S STORY

Soon after I started riding in 1999, I thought I had found my perfect bike position and saddle height. I quickly memorised the key measurements, transferring them to any new bike that came my way. After two or three years, and with a bit more strength in my legs, I thought that 'long and low' was the way to go, and so I put myself on a very long (140mm) stem to replicate the pros' machines. I kept this position into my late 30s, but a work-related back injury in 2009 severely compromised my normal riding position – I just couldn't get past 45 minutes in the saddle without severe hip flexor pain.

I went to see a former professional racer-turned-bike -fitter and was shocked when he made what I considered to be a significant drop in my saddle height of 6mm. I tried it, but in hindsight didn't give it enough time before returning to my tried-and-tested saddle height. With big races and team pressure, I felt that the position change was too much of a risk. At this stage I was considering retiring from racing due to lack of progress following the injury. The pain returned and so I decided to approach the problem from a different direction. I invested a significant amount of my weekly training schedule in improving my core strength. By 2011 I was back at full race speed. Despite being into my 40s, I was again able to hold my own with riders half my age.

By 2012, I found myself hitting a plateau yet again but was convinced that I wasn't ready to hang up my race wheels. I visited a bike fitter who had been recommended by a friend. After a long discussion about the road taken up to that point we made what I considered to be huge changes to my position: stem shortened by 20mm, saddle lowered by 10mm (even lower than it went in 2010), shoe cleats pulled forward, hoods rotated slightly forward. This time

Martin Smith in action

around, I had no big races on the horizon; I gave my body time to adjust to the radical changes. After just one month I was surprised to find that I'd not reverted to my old set-up, and, more significantly, riding had become quicker and less painful. A year later, I was back to winning ways, taking my third National Masters title and, in 2014, winning three National titles in less than a month of intense racing.

To this day, I still find myself making minor changes to my position. Our bodies, and the demands of our cycling, are constantly changing such that ongoing evaluation – and adjustment where necessary – is probably essential for success.

Martin Smith, eight times' National Masters and Veteran Champion across road, track and cyclo cross-disciplines

>> In the never-ending quest for performance improvement it is easy to be overwhelmed by the sheer volume of advice available. >>

HOW IMPORTANT IS RIDING TECHNIQUE IN ULTRA-DISTANCE CYCLING?

Some sports are heavily dependent on technique. Get it right and you're in the game; get it wrong and you become a spectator. For example, if you were a high jumper with the world's most impressive scissor kick, you would still lose every time to those elite high jumpers who use the Fosbury Flop, such is the difference in effectiveness of the two techniques.

The advantages of technique development in cycling appear less dramatic, but the combination of many small improvements can really add up. A more aerodynamic riding position might save you several seconds per kilometre; a more efficient pedal action might save a handful of calories per hour; and a more consistent power delivery might mean that you go 'into the red' less often. All of these things will save time and, therefore, improve performance during standard cycling time trials and road races. But imagine how these small gains really add up for the ultra-distance cyclist who is on the road for days rather than hours. In this chapter you'll discover ways to improve your ultra-distance cycling performance through developing your riding technique.

ULTRA-DISTANCE CYCLING: IT CAN'T BE THAT COMPLICATED, CAN IT?

In the never-ending quest for performance improvement it is easy to be overwhelmed by the sheer volume of available advice. From books written by your cycling heroes, to monthly and weekly cycling magazines, and innumerable internet articles and discussion forums, the advice is nearly endless. It is, therefore, easy to strike out in the wrong direction. Equally, it is easy to be stymied by the range of conflicting views with, in Herbert Simon's words, the 'wealth of information creat[ing] a poverty of attention'.

A filter of some kind is required to separate the helpful advice from the unhelpful. Sports scientists provide one of the best filter mechanisms by carrying out research on groups of cyclists under controlled conditions. The problem of course is that the conclusions of such research are constrained by this very control. A particular supplement or training regimen may work in the laboratory, but will it work for you as you juggle the demands of family, work and your cycling aspirations?

Intuition and the experience of others is often relied upon to fill in the gaps left by the scientists. In many cases this is a good thing; you and your coach (if you have one) must walk the fine line between the science and the art of cycling. It can, however, be risky as intuition and experience may lead to the proliferation of myths; myths that might be benign but could also damage your performance. Do you really need to adopt a super-high cadence? Should you recover on the downhill? Does it really matter if you climb in or out of the saddle? This chapter will shine a scientific light on some of the riding technique 'tips' that have proliferated within the cycling press.

>> At cadences above 90rpm the nervous system is unable to activate and deactivate the muscles fast enough to produce power efficiently. >>

CADENCE

Your pedal cadence (the speed at which you turn the pedals) can influence both your power output and how efficient you are in delivering this power. Some researchers have suggested that moderately high cadences of ~90rpm are preferable as they minimise muscle activity and neuromuscular fatigue. In direct contrast, other researchers have reported that low cadences, i.e. below 60rpm, are more economical. The contradiction is explained by the fact that different research studies look for cadences that optimise different physiological variables. Thus, a low cadence is probably 'energetically' optimal, while a high cadence is probably optimal for the neuromuscular system.

If you are simply seeking to maximise your power output, in a situation where your efficiency doesn't matter, a cadence of 120–130rpm will be preferable. This is why track sprinters and BMX riders pedal at very high cadences. Because races in these disciplines are so short, it doesn't matter how much energy is wasted. In these disciplines, raw power is everything.

As an ultra-distance cyclist, however, you must find a good balance between energy use and power production. For a given power output, your muscle forces per pedal revolution will reduce as your cadence increases. This will lead to an increased reliance on your slow-twitch muscle fibres and reduced use of your energy-hungry fast-twitch fibres. A higher cadence may also reduce intramuscular pressure, reducing blood flow occlusion, thereby improving oxygen delivery to the working muscles. Thus, by adopting a high cadence you may optimise nutrient delivery and preserve carbohydrate stores.

There is, however, a trade-off between muscular and non-muscular components. Though muscular forces are reduced as cadence increases, non-muscular forces increase. The best compromise between these competing forces appears to arise at a cadence of ~90rpm; an interesting research finding when noting that many riders self-select just such a cadence. Joint torques appear to be minimised close to this preferred cadence, which suggests that the minimisation of muscular forces is a priority for the nervous system.

Another mechanical variable that appears to influence the selection of preferred cadence is the production of (inefficient) negative muscular work. Researchers have shown that there is a significant amount of negative mechanical work above the preferred cadence of 90rpm. It seems that at cadences above 90rpm the nervous system is unable to activate and deactivate the muscles fast enough to produce power efficiently.

That the preferred cadence for many riders is ~90rpm appears to contradict the oft-quoted research finding that the most efficient cadence is in the range of 50–60rpm. In part, this shows that the selection of preferred cadence is driven more by mechanical factors than by the maximisation of efficiency. A preferred cadence is adopted to minimise muscular forces, muscular stress and inefficient, negative muscular work, possibly with the goal of avoiding or delaying muscular fatigue. Having said that, the most efficient cadence is strongly influenced by intensity. While 60rpm might be the most efficient cadence at power outputs of 200W or less, as power increases above 300W the most efficient cadence is likely to be in the 80–100rpm range.

>> Your self-selected (preferred or natural) cadence is probably close to optimal. >>

With many competing cadence-related messages out there, the best advice is not to worry about it too much. Your self-selected (preferred or natural) cadence is probably close to optimal. There is certainly no need to force yourself to spin at 100rpm+ during an ultra-distance training ride when you would naturally adopt a cadence of 75rpm.

PEDALLING: HOW HARD CAN IT BE?

The formula for fast cycling is very simple: maximise power output and minimise resistance. The latter can be achieved by adopting an aerodynamic riding position (discussed below), by using aerodynamic equipment or even just by adjusting your tyre pressure (discussed in Chapter 4: Equipment, page 101). Increasing power output is one of the main goals of your training programme as you seek to maximise the amount of force that you can produce while minimising the amount of energy required to produce this force. Improving your cycling efficiency (see Chapter 5: Fitness, page 133) is, therefore, an important means of improving

your ultra-distance performance. In the quest for improved efficiency, many cyclists agonise over their pedal actions. Should you ride with heels up? Toes down? Cleat forward? Cleat backward?

POINT THOSE TOES (OR NOT!)

There are three main toe/heel position types. Most cyclists adopt a 'horizontal' pedal action, where the heel is level with the toe 90 degrees into the pedal stroke. The 'toe dipper' points the toe throughout the pedal stroke, whereas the 'heel dropper' drops the heel below the level of the toe during the downstroke.

These variants have implications for overall body position. Compared to the normal horizontal style, the heel dropper must reduce saddle height due to increased knee extension, whereas the toe dipper must increase saddle height due to what amounts to an increased leg length. The toe dipper will need to sit back to counteract the forward body tip resulting from the predominant posterior pedal vector. The heel dropper will sit slightly forward to counteract the fact that the anterior pedal vector will push them back in the saddle.

All cyclists do a bit of toe pointing and a bit of heel dropping. At low power outputs there is a tendency to toe point, but a shift towards heel drop occurs as power output increases, probably because of the need for increased downward torque. Nevertheless, there are riders at all levels – including Tour de France winners – who have an exaggerated style. The key point to note is that this exaggerated style could be in either direction. There is no convincing evidence to suggest that a toe-pointer or a heel-dropper style is beneficial for performance. The key message then is that you do not need to force yourself to adopt a different toe/heel pedal action. Indeed, allowing your pedal action to naturally vary to suit the situation (terrain, fatigue, etc.) will likely result in optimal performance and reduced injury risk.

Similarly, there is no conclusive scientific evidence to support a particular fore/aft cleat position. When comparing fore and aft cleat positions in groups of cyclists, cycling efficiency does not appear to be affected. It should be said, however, that scientific studies mask individual differences, so it's not impossible that you would

benefit from a change. The key message is that, on average, this particular opportunity for a marginal gain is marginal indeed!

PEDALLING IN CIRCLES

Biomechanical analyses have provided a detailed understanding of how the muscles of the leg work in synergy to deliver force to the crank. Using instrumented force pedals and motion capture camera systems, scientists have been able to determine the mechanical effectiveness of the pedal stroke and the magnitude of the rotational forces that muscles generate around the ankle, knee and hip joints.

Different types of pedal action can be evaluated by measuring pedal force effectiveness, which is the ratio of the force applied in the direction of movement (the effective force) to the force applied to the pedal (the resultant pedal force). Several research studies have shown cycling efficiency improves with increases in pedal force effectiveness. Intuitively, greater pedal force effectiveness should result in improved cycling efficiency and, therefore, improved performance. In reality, however, the physics

of pedalling adds some complexity. The simple ratio between effective and resultant forces is not able to account for gravitational and motion dependent influences, with the result that only a fraction of the measured pedal force can be attributed to muscular effort. In addition, maximised pedal force effectiveness would depend on the elimination of radial forces; however, radial forces are actually essential for the efficient working of the muscles.

Findings from laboratories have suggested no association between cycling efficiency and pedal force effectiveness. Indeed, when researchers have evaluated acute adjustments of pedalling style aimed at increasing pedal force effectiveness (e.g. 'pedalling in circles'), cycling efficiency has actually declined.

Perhaps it is no surprise that benefits are not seen during short-term adjustment of pedal action. Similar results have, however, been reported following longer-term adjustments. By using decoupled cranks, cyclists are forced to actively pull on the pedal during the upstroke and, therefore, increase their pedal force effectiveness. Taken as a whole, the experimental evidence suggests that the acquisition of new pedalling techniques does not result in significant increases in efficiency.

Spin sessions and one-legged cycling sessions may be helpful in the development of some aspects of your physiology. They are, however, probably a waste of precious training time if you're doing them in an attempt to make your pedal style more *effective*.

>>The mantra is simple; you're either pedalling or braking.>>

THERE ARE NO HILLS

Once you know your cycling vital statistics (your V̇O2max, functional threshold power and so on; see Chapter 5: Fitness, page 133), the next step is to use these statistics to good effect. This means riding to your numbers and not the terrain. Many recreational cyclists ride steadily on flat sections, which allows them to work hard going up the hills, and then freewheel, and therefore recover, down the other side. Thus, the level of riding effort is a mixture of Level 2, Level 4 and Level 1 (see Chapter 5: Fitness, pages 135–136 for a discussion about training 'levels'). This strategy is a sure-fire way of reducing the distance you will be able to ride. For endurance riding, the key is to maintain the same level of power output at all times, at no time going into the red. Thus, if your optimal power is 230 watts for an endurance ride, this means riding up *and down* hills at 230W. The mantra is simple; you're either pedalling or braking. The only time you are doing neither is if you have run out of gears. This is a surprisingly hard skill to learn. In the early days it requires vigilance. What it means in practice is going far more slowly up the hills than you might feel comfortable with, and when you crest the hill, maintaining the effort and working surprisingly hard down the hill. When you first start training with a power meter it's a bit of a shock to find that what you thought was steady riding has a much greater range of effort than you imagined. In time, you will learn what your endurance power feels like and be able to maintain it almost without looking at the bike computer screen. But until then, vigilance is the key. There are some things that can help.

RIDING UPHILL

- However you choose to remind yourself, whether it's setting an alarm on your power meter to indicate when you are out of zone, or just keeping an eye on the screen, stay focused.
- Practise alternating between seated and standing climbing without your power output changing.
- Watch what happens when you take your water bottle out for a drink – sometimes people speed up as they do this. Are you maintaining your power output at the right level? Can you drink and eat while holding a steady power output?
- Read the terrain in front of you. If you can see it easing slightly ahead, change to a harder gear in readiness to keep your power output the same as the gradient eases. This is critical when riding over a crest. Similarly, if you can see that the gradient steepens ahead, change to an easier gear in enough time to maintain the same power output. While riding a single-speed bike does very little to help you learn to ride to a constant level of effort, it is an excellent way of learning to read the terrain, as you get a very clear sense of what you are travelling over when you only have one gear to choose from!
- When riding up hairpin bends, use the outside of the curve, where the gradient is often gentler, to make it easier to manage your effort. As it steepens, slow down to ensure you stay at your required power. It's not about constant speed, but constant effort. It may feel like you are hardly moving on the steepest of gradients and your cadence may be very slow indeed, but you will benefit when you get to the top in great shape, able to continue the effort during the descent and on towards the next climb.

• Because you are riding up the hill at a steady manageable effort and won't be out of breath, this is a great time to eat and drink or to re-organise the contents of your pockets, stretch and generally sort yourself out, leaving you ready to make the most of the descent.

RIDING DOWNHILL

Getting the most out of the downhill sections of any ride requires good bike-handling skills. In many ways, it is harder to descend at the required power output than it is to climb. You may be excellent at climbing, but if your ability to descend is weak, all your hard-won gains may be lost in just a few minutes on a long technical alpine descent. The most important skill is to look a long way forward to plan your line down the hill. Look at where you want the bike to go rather than what you want to avoid.

• Ride with your hands in the centre of the curve on the drops. There are two reasons for this: first, it keeps your centre of gravity lower, which helps with stability, and second,

if you hit a pothole at speed your hands will be pushed into the bars. If they are on the hoods, they will be pushed off and you will likely crash.

• When going into a corner, point your hips and your eyes at the exit point. Keep your outside leg extended and the inside leg bent (i.e. when going round a left-hand bend, the right-hand leg is extended straight, and the left-hand leg is bent with the pedal at the top of the stroke).

• Do all your braking *before* you go round the corner. Start pedalling as soon as you can coming out of the corner, but be careful to avoid pulsing your power output out of your endurance zone.

• Follow the racing line down the hill if safe to do so. This straightens the road by using all of the space and thus enables you to go faster as it is easier to maintain power. Be aware that there is no such thing as the perfect racing line as it depends on the conditions, the nature of your bike, the properties of your tyres and how brave you are.

- While the aim is to maintain a constant effort, and this may mean some very fast riding, you can't win if you crash out of the race. As you become tired, your ability to concentrate and process information is diminished. Adjust your approach accordingly.
- There is no such thing as *risk-free* riding. Descending, by its very nature, is inherently more dangerous than ascending. What is an acceptable risk for you may be less than others are prepared to accept. Don't get caught up in stepping outside what you can cope with. Similarly, be wary of others who may be riding outside of their ability; their errors could cause trouble for you.
- If you have to stop pedalling because of the nature of the terrain, do not try and make up the lost time by working harder on the next hill. Instead, focus on getting back to the target number and staying there.

When you master this skill, there are no hills – there is only your target power output. It can get as steep as it likes, but your power output will remain the same *whether going uphill or down*. The feeling of mastering this constant effort is incredible. The kilometres will disappear under your wheels with seemingly no effort. But be warned, it can feel like an antisocial way of riding. Less experienced riders will drop you on the hills and struggle to stay with you on the descents. The relentless nature of such riding means that unless their fitness is good enough to sit on your wheel, they will eventually get left behind.

SIT, STAND, SUPERMAN?

You won't see many riders in a standing position at 50kph on a flat road. Conversely, you won't see many riders in a seated position when riding up a steep climb. The difference, of course, is that wind resistance is far lower on the climb compared to the flat, such that there is no need to minimise frontal surface area, i.e. the 'hole' that you are punching into the wind. Most riders feel that they can put out more power in a standing position. But is this really true? Where you have

the choice – that is, when wind resistance is not a major issue – should you sit or stand?

Research actually suggests that riders are more efficient in a seated position at low to moderate intensities – anything below mid-Level 4 (see Chapter 5: Fitness, page 135). As you move from a seated to a standing position your centre of mass shifts. This results in a reorganisation of your muscle recruitment patterns, in particular, increasing muscle activity in the muscles of your upper leg. Simply put, more muscle activity at the same power output means you are less efficient.

The difference between seated and standing positions reduces as cycling intensity increases, eventually becoming negligible. Thus, if you are pushing at near maximal levels on a reasonably short climb, you should adopt the position that feels most comfortable. On longer climbs, however, that 'negligible' difference will add up over time. Therefore, on such climbs you will probably benefit from adopting a seated position, even if riding at very high intensities (e.g. the final *hors catégorie* climb of a Tour de France stage). Of course, few ultra-distance events involve bunch racing and can instead

be considered as ultra-time trials. There is, therefore, no need to bounce between low- and high-intensity sections; a sustained, seated, moderate intensity ride will be the optimal approach in most cases.

Aerodynamics is an incredibly complex area. Evidence from wind tunnel tests is useful to provide comparisons between different pieces of equipment and when assessing the aerodynamic efficiency of your riding position. Of course, riding on the road is a much more complex business. The wind can come from any direction and local features will impact the wind direction and force. You will know from riding along a country road with high hedges that conditions can change dramatically when riding past an entrance to a field. The capillary action of the hedge and narrow opening accelerates the force of the wind, and if you're not ready it can push you across the road, or, worse, blow you over.

If you've ridden along a very busy main road, the impact of vehicles going past you can provide a positive force that pushes you along. At the same time, the bow wave of air from a large vehicle can push you to one side and then suck you in towards

>> Adopting a aerodynamic position is only worth it if you can sustain that position for the duration of the ride. >>

the vehicle as it passes. In such conditions, safety outweighs the demands of aerodynamic efficiency. For example, a wider hand position on the hoods will improve bike handling when compared to using tri-bars. Aerodynamic decisions require you to balance the demands of the conditions in which you will be riding and the aerodynamic gains that might be achieved by equipment and position adjustments.

The faster you go, the more significant aerodynamic effects become. Estimates vary: at 26kph somewhere between 70 and 90 per cent of your effort is expended in overcoming wind resistance. Of all the variables involved, you, the rider, are the source of most of the resistance, significantly more so than any other variable. After you come wheels, frame, forks, and helmet matter. In one experiment, Mark Cote at Specialised Bikes estimated that in order to maintain a speed of 40kph he needed roughly 60 watts less effort when wearing an aerodynamic helmet on a time trial bike, compared to riding on the hoods on a road bike wearing a road helmet. In an ultra-distance cycling event you are unlikely to average 40kph, but there is free speed to be had from thinking a little about your set-up.

There is one significant and very important caveat. Adopting an aerodynamic position is only worth it if you can sustain that position for the duration of your ride. If halfway through you are sitting up, maybe even riding no-handed to give your back a rest, you will erode any gain from the position. Do it enough and your aerodynamic efforts will have been pointless, and you would have been better to ride slightly less aerodynamically but more comfortably. There are a wealth of stories about cyclists who have invested in a wind tunnel session to determine their optimal riding position, only to find this is not something they can sustain in a race.

From an ultra-distance perspective, probably the single most important thing you can do is add tri-bar extensions to your bike to reduce your frontal area. In Mark Cote's research, approximately 30 watts of benefit came from using the tri-bars. Deep section wheels can help if the course is relatively flat, whereas the extra rotational weight of deep section wheels and the slower speeds involved means shallow section lightweight wheels will be better in the mountains. An aerodynamic helmet can provide

> **The greater your power -to-weight ratio and the smaller your frontal surface area, the faster you will go.** »

an advantage as long as it provides sufficient ventilation for the temperatures in which you will be riding. Clothing has been developed that improves aerodynamic performance, with much attention focused on the location of seams and the profile of those seams to 'trip' the air. Even your choice of gloves can have an impact, with fingerless gloves seemingly creating more drag than wearing no gloves.

It's important to be cautious about kit: many wheels have a carrying capacity of 100kg, which can easily be breached when everything is taken into account (e.g. 82.5kg rider, 9kg bike, 2kg clothing, 2.5kg of kit, 2 litres of fluid, 0.5kg of food and 2kg of lights). Kit that would work well in a short-distance time trial may not be suitable for ultra-distance events. This is discussed in more detail in Chapter 4: Equipment, page 101.

Developments in equipment are such that what is considered a leading performer today will be an also-ran tomorrow – apart from you. The greater your power-to-weight ratio and the smaller your frontal surface area, the faster you will go. That will always be the case. Whatever you choose needs to be reliable.

TRY THIS FOR SIZE

BIKE FIT

There is undoubtedly such a thing as a bike fitting a rider. Rather obviously, if you can't reach the pedals because the seat is too high, or if the saddle is so low your knees are around your ears, you won't be going very far, nor very fast. In short, the bike needs to fit you. A proper-fitting bike is one that allows you to ride sustainably as fast as possible without pain or injury, whatever the measurements that entails. While some of the critical factors in getting a bike sized correctly are explained, it is recommended that you seek the services of a bike fitter as a *starting point* from which to then adjust and tweak to suit your real-world experience of riding your bike. Cycle fitting is an area of cycling where there is limited rigorous research in support of the many claims made.

There is a wealth of 'bike fit' services available. For a fee, and using their own proprietary tools and techniques, bike fitters will prescribe a set of measurements. Attending a bike fit will often result in measurements recorded in millimetres. A bike fit sits within a context and depends on

>> A bike fit provides a starting point that will need to be adjusted in the light of the real-world experience of riding your bike. >>

the type of riding you do and time you spend doing it. What you can cope with on a bike will change according to the duration of the ride. For a short 10-mile time trial it is possible to hold an aerodynamic position that would be simply impossible for most people to maintain for 24 hours. While the length of your bones doesn't change, fatigue impacts the ability of the body to hold certain positions, which means that what is correct at the start of an event can be uncomfortable by the end.

There are many examples of elite cyclists whose bike positions seem to contradict those advocated by the various bike-fitting systems. There are plenty of others who spend hours tinkering with a few millimetres here or there, on the basis of getting things just right. A bike fit provides a starting point that will need to be adjusted in the light of the real-world experience of riding your bike. There is, however, a simple rule of thumb about bike set-up: riding a bike should not hurt. If it does, something in the set-up is not right. Knee pain, back pain, numb hands and hot feet are all symptoms that should not be attributable to the bike if it is set up correctly.

Positions and techniques you can hold and undertake without difficulty during normal training, including long-distance training rides, can become unbearable during ultra-distance due to the incredible levels of fatigue experienced in such events. For example, the amount of resistance the pedal provides upon unclipping can have a significant negative impact over time. The aim of the spring-loaded resistance is to stop the shoe accidentally coming adrift from the pedal when riding, while enabling the rider to overcome the resistance when they wish to unclip. On a long ride over

many hours that will inevitably include many junctions, the number of times you will need to unclip will be significant. That rotational force on the knee when unclipping can cause pain in the knee and become acutely uncomfortable. It is worth putting the resistance on the quick-release set as low as you can get away with in order to avoid this pain. Some pedal systems require considerably less 'unclipping' force than others.

ULTRA-DISTANCE FACTORS
Belinda was mid-training ride from her UK home to Geneva, a journey of nearly 1,000 kilometres over two-and-a-half days. Midway through day two, what had been an exceptionally comfortable position on the bike was simply too difficult to hold. The muscles in Belinda's upper body were just as tired as her legs, and holding a position with her hands on the hoods was just too much. She kept sitting upright and riding no-handed to get comfortable. With over 240 kilometres to go, riding no-hands the rest of the way was never going to work. Stopping by a beautiful river, she flipped the stem to maximise the angle and put all the spacers above the stem underneath. She also rotated the brake hoods up a touch. The result was a much more upright riding position that she was able to hold until the end of the ride.

You can influence comfort in other ways. For example, if you have a helmet-mounted light, you have in effect mounted a weight at the end of the lever where the fulcrum is your neck. Lifting your head up and down many times during the course of a night adds a strain to your neck that can be avoided by positioning the light on your handlebars. The same applies to wearing a rucksack or having your pockets full of stuff.

>> Pay attention to the speed at which you are travelling, and the terrain over which you are riding, and adjust your position accordingly. >>

Each time you get out of the pedals you then lift the weight of the contents of your pockets or rucksack as well as yourself. If you really need the contents, get them into a bag on your bike and let it do the work of carrying the goods.

POSITIONING FOR SUCCESS

Using a variety of riding positions that respond to the terrain can assist with comfort, as the changes alleviate the fatigue experienced when trying to sustain one particular position for the duration of a ride. For example, aerodynamics become an issue when speeds begin to exceed about 26kph. When climbing, speed can drop to single figures, where aerodynamic factors make very little difference. In this case, climbing out of the saddle for a while can ease the lower back and neck. Similarly, when descending, getting low and on the drops can aid stability and speed, while resting on the tri-bars when riding on the flat can alleviate pressure on the shoulders. Varying your riding position can extend your ability to hold an appropriate position for the terrain. Pay attention to the speed at which you are travelling, and the terrain over which you are riding, and adjust your position accordingly.

THINGS TO THINK ABOUT WHEN FITTING YOUR BIKE

SADDLE HEIGHT

In terms of bike fit, saddle height is popularly considered to be the most important factor in determining the power you can generate and the efficiency with which you can do it. As a crude measure, when the foot is at the bottom of the stroke, the angle of the knee should be somewhere between 30 and 35 degrees. The correct height, however, is complicated by a

number of factors including the length of the feet (a longer foot is the equivalent of increasing leg length), the stack height (the distance from the centre of the pedal spindle to the bottom of the shoe), the thickness of the rider's insoles, how fat they are (soft tissue compresses over time), and the amount of clothing they are wearing (padded shorts and winter tights add additional height).

When determining the right saddle height, it is important therefore to do it in the kit you will be wearing. Discrepancies in leg length can also impact the appropriate saddle height and may necessitate the use of orthotics to overcome the imbalance. A bike fit service will help you balance up all these variables to find the right saddle height for you. Incorrect saddle height can lead to knee pain and also compromise the power delivered through the pedals. It is worth taking the time to get your saddle height just right.

SADDLE CHOICE

There are a wide range of saddle designs on the market, from the classic B17 leather saddle made by Brooks, to carbon-fibre shells with almost all of the seat cut away apart from a few contact points. This diverse range of saddles points to the issue that many people have of getting comfortable on a saddle for long periods of time. As discussed in Chapter 4: Equipment, page 101, the use of a good-quality chamois cream will help, whatever the saddle choice. It is possible to find a saddle on which you can be comfortable for hours and even days. Eventually, whatever the saddle, the repeated action of pedalling will take its toll and discomfort will set in. The challenge is delaying that for as long as possible. As participants in the Race Across America can attest, this can be for as long as 12 days of virtually 'non-stop' cycling.

>> **The more often and the longer you ride, the more you become used to the position and the less you suffer.** >>

When seated on a bike there are three points of contact. The first two are your sit bones *(ischial tuberosities)* – the bony protrusions at the top of your legs near the base of your buttocks. The third is the perineum (the area between the genitals and the anus). Your choice of saddle should be of the appropriate width to support the sit bones, and the shape and length of the nose of the saddle should not create undue pressure on the perineum when in your preferred riding position.

The choice of saddle and riding position can indeed impact your health. Saddles can place great pressure on the perineum. For men, the consequence of this pressure on the nerves and blood cells when riding bent over on a saddle that's too narrow causes compression of the perineal arteries, reducing blood flow to the penis and contributing to the risk of erectile dysfunction. It can also lead to tingling sensations and numbness. In women, poor saddle choice can result in 'Bicyclist's vulva' (a chronic swelling of the *labium majus)*, frequent bladder infections and irritable skin problems.

If you want to avoid all these problems, the best option is to ride a recumbent bike, where the rider is seated in a chair in a recumbent position. The next best option is to sit upright at 90 degrees on a wide saddle in order to spread the weight more evenly. Assuming you wish to remain competitive and ride in a more bent-over position, choose a saddle that suits your body shape and the way you ride. Women have a wider pelvic width than men, so what's right for him is unlikely to be right for her. Many saddles have a cut-out section to relieve pressure on the perineum, although some find the edges of the cut-out create pressure points in and of themselves. It is worth experimenting to find what works. A saddle that's too wide is just as problematic as one that is too narrow as it will, at the least, cause chafing.

If you ride mainly on the hoods in one position, the Brooks B17 is probably one of the most comfortable saddles. Over the kilometres, the leather stretches and adapts to your shape. The leather is suspended across a frame and this gives a little as you ride, acting as a very subtle suspension. The overall effect is extremely comfortable, assuming it is the right width for you. The downside is that such saddles are not so comfortable when it comes to riding in a more aerodynamic position, as the nose of the saddle digs into the perineum. If you can sustain an aerodynamic position for a long period of time, a longer, flatter saddle may be more comfortable. There is significant evidence that suggests that saddles without a protruding nose, such as the Adamo ISM, can reduce the amount of perineal pressure.

One factor frequently ignored is the choice of material out of which the saddle rails are made. The rails form the frame onto which the saddle is mounted. Whereas hard rigid rails provide a stiff, solid feel to the saddle, more flexible rails provide a bit of give and additional comfort. While heavily-padded saddles can appear at first to be very comfortable, over time they can make things worse. Your body weight will compress the padding and distort the saddle shape, increasing pressure on the perineum. Some padding is helpful however, as the evidence suggests it aids blood flow.

Bear in mind that, the more cycling you do, the more you will become accustomed to riding on a saddle. The more often and the longer you ride, the more you become used to the position and the less you suffer. In other words, you need to work out, based on experience, whether the discomfort you are experiencing is because the saddle is the wrong shape, or because you have ridden further than you are used to doing and are simply uncomfortable due to the stress of training.

SADDLE POSITION

Trimming the saddle forward or aft affects the position of the knee over the pedal spindle. Time trial riders on bikes with steeper seat tube angles (76–90 degrees) will have their knee in front of this position, and those riding much slacker angles, such as on touring bikes (~72 degrees) may find their knee is a little behind. You will naturally vary the position by where you sit on the saddle. During a long climb you may sit to the back of the saddle as it is easier to push a big gear from this position. When trying to get low and aerodynamic on the flat, you may shuffle forward on the saddle and thus move your knee, in relation to the pedal spindle, further forward. Riding an aerodynamic position may benefit from the saddle being angled ever so slightly downwards.

Your level of flexibility, the way you like to ride and your posture will all impact what feels comfortable. Don't be afraid to experiment with your position. Getting further back can be achieved by moving your saddle and by using a laid-back seat post. Getting further forward can be achieved by moving the saddle forward and with the use of a zero-degree angled seat post.

❯❯There is a myth associated with the need for the ball of the foot to be over the axle of the pedal to maximise the power available.❯❯

The saddle can also be angled either horizontally or with the nose angled up or down. When riding aerodynamically, angling the nose down can be more comfortable as it spreads the pressure over the perineum more evenly, which improves comfort. A more upright position may be a bit more comfortable if the nose is angled ever so slightly upwards. A practical indicator that the saddle is at the wrong angle is if you find yourself shuffling forwards or backwards all the time in order to stay in the right position. If you continually have to shuffle backwards, consider angling the nose up a degree or so, or moving the saddle back a few millimetres. If you are shuffling forwards, try angling the nose downwards, or moving the saddle forward.

PEDAL FOOT INTERFACE

The position of the cleats on the soles of your cycling shoes matters. Stand on the spot. Jump up and down once. Don't move! Look down at your feet and you will see that, rather than pointing North–South, they are splayed. When riding, your position on the pedals should reflect this variation from North–South. Forcing the foot into a North–South line can impact on the knee joint, causing pain. Getting the right angle of the foot to the pedal can be achieved through adjusting the alignment of the cleat on the sole of the shoe. During a bike fit, much effort will be expended in determining the right angle through the use of sensors or laser beams to determine movement in the knee that corresponds to the angle at which the foot is placed.

There is much discussion about the optimal placement of the cleat in terms of aligning the foot appropriately over the axle. From an ultra-distance perspective, it is important to avoid 'hot foot'. This is not, as is often thought, caused by the foot being too hot as a result of ill-fitting shoes, but rather by the nerves in the foot being squeezed between the heads of the metatarsal bones in the foot and causing pain that feels like the foot is hot. The medical term for the condition is *metatarsalgia*. Eventually the sole of the foot goes numb, but the pain when the pressure is relieved can be intense.

There are two solutions to help with this problem. The first is moving the cleat such that the ball of the foot is behind the spindle of the pedal. The second is the use of metatarsal pads – small pads placed in the shoes that help spread the arch that runs behind the ball of the foot and runs across the width of the foot (the transverse arch). The pads need to be positioned behind the ball of the foot as, if positioned under the ball, it will make the problem worse. Use some double-sided sticky tape on the pad to find the right position before fixing permanently. If you have bought shoes a size larger than you would ordinarily use to allow for the fact your feet swell over time, you may need to purchase an extension plate to bring the cleat back into the right position. Not all manufacturers offer this capability.

There is a myth associated with the need for the ball of the foot to be over the axle of the pedal to maximise the power available. In reality there is evidence to suggest that VO_2 (a surrogate term for energy use) is the same when the cleats are positioned further back as when positioned directly over the axle. Not all cycling shoes have options for where the cleats can be placed longitudinally on the shoe.

One way around all these problems might be the use of flat pedals, as used in mountain biking. As of the time of writing there is no robust evidence to suggest a degradation in performance for the ultra-distance cyclist using such pedals. The foot can be positioned in whatever place feels most comfortable, and this can be changed whenever the rider wishes. It also allows a much broader range of footwear to be used when riding.

REACH

When riding in a comfortable position on the hoods, a good baseline 'reach' set-up would result in a plumb line, dropped from your nose, landing at the intersection of the bars and the stem; your elbows will be just in front of your knees when pedalling, just avoiding your knees hitting them. This will all be significantly influenced by what you've become used to, your flexibility, the strength of the muscles in your trunk, and your flexibility. If you've ever tried touching your toes, you will know that at first it can be difficult to do, but if you hold the position for 30 seconds or more, gradually your reach will increase as your hamstrings begin to relax. The gain can be several centimetres as your muscles begin to give a little more. Thus your reach, when cold, may be less than when warmed-up. Reach is, therefore, an area of bike fit where trial and error is probably the most reliable method.

The lower the bars the more aerodynamic you will be. However, if you are too low you will find yourself having to sit up because you cannot maintain the position, thus losing any aerodynamic advantage. Allow for the fact that, when descending, you may wish to go onto the drops, in which case the overall bar height needs to be sufficient to allow you to do this. The bars should be as low as you can maintain for the distance of the event in which you intend to participate.

To help you, there are three variables you can play with: the choice of handlebar, the stem, and the use of spacers. Many different types of drop handlebars are available. The key dimensions are:

- width (generally accepted as needing to be the equivalent of your shoulder width, but more aerodynamic if you can ride 'narrow' as this reduces your frontal surface area);
- reach, which is the distance from the centre of the handlebar in a horizontal line to the point furthest away, i.e. where the brake hood is mounted; and
- drop, the vertical distance from the centre of the bar to the bottom of the drop.

Other factors include the shape of the bend and the angle by which the bar drops away from the horizontal. Thus, it is possible to have a shallow drop bar (125mm) with a small amount of reach (80mm) that is narrow in width (400mm). This means there is only a small transition from the hoods to the drops and thus the relative position on the bike would remain the same. The narrow width also aids aerodynamics. The overall height of the bars can be adjusted using spacers underneath the bars and by the choice of stem angle. The position of the horizontal section of the bars can be adjusted using different length stems, and the height varied by using stems set at different angles. Experiment also with the positioning of the hoods on the bend. Too far around the drops and your wrists may be at an uncomfortable angle; too close to the horizontal bar and the brakes and gears could be difficult to operate when on the drops.

Much can be done to get comfortable on the bike by adjusting the handlebar–stem combination. Experiment to find what works best for you. Over time you may find you can train yourself to ride a little lower and more aerodynamically.

One final thing to think about is the choice of bar tape. If you have larger hands you may wish to double wrap the bars with bar tape to increase the diameter and so improve comfort. You can also get gel pads that sit beneath the bar tape and provide additional cushioning.

CRANK LENGTH

A crank that is too long may feel uncomfortable at the top of the pedal stroke, whereas very short cranks impact cadence (the shorter the crank, the faster the cadence at a given speed and gear). A crank length variation of 2.5mm is neither here nor there. The differences only really become significant at the extremes of crank length, e.g. 160mm vs 185mm. A difference of 2.5mm between 172.5mm and 175mm can occur as the pads in your shorts and the insoles in your shoes compress over time. If you like to spin, use shorter cranks. If you like to push a big gear, use longer cranks. Generally speaking, most bikes are sold with crank lengths commensurate with the frame size.

RIDING A TANDEM

A tandem bike is one that will take more than one person. Typically comprising two seats, they can have three, four or many, many more.

It is one of the most enjoyable ways of cycling. You can never drop the person you are riding with, and the challenge of becoming a highly efficient and fast team is immensely rewarding as it requires communication, technique, trust and teamwork. Tandems can cover ground very quickly and descend at speeds that are exhilarating. It is very common for a tandem to get to 80–110kph on a long descent. Even more enjoyable is when the Captain (who normally rides at the front) and the Stoker (who usually sits at the back) can swap places. The assumption is that the bigger, stronger rider takes the front seat because of the strength needed to control the bike, but this is something of a myth. A tandem, when ridden well, feels no different to a single bike, other than being a bit longer. Being able to swap positions provides you with very useful insights into what the other person experiences, and means you can be more empathetic and, as a result, a better team.

There are some technique challenges specific to a tandem. A chain connects the front and rear sets of pedals, thus you both have to pedal at the same time. The Captain is responsible for choosing the line on the road and the choice of gear, and for operating the brakes. There are three brakes on a tandem; the front and rear like a single bike and a third drag brake. This can be pulled on and left, and will remain on until it is released. It is used on descents where it is helpful to lose some speed all the way down, using the normal front and rear brake to moderate the speed commensurate with road conditions. It reduces the pressure on the Captain to have to hold a brake on the entire time. Of course, if you want to go as quickly as possible, it's best to leave the drag brake off.

PEDALLING TOGETHER

Your riding style is unique to you. When riding a tandem this poses a challenge. The intensity and timing of when you introduce power into the pedal stroke, if different to the other rider, will mean that one of you will waste effort to overcome the resistance of the other person's leg in addition to the resistance offered by the bike. This is a waste. Through practice you can get better at feeling when you are in sync in terms of power delivery. Being out of sync feels like pedalling through treacle, whereas being in sync feels no different to riding your normal bike.

There are several ways you can overcome the difference. The first is to communicate to the other rider how it feels, noting when the pedalling action feels light and when it feels heavy. Secondly, build in some very high-intensity drills to your training. These strenuous efforts give an even greater sense of when you're aligned, and it's easier to get it right when working hard than when riding with little or no pressure on the pedals.

CADENCE

Preferred cadence is likely to differ between tandem partners. One rider may have to increase and the other decrease their cadence in order to find a speed at which you can both work. When riding on your own you may not even realise how you change and adapt your cadence to the terrain. Some people spin up going into a hill; others go through the gears slowly, clicking up through the block as the speed wanes. If you are one of the

latter, a sudden frenetic spinning of the legs can be uncomfortable for your riding partner. Similarly, if you are used to spinning your way up the hills, a big slow gear may be unbearable. The teamwork required on a tandem is all about working through these differences to find the happy medium.

CHANGING GEAR

It is very common for a tandem retailer to have new riders return to the shop, complaining that the gears don't work. The front mechanism on a tandem is unable to overcome the power of the chain when two people are pedalling, and consequently will not shift from the inner to the outer ring. Once the riders learn to back off the pressure on the pedals momentarily when shifting, the change becomes as smooth and easy as on a single bike. Similarly, changing down benefits from a slight reduction in pressure. Once mastered, it becomes second nature, but until then it can cause frustration.

TRUSTING YOUR PARTNER

There is a much-cited myth out there that *the Stoker can do no wrong*. The thinking behind this statement is that the Captain should take into account the Stoker's wishes and comply in order to remove fear and uncertainty from what is a position devoid of much control. In fact, the Stoker can do a lot wrong.

If, when approaching a junction, the Captain is preparing to turn left and begins to lean to the left but the Stoker thinks it's a right turn and starts to lean to the right, the bike will simply go straight on and both riders run the risk of falling off, or worse, placing themselves in a dangerous position in front of traffic.

If, when descending a technical hill, the Stoker does not like the line the Captain is taking and tries to lean away from the line, the impact on the bike is to move it across the road. If done aggressively enough, the bike can move metres the other way. If the Captain has planned the line through the corner and is now thrown off course, at best they can brake to get out of trouble (thus wasting valuable speed) and, at worst, the bike can end up on the wrong side of the road in the face of oncoming traffic. Stoking means learning to relax and going with the flow. If aiming to go fast, this means tucking up behind the Captain, getting out of the wind and helping make the bike more aerodynamic. This will probably mean having no idea what lies ahead, or in which direction the bike is going to go. Thus it is essential to be relaxed to allow the Captain all the freedom to put the bike where they wish.

ANTICIPATING AND TAKING DECISIONS

We all have different appetites for risk and different levels of confidence. There are few places where this is more apparent than road junctions and roundabouts. Brave, confident cyclists flow into the traffic, adjusting their speed a little to match the ebb and flow of the vehicles around them. Timid riders prefer to brake and if necessary stop to be absolutely sure it is safe, and will only get going when a sufficient gap presents itself that is commensurate with their confidence. Ultra-distance riding is all about maintaining momentum and the stop–start nature of junctions can be tiring, as well as detrimental to average speed. The more confident Captain may be prepared to keep going at a junction when a less confident Stoker would otherwise stop. If the Captain is relying on the Stoker for the power to make the manoeuvre and the Stoker ceases to pedal, thinking they are going to stop, the outcome can mean the bike is left stranded in the middle of the road.

Similarly on descents, the more timid rider may not be ready for the speed and dexterity at which the Captain can operate the bike on a descent. If they slow down, it can affect the handling. The principle is simple: the Stoker keeps the power on the whole time, unless otherwise instructed by the Captain. The Stoker will learn to sense what the Captain is doing and respond accordingly – but this takes practice.

IT'S ALL ABOUT COMMUNICATION

Teamwork comes from a concerted effort to work together effectively. This means talking and listening to each other about what's happening, how it feels and how it can be improved. While anyone can ride a tandem, riding a tandem well, for hours at a time, takes thousands of kilometres of team-building.

WORK TO YOUR STRENGTHS

If you are able to swap positions, play to your strengths. If one of you is excellent at descending or riding through traffic, change places to allow that rider to pilot the bike through these sections. If the other rider is brilliant at maintaining an aerodynamic position for hours at a time, put them on the front on the long flat sections. Even if one of you is more technically proficient than the other in all aspects, swapping places still means one of you can have a rest from piloting the bike, to stretch, eat and have a mental break from the pressure on the front. There is no law that states the Captain position must be retained by the same person, or that the role has to be shared 50:50. If you are able to swap positions, you may find that you both have a preference for being Stoker as this position carries the least stress (but the same level of effort).

CLIMBING

Getting out of the saddle on a tandem becomes no different to getting out of the saddle on a single bike. Once you become sufficiently proficient, either one or both of you can get out of the saddle whenever you wish, without having to tell the other person. To get to this stage, begin by agreeing when you will get out of the saddle, count down and rise up when starting a downstroke on the pedals. At first you may only manage a few seconds, but over time this will increase. Once you get to the stage where you can stand whenever you wish, the Stoker should always check where the Captain's hands are before getting up. If the Captain is midway through eating a banana and has one hand loosely holding the bars, the movement of the bike as you stand may cause a severe wobble. Similarly, if the Stoker is halfway through unwrapping a sandwich or removing a coat and the Captain suddenly stands, it can unsettle the bike. If in doubt, let the other person know so they can be prepared, or ask you to hold on for a few moments while they sort themselves out.

SHARE THE ROLES

While the Stoker cannot control much on the bike, they can provide help in indicating to other road users when you intend to turn. They can also do the navigation. Freed from the constraint of having to look where they are going, the Stoker can read a map for as long as it takes to work out the right route and feed this information to the Captain. They can also do on-the-fly navigation to get around road closures. If working with a support team, they can take responsibility for communicating with the support vehicle.

IT'S WARMER BACK THERE!

Because the Stoker is sheltered by the Captain, it can be several degrees warmer than on the front. In winter this often means the need to wear one fewer layer than required in the Captain position. It can also mean the Stoker has no idea how hard or otherwise the headwind is into which they are riding, which can sometimes lead to tension if the Captain is slogging away into a gruelling headwind and the Stoker has mistaken the sedentary speed for a more relaxed effort!

SUMMARY

The aim is to ride as aerodynamically as possible in a position that you can sustain for the duration of your ride. Riding a long way is a tiring business, but it shouldn't be painful. If it is, change your bike set-up, remembering that saddle choice and seat height are perhaps the two most critical factors to get right. Ride at a cadence that works for you and don't worry about having to 'ride in circles'. There is much to gain from improving your bike-handling skills, in particular your ability to descend. The key skill to master is the ability to maintain a constant power output, whether riding along the flat, uphill or downhill. This takes some practice and discipline, but the reward – being able to ride faster and for longer – is well worth it.

CHAPTER 2:
IN BALANCE: LIFE, WORK AND CYCLING

To win races but fail in relationships and at work is no success.
Keeping work, home and training in balance is the challenge.

You cannot save time. You can only spend it. Time is perishable. Just as a hotel cannot save a room that has not been used for another occasion, neither can we recover a missed training session later. Once a session is missed, it can never be done at that time again. The moment has passed. This doesn't mean you cannot spend time doing that session at some point in the future; it just means you chose to spend the time doing something else other than training.

In just the same way, if you choose to train instead of doing something with the family, that time too can never be recovered. That moment has passed too. Achieving a balance between work, family/home and training is about deciding how you wish to spend your time in a way that is acceptable to you and those around you without causing a breakdown in any of the important elements that make up your life. It will also mean compromising in other areas. For example, a night out with family and friends may entail compromising what you eat and drink. While eating a supremely healthy diet may mean choosing water instead of wine, to those who do not have sport as a major priority in their life it can feel a bit puritanical and engender a sense of guilt. Similarly, a 4.30 a.m. start in order to fit in

a big training session is not conducive with late-night socialising. Getting the balance right is not easy. For the enthusiastic amateur, these are the everyday decisions you have to make.

This is not a chapter on time management; there are plenty of good books out there that cover this. The focus here is on some tips and techniques that will help you consider how to get the balance right.

The harder you wish to train, the more unreasonable you will need to be. Fitting in an average of 20 hours' training a week, within a range of 10-30 hours, alongside a full-time job and a home life requires a great many compromises to be made by you and those around you. There are some things you can do, however, to ensure that you keep everything 'in balance'.

Unless you're a professional athlete, your sporting ambitions will be compromised by everything else going on in your life. The challenge is working out what to compromise and when. Just because you are training doesn't mean you're not working. There is plenty of evidence to suggest that the process of defocusing is a great way to achieve insights and epiphanies: ideas or solutions to work challenges may drop into your mind while out training.

>> If your life is
already full
of activities,
adding
in more
training is
not possible
unless you
stop doing
something
else. >>

STOP!

There are only 24 hours in a day. If your life is already full of activities, adding in more training is not possible unless you stop doing something else. Given that you have to work and sleep, there are few places where the extra time can be found. One obvious place is to stop or significantly reduce time spent watching television or surfing the internet; both activities are incredible thieves of time. They are also poor-quality activities in terms of family time. Sitting on the sofa watching TV is not as effective as spending time doing things together. The downside of reducing or eliminating TV is that you may find yourself unable to join in the latest conversation about a popular TV programme because you were engaged in other activities. The upside is that you will be able to fit in activities that will allow you to achieve your sporting aims.

Taken to an extreme, life becomes one of three activities:

- Work
- Training
- Family/partner/home activities.

Everything else is a distraction. There will be times when after a long, hard training session, you are incapable of doing much, in which case slouching in front of the TV may be all you can muster the energy to do. In this scenario, might you be better off in bed, resting properly? As you can see from Figure 2, this approach can seem a bit brutal. It all depends on how successful an athlete you want to be. For very arduous events, such as the Race Across America, this level of focus is essential.

YOU NEED GOOD SUPPORT

Training for ultra-distance cycling is a family business. You might be the person doing the training, but everyone around you is affected by what you have to do. Without the support of those around you, the chances are that either your relationship will fail or your training will come to a grinding halt in the face of a necessity to do other things. Go into ultra-distance racing with your eyes wide open. It is a way of life, not just a hobby. You will have to make a whole series of compromises, the cost of which may not be worth

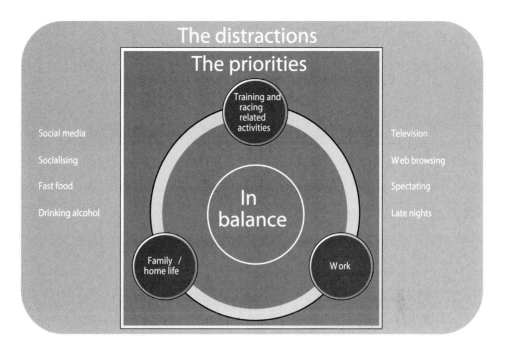

The distractions

The priorities

Training and racing related activities

Social media

Socialising

Fast food

Drinking alcohol

Television

Web browsing

Spectating

Late nights

In balance

Family / home life

Work

Figure 2: In balance – examples of activities that help and those that distract

the price. Better to have an honest discussion about how you will fit it all in than hope that somehow it will all work out in the end.

THE EMOTIONAL BANK ACCOUNT

Spending all your time training and working can mean you pay a heavy price in terms of your relationship. It is like a bank account: there are things you do that put you in credit, and things that you do that will put you in the red, such as training when you should have been doing something else. If the account ends up too much in the red, you threaten the existence of your relationship. It is important to keep the account healthy by making sure you're doing the right things. That may mean dropping a training session from time to time.

PLAN YOUR SESSIONS WEEK BY WEEK (NOT MONTH BY MONTH)

Whether you work with a coach (recommended) or you devise your own training schedule, plan your sessions on a weekly basis. Unless your job is very predictable and you know exactly when and where you are going to be months

in advance (such as a teacher who will know their timetable for the year ahead), you may have no idea where you will need to be in two or three weeks' time. Trying to complete a pre-determined schedule may become impossible and, therefore, demotivating when no allowance is made for work or family commitments.

On the other hand, most people have a reasonable idea of where they will need to be next week. Sessions can then be planned around your availability to train. For example, a rest day can be scheduled for a day when your commitments preclude any time to train, and a session can be split across the morning and evening rather than in one big block. In this way, you stand the best chance of completing the training schedule because it fits in with everything else you have to do. Whether you write your training plan or your coach does, make sure your schedule contains enough sessions and enough rest to achieve your race goals.

FITTING TRAINING INTO WORK

GET UP EARLIER

You need sleep; sleep deprivation helps no one. Getting up earlier may mean you need to go to bed earlier. You can work out how much sleep you need by monitoring your sleep requirements over a month and averaging the sleep you get. That will give a crude estimate of the target amount you should be aiming for each night. If you need seven hours and wish to get up at 5 a.m., you need to be asleep by 10 p.m., which may mean being in bed by 9.45 p.m. to allow yourself time to settle down. A 5 a.m. start may allow you a couple of hours' training before having to head off to work.

If you need to make radical changes to your sleep pattern, take it slowly. Rather than set the alarm on day one for 5 a.m. when you are used to getting up at 7.30 a.m., build up to it, with progressively earlier alarm calls over a period of several weeks. Spend a week getting up at 7.00 a.m., then move it back to 6.45 a.m., 6.30 a.m. and so on until you get to your desired wake-up time. The advantage of early starts is that most people are not up and around and, therefore, you are unlikely to be distracted by phone calls and emails. The disadvantage is that very demanding sessions may be more difficult to complete compared to the same session later in the day. Going from sleep to Level 7 (discussed in Chapter 5 on Fitness) within 30 minutes is a challenge.

PLAN AHEAD

If you have to attend a meeting somewhere other than your usual place of work, can you ride there? The ride to and from the meeting may provide a bonus opportunity to train. Colleagues will often be supportive, sometimes even locating meetings at places that enable you to fit in your training. If staying away for a few days, take your bike with you. Spend a few moments before departure planning routes that fit in with your training schedule and download these to your bike computer or mobile phone. It is often easier to train away from home, as fewer of the usual tasks or duties need to be done in the morning prior to starting work.

>>It is all about planning.>>

Do not rely on hotel leisure facilities for adequate equipment. The quality tends to be hugely variable and almost none of it fit for ultra-distance purposes. The riding position of gym bikes is often unsuitable, with too little adjustment and the data provided from the device inadequate for proper sessions (the power output measurement may not be properly calibrated and often there is no ability to create lap times or show lap power output).

GETTING CLEAN

If planning to cycle to a meeting or place of work, be aware that the venue at your destination may not have showering facilities. The prospect of sitting in a meeting, sweaty and probably smelly, is not pleasant for you, or those around you. There are a couple of solutions. The first is to find a leisure centre or a health club nearby. Public leisure facilities will allow you to use their changing facilities at either no cost or a modest fee. All it takes is five minutes on the internet to establish what is available and a phone call to check whether you can use the facilities.

Have a 'bike wash kit' prepared and ready to go for such training opportunities. Use travel-sized toiletries to minimise what you need to carry. Take a microfibre sports towel. These pack incredibly small and, while perhaps a less satisfying drying experience than using a full-sized luxuriant cotton towel, they do the job just fine. Buy a set of clothes that pack

right down – mountaineering clothing is particularly suitable. The advantage of clothing designed for the outdoors is that it can act as an emergency layer in the event you get cold or have to stop due to a mechanical problem, thus reducing the need to carry spare cycling kit and a change of clothes. Some companies manufacture shoes specifically designed to pack small for travel purposes. The result of this is that you need not be laden down with luggage. It is possible to fit a complete change of clothes, wash kit and towel into a saddle bag or pannier top bag.

The second option is 'dry showers' – liquid products you rub on your body to clean yourself. They work primarily due to the rubbing action of the fabric of the cloth or towel used against the skin.

HAVE A CREED

Having a simple creed to guide the decisions you take about training can be very helpful. It enables you to make the right decisions about what to do and when. An example of a creed might be as follows.

Principle	Meaning
Stay married/together	If what you are about to do is going to place an unreasonable strain on your relationship, do not do it. Nothing is worth the breakdown of your relationship.
Work first	Going to work pays the bills. Sometimes things happen at work that mean training has to be abandoned. That is just the way it is. Assuming you have explored every option that would allow you to fit in a training session, and this has simply proved impossible, miss the session. Having a job makes our hobbies possible. Being fired severely compromises what we can do.
Leave no stone unturned	A useful principle for encouraging you to look at every aspect of your performance to find opportunities for improvement, or to find additional ways in which training can be squeezed into your schedule.
There is always 10% more	The human body has an incredible capacity for work. Whenever you think you cannot achieve the aim of the session, remind yourself that there is always 10 per cent in reserve; you will endlessly surprise yourself with what you can do.
It is not worth dying for	Carried away by circumstances, occasionally you can find yourself taking undue risk; whether that be pushing the limits on a descent, carrying on riding when massively sleep-deprived, or running the gauntlet of heavy traffic. It is useful to remind yourself that this is just a hobby and not worth dying for. The consequences for your family and friends do not justify the extra 1kph on a descent or getting through a town 30 seconds faster.

You can have whatever principles you wish. Keep them to just a few easy-to-remember key points that work for you. Remember, a principle is nothing unless it is applied.

IT IS EXPENSIVE!

There is an overwhelming range of equipment upon which you can spend your hard-earned money to help achieve your ultra-distance goals. Many products promise significant gains in speed, but at what price? On what else should your money be spent? How often will you get the benefit from the equipment?

Ultra-distance racing is expensive. There are only a relatively small number of races across the world when compared to shorter-distance races. This means that participation will involve the race entry fee; mileage to and from the airport; flights, plus any extra costs for bike transport; transfers/taxi/car rental; accommodation, meals and the almost inevitable panic purchase of things you do not really need. This is in addition to all of your training costs. As a result, it can be useful to tie a race into a family holiday. Ideally, the race should take place at the start of the holiday, allowing you time to relax and recover, freed from pre-race nerves, a controlled diet and the need to get lots of sleep. Choosing which race to enter therefore becomes a family decision.

TRAIN ON HOLIDAY

RIDING TO AND FROM THE DESTINATION

One technique that is very useful – provided it works for all – is to ride while your partner drives. This is useful for holiday destinations within rideable distance. For example, a weekend away could mean leaving work on Friday lunchtime and cycling to the destination. You can then leave mid-afternoon on Sunday, a few hours before your partner departs, arriving home a few hours after they get there. In extremis, an overnight training ride can fit well with such arrangements, leaving after work on a Friday and riding through the night to the destination. Just be prepared to be sleep-deprived on the Saturday, with all that entails.

HOLIDAYS FURTHER AFIELD

If you have trained yourself to get up and ride early, the same technique can be used on holiday. An early start involving two to three hours of training need not disrupt holiday activities too

LIKE PIECES OF A JIGSAW – AN ANECDOTE FROM JULIAN

The late afternoon sun bathed Exmoor in a luxuriant light that accentuated the features of the landscape around me: 325km done. Just another 100km to go and I would join my wife, daughter and some friends for dinner in a local restaurant. I had left at the crack of dawn, leaving them asleep at home. The car was packed and later that morning they would leave for Cornwall. Our paths would cross in Exeter for a quick coffee together before we both continued our respective routes South-West. Later in the week we drove to West Wales to see some relatives, and a day or two later I was once again up before the birds, heading the 325km home on my bike. As I rode across the old Severn Bridge, my wife and daughter drove across the new Severn Bridge. Arriving home sweaty, tired and hungry, I fell into a plate of food as we swapped stories of our respective journeys. This has been my life for years. My colleagues tolerate my obsession and meetings are held in places I can get to by bike and have a shower before we start. The key is fitting the exercise into everyday activities in a way that allows you to integrate normality as much as possible.

much. Out at 6 a.m. and back by 8 a.m., ready for a relaxed breakfast and whatever is planned for the day can meet everyone's needs.

SUMMARY

Ultra-distance is a way of life. It's about choices and compromises. Very few ultra-distance cyclists are professional athletes, which means that life requires constant juggling of the demands of family, work, training and racing. Getting the balance right means working out what's important, doing those things, and avoiding the distractions. Easy to say, hard to do. Be aware of the price you are paying in choosing to do what you do, and ask yourself if it's worth it. The amount of training you will have to do, as well as the racing, means that you need the support and cooperation of those around you. Spend some time working out what is acceptable to all to enable you to have a rewarding and fulfilling ultra-distance career.

CHAPTER 3:
DIET AND HYDRATION

Eat and drink your way to success. The demands of training and racing require a disciplined approach to how you fuel yourself for performance and recovery.

DOMINIC'S ELECTROLYTES EXPERIENCE

If there is one thing that has plagued my performance more than any other, it is getting the electrolyte balance right. (An electrolyte is a substance that carries electrical charge, such as sodium (also known as Na+). The unequal distribution of charge throughout the body's cellular environment allows the production of concentration gradients that give the body control over the location and movement of key substances such as water and energy.) In almost every race I have ever entered, at some point I have found myself unwell. I first experienced it during the Race Across the Alps where, as a consequence of having been sick halfway through the race and, consequently, feeling unable to eat very much, I rode for over 12 hours eating little more than a handful of boiled sweets. I didn't know it at the time but it was caused by simply not having sufficient electrolytes. My first attempt at the UK End-to-End almost came to a premature end after little more than 12 hours when, once again, I found myself struggling to ride, and vomited. This was rectified by restoring the electrolyte balance. After this, despite undertaking analysis of my sweat and managing my in-ride electrolytes intake much, much more carefully, I still find myself feeling unwell during races. The difference is that I have learned to spot the early signs and to adjust my electrolyte intake until I feel fine again. Sometimes this means a little less, sometimes a little more. While in theory I know how much salt is excreted in my sweat, this does not accurately translate into real-world performance, and I find I need to fine-tune the amounts on the go. What is overwhelmingly clear is that you get electrolytes wrong at your peril.

Dominic

ULTRA-DISTANCE NUTRITION

Many believe that cycling success is dictated by natural talent (i.e. genetics) and the amount and type of training completed. These factors are undoubtedly important; they determine the size of the engine that will drive the bike forward. However, engines do not function without fuel.

The fuel that we consider in this chapter comprises the food and drink that you consume during discrete time phases pre-ride, in-ride and post-ride. The optimal function of your cycling 'engine' will depend upon getting your 'fuelling' just right in each of these phases.

Finding the best nutrition strategy is difficult; the demands of athletic training and competition only increase the challenge. All cyclists have dietary needs that are specific to their body size, composition and physiology, and to their cycling discipline. While relatively

short cycling disciplines such as BMX and track sprinting present novel challenges because of their reliance on anaerobic energy supply, they present no physical barriers to food and drink intake because of their short duration. In contrast, ultra-distance cyclists are, by definition, in the saddle for a long time, making it virtually impossible to eat large, complex meals.

As an ultra-distance cyclist, you need a good understanding of the nutrition demands of endurance sport. Many of the general principles of sports nutrition are applicable here, for example, considering both your macronutrient (carbohydrate, protein and fat) needs and your micronutrient (everything else!) needs. A vast amount of information is available on this topic but it's important to remember that much of this information has been derived from non-ultra-distance research. Many standard recommendations will be appropriate, but some will not.

This chapter combines diet and hydration information derived from academic research with advice from the authors' experiences of ultra-distance cycling. There is, however, no substitute for trying it all out yourself, during training and non-priority races. While some riders will happily tolerate energy bars for breakfast, lunch and dinner, others will feel nauseous after two mouthfuls. For the ultra-distance cyclist, palatability is as important as the scientific complexities of the event's nutritional demands. Sports foods are all well and good when the sun is shining and you've been on the road for two hours. However, when riding over a mountain top in freezing mist at 4 a.m. after 24 hours of pedalling, all you really want may be a bowl of hot porridge!

REAL FOOD FOR REAL PEOPLE

Cycling literature is awash with recommendations about how many grams of this and how many millilitres of that should be consumed for optimal training and racing performance. This is fine if you have your scales with you at all times, as well as constant access to just the right foods and supplements. Chances are, however, that this is not the case as you juggle the demands of a busy family life with those of a busy work life. A business trip to the next county might make it difficult to find your preferred carbohydrate options, while a business trip overseas could mean that you simply struggle to find enough calories, especially if you are vegetarian or vegan.

It is a good idea, therefore, to keep your nutrition options open. If your training nutrition is based on real food, there is a good chance that you will be able to maintain an appropriate balance of key nutrients even when you're 1,500km away from the nearest sports nutrition outlet. Variety is the spice of life. Try to ensure that while your ultra-distance cycling nutrition is underpinned by science, it is delivered by a range of foods that will, more often than not, give you a boost rather than a grimace.

FOOD FOR HEROES

Have you eaten kale this week? Blueberries? Chia seeds? All in the belief that they are 'superfoods' and so they must be doing us some good. Over the last few years, the term 'superfood' has become a staple in our vocabulary; it refers to those foods identified as being extremely high in a particular nutrient thought to have a positive benefit on our health and performance. Celebrity endorsements and media claims lead us to believe that such items exist. But is it all just hype – a marketing ploy – or is there some truth to the claims?

Research evidence to support the idea of superfoods is very limited; it is, unsurprisingly, nigh on impossible to demonstrate that one specific food item can transform your health. As a nutritional professional, regulated by a governing body, all advice I provide needs to be evidence-based. So from that perspective a superfood cannot exist – no individual food item is really able to provide all the components you need for a healthy diet. Indeed, the whole drive towards a superfood provides false hope: eating a punnet of blueberries can't offset that burger you chose to have at lunchtime.

That said, I do believe that individuals should aim to eat a 'superdiet' – one high in foods that, when combined, provide a diet rich in nutrients that optimise good health. A cheeky burger no longer needs to be a guilty secret. No food should be off limits, but moderation, being mindful of choice and portion size, is key for those wanting to follow a 'superdiet'.

No matter who you are – elite, amateur or recreational athlete – the key is to tailor your nutritional intake to your training, lifestyle, family commitments and budget. Many of the so-called superfoods on the market are costly; you need to eat an awful lot of kale to get the rich nutritional value quoted for health benefits. Throughout this chapter you will instead find a number of 'hero foods' – foods that are affordable and attainable, that provide a big nutritional punch, and that should be on every cyclist's shopping list.

Renee McGregor, registered sports and eating disorder specialist dietitian/nutritionist

STAY FUELLED

Ultra-distance cycling requires a lot of energy, which can be provided by carbohydrates, fats and/or proteins. Sometimes this energy is stored up for later use. At other times it is needed 'right now'. Ultra-distance cycling, as with any athletic training, also requires the raw materials to repair damage to the body and to build new muscle and connective tissues. The main such raw material is protein.

This means that there are some key questions to answer. For example, how much energy and protein do you need? When is the best time to consume it? A good way to think about all of this is to consider your food and drink requirements in three key periods: pre-ride, in-ride and post-ride.

STAY FUELLED: PRE-RIDE

Performance improvement doesn't occur only when you are on the bike. Many cyclists are now aware that recovery is just as important as turning the pedals, but few give serious thought to what they do before getting on the bike.

Good preparation for training and racing is, of course, essential, but have you really optimised your preparation routine? A major part of your preparation will revolve around the food you eat. A good pre-ride nutrition strategy can make a ride feel easy, while a bad strategy can make it feel difficult or just plain impossible!

Your main aim prior to a competition will be to maximise your body's carbohydrate stores, as carbohydrate will be the most important fuel during the event. This necessitates some form of carbohydrate loading, with loading protocols lasting anywhere between one day and one week. Standard loading protocols require an exhaustive training session several days prior to an event in order to deplete the body's carbohydrate stores. This is followed by several days of very high carbohydrate food intake, which causes the body to 'super-compensate', storing higher than normal levels of carbohydrate in preparation for the possibility of another period of carbohydrate starvation. Such loading protocols can, however, cause gastrointestinal distress, the symptoms of which might include stomach cramps, nausea, bloating, vomiting and diarrhoea.

> > Despite being an ultra-distance cyclist, none of your training sessions will last for more than an hour. > >

The good news is that more moderate approaches appear to stock up carbohydrate stores to a level almost as high as the radical loading protocols. In order to maintain quality training and to limit gastrointestinal problems, a gradual increase in carbohydrate intake, accompanied by a gradual tapering of training in the week leading up to competition, results in a compromise that is more manageable for most riders.

Simply stocking up on carbohydrates with a large carbohydrate meal three to four hours prior to your event can also have a big positive impact on your performance. Three to four hours is required to allow time for the carbohydrate to be absorbed into your blood and muscles and for you to get rid of the waste. Any closer to the event and you risk gastrointestinal distress and, therefore, reduced performance.

Careful planning of your pre-ride nutrition strategy is, therefore, required. Eating a big meal four hours prior to an event that starts at midday is not a problem, but doing the same for an event that starts at 7 a.m. probably will be. Try some different strategies in your training. Some cyclists will need four hours between meal and event while others will have no trouble with a

HERO FOOD: SWEET POTATO

Sweet potato has taken the space of the humble white potato in many an athlete's food box due to its high beta-carotene antioxidant content and because it is a great source of complex carbohydrate and, therefore, slow-release energy. All of this makes the sweet potato an ideal fuel option pre-, in- and post-ride. They are great when added to a risotto for a pre-endurance training meal, or when baked and served with oily fish as a recovery meal. They can be added to salads or used to make soups for lunchtime options, helping to prevent the 4 p.m. sugar slump. Some riders even make them into wedges, add salt and take them out on long training rides.

meal taken two hours before the start gun.

Despite being an ultra-distance cyclist, many of your training sessions will last for no more than one hour. For such sessions, there is little or no benefit in consuming carbohydrate during the ride. By the time such carbohydrate has become available to the muscles you will be in the shower. For such sessions, it is far more important that you get the pre-ride fuelling just right.

>> During training you may burn 500–800 calories per hour, with most coming from your body's carbohydrate stores. >>

STAY FUELLED: IN-RIDE

Your pre-ride nutrition strategy should put you on the start line with a full store of carbohydrate. As soon as you start riding, this store will begin to deplete, with the rate of depletion being dependent on how hard you are riding. You therefore need to keep your carbohydrate stores topped up. These top-ups will spare your reserves for times of real need and help to maintain high concentrations of glucose (the most important form of carbohydrate in the body) in the blood. The supply of glucose in the blood needs to be kept high in order for your muscles to use carbohydrate at an optimal rate.

During training you may burn 500–800 calories per hour, with most coming from your body's carbohydrate stores. Good in-ride nutrition means that you work hard to replace these calories as you ride but, try as you might, it will never be possible to replace all the calories when you are working this hard for ultra-durations. Depletion simply happens more quickly than replenishment. Don't, therefore, try to force too many carbohydrate calories back in; if you do, gastrointestinal upset is likely.

HERO FOOD: OATS

We've all been told, time and again, that porridge is the best start to the day. It is low in fat, high in soluble fibre, as well as being a great source of complex carbohydrate. This means that it releases energy slowly throughout the day, preventing blood-sugar fluctuations and energy crashes. Of course, oats don't have to be eaten as porridge. You can enjoy them cold in the form of Birchers, standard muesli or oaty pancakes. If you are not a morning oat person, you could have oatcakes or even make your own energy bars to eat as a pre- or in-ride snack. Whichever way, oats should definitely be in your food box for long endurance training rides.

Accepting that you have to slow down a little as your carbohydrate stores run low will often be better than having to stop to deal with stomach cramps and nausea simply because you have tried to overdo your in-ride calorie intake.

How many carbs do you need to carry?

Consuming carbohydrate while racing is clearly a good thing. But just how much should you have in your musette? The highest rates of carbohydrate oxidation occur with a consumption rate of 72g of carbohydrate per hour. In real money this is approximately three energy gels, one litre of sports drink or three bananas. Where sessions continue for more than an hour, intake of 60–70g of carbohydrate per hour is recommended. A four-hour training ride will therefore require consumption and, perhaps more importantly, carrying of 12 bananas! While simple, this plan will certainly lose palatability as you enter hour three, and so you need to carefully plan a combination of foods that will deliver the required amount of carbohydrate, palatability and portability.

WHAT'S IN A MUSETTE?

Charlie Mitchell, an ultra-distance rider who partnered Dominic in his successful End-to-End challenge, has in his musette enough food for two to three hours of riding. This might include a sandwich containing either cheese and ham or peanut butter, providing slow-release energy and protein. In addition, he will have a small portion of sweets, particular favourites being Liquorice Allsorts and Jelly Babies. These provide fast-release energy. Finally, there may be a cube or two of fruit or Christmas cake – the fruit, icing and sugar content providing an instant boost as well as tasting delicious. Each portion will last 20–40 minutes. In addition to the food will be a bottle of flavoured water mixed with an appropriate amount of electrolyte.

>>In practical terms, the glycaemic index translates into consuming a range of food on the bike.>>

You may not even need to swallow carbohydrate for it to have a positive influence on your performance. Research evidence suggests that simply rinsing a carbohydrate solution around the mouth stimulates receptors to activate brain areas that cause feelings of pleasure and reward. This reduces your perception of effort, making your ride feel easier. Much of the research support for carbohydrate mouth-rinsing is based on relatively short bouts (e.g. one hour) of cycling exercise. However, it could also be particularly helpful for those ultra-distance cyclists who have difficulty maintaining the high levels of carbohydrate intake suggested above for long periods without experiencing feelings of nausea.

Food choice?

In many ways it does not matter where your carbohydrate comes from, as long as you are consuming enough of it to fuel muscular contraction and, therefore, forward motion, at the highest possible rate. There are, however, some key issues to consider when deciding what goes in your food box, your musette and your fridge, such as glycaemic index, weight (how heavy it is to carry on your bike) and palatability.

The glycaemic index (GI) is a measure of how quickly an ingested carbohydrate is absorbed into the blood. The GI rates foods on a scale of 0–100, where 100 is equivalent to the blood-sugar response following ingestion of glucose (i.e. pure sugar). A high GI food will cause your blood-sugar levels to rise more quickly than a low GI food. A simplistic reading might suggest that low GI foods are preferable to high GI foods on health grounds, given that they impose a lesser disturbance to the cellular environment. Low GI

foods might also be preferable during training and competition as they 'release' carbohydrate more slowly. Don't be fooled, however, by the apparent simplicity of GI: chocolate cake has a lower GI than watermelon and parsnips, a clear indication that GI is not a straightforward index of food 'health'. In addition, there are many times when, despite your ultra-distance credentials, you will need a quick (high GI) carbohydrate boost during training and competition, such as is obtained through gels, sweets and biscuits.

In practical terms, the glycaemic index translates into consuming a range of food on the bike. A sandwich made with wholemeal bread and filled with cheese or mashed banana provides some slow-release energy. A handful of sweets provides an instant hit of energy. By mixing up the range of food, you can match what you consume with how you feel. If you are feeling a bit flat and lacking energy, the kick of a few sweets can get you going again. This can be followed up with a sandwich to provide a more sustained slow release of energy. The key thing is that the food is something you want to eat. By choosing 'normal' food that you are used to eating day in, day out, you can have confidence you will be able to consume it, and if you make sure it's food you like, it's something to look forward to as well. Just as we don't consume energy bars for most meals when off the bike, avoid making them your 'on the bike' staple. They can be a helpful addition to your diet but they should not be your only source of energy. Mix and match.

Containing macronutrients (typically carbohydrate and/or protein), micronutrients (e.g. electrolytes) and water, sports drinks allow you to keep fuel depletion, dehydration and cramp at bay. They,

> **»Post-ride fuel intake is just as important as pre- and in-ride fuel intake.»**

therefore, appear to be the perfect nutrition solution for the ultra-distance cyclist. However, the volume of fluid required – sometimes in excess of two litres per hour – often causes gastrointestinal discomfort and, just as importantly, is heavy. In a training situation, extra weight is great as it provides extra resistance for you to work against. But in a race situation you need to minimise every bit of resistance you can to go as fast as possible. Sports bars or energy gels contain concentrated carbohydrate, weigh less than many 'normal' foodstuffs and limit the amount of material that is moving around in the stomach. They are, however, very sweet and can quickly become unpalatable.

Every in-ride nutrition option has its relative strengths and weaknesses, which will themselves be different for every rider. In all likelihood, a combination of sports drinks, sports bars, energy gels and real food will provide the best solution. The trick is to practise with different strategies during training. It's probably not a good idea to hoard all of your shiny, vacuum packed *CycleFast* products for your focus race, only to realise, 20km in, that you abhor banoffee-flavoured goo!

STAY FUELLED: POST-RIDE

The causal link between pre-ride/in-ride food intake and performance is short. If you don't take in enough fuel during one or both of these key periods you will know about it very quickly as you begin to wonder why you can no longer hold your training partner's wheel, why you are dreaming about chocolate bars, and why your speed is dropping to single figures!

Post-ride fuel intake is just as important as pre- and in-ride fuel intake. The difference is that the causal link here is a bit longer, making it easy to ignore good nutrition post-ride. You won't notice the negative effects of poor post-ride nutrition until subsequent training sessions, by which time you will be attributing a weaker than expected performance to the weather, a bad night's sleep, a bad training programme – in short, everything but your poor post-ride nutrition.

There are two essential elements to the training response: (1) stress and (2) recovery. Your training sessions are designed to cause stress on and, therefore, damage to, your body's tissues (e.g. muscles). Continued training causes continued damage. Recovery time is essential to allow the body to respond to this stress, replacing damaged tissues and, crucially, developing more effective tissues (e.g. stronger and/or more efficient muscles) to ensure that the same level of stress will not cause damage in the future.

Post-ride protein intake

Protein is particularly important during the post-ride recovery phase, as its component parts – amino acids – constitute the building blocks of body tissues (muscles, etc.). Irrespective of the amount of recovery time given, without protein your muscles will not bounce back from the damage caused during training. Instead of training-induced improvement occurring, fitness and performance will actually decline.

Optimal recovery and adaptation to training requires a daily protein intake of 1.2–1.8 grams per kilogram of body mass (i.e. 96–144 grams for an 80kg rider). The top of this range is usually reserved for those cyclists actively seeking to increase muscle mass (e.g. track sprinters), with endurance cyclists typically falling in the low to middle part of the range. This will be the case for much of your year but, as an ultra-distance cyclist, your protein needs may, at times, approach the top of the range. After several hours of riding your body's carbohydrate stores will be running down. As such, your body will start to use protein and fat as alternative fuel sources. A typical endurance cyclist may start to

dip into this reserve from time to time; however, as an ultra-distance cyclist, you may dip into these reserves on a regular basis. It is, therefore, a good idea to increase your protein intake following very long training rides and races.

Despite the need to increase your protein intake occasionally, a balanced diet should, for the most part, allow you to meet your

HERO FOOD: EGGS

They may be small, but eggs really pack a punch when it comes to nutritional value. Two medium eggs provide you with around 15g of protein and 100 per cent of your daily requirement of Vitamin B12, which is essential for the formation of red blood cells. Eggs are also packed with selenium, a powerful antioxidant. Many people avoid them due to cholesterol concern but, in reality, a medium egg contains only 4.6g of fat, of which only 1.3g comes from saturated fat. Studies have also shown that individuals who consume two eggs for breakfast every morning eat 300 fewer calories through the rest of the day, making eggs a really good start on low-intensity or rest days!

HERO FOOD: GREEK YOGHURT

Yoghurt is a great recovery option. Fat-free Greek yoghurt is particularly helpful due to its very high protein content. Most natural Greek yoghurt provides 10g of protein per 100g serving, double the amount found in standard yoghurts. Greek yoghurt is an ideal choice due to its versatility; it can be mixed into fruit, added to smoothies and eaten with cereal such as muesli or granola. It can even be used as a base for a more decadent dessert, meaning you can enjoy your pudding guilt-free, knowing that it is also the perfect recovery food!

protein requirements without the need for supplementation. A 'normal' diet of three meals and the odd snack will comfortably place you in the middle of the recommended protein intake range. For example, a breakfast of cereal, milk and toast; a yogurt snack; a lunch of two chicken sandwiches and a milkshake; a cereal bar snack; and a dinner of beef stir-fry would comfortably provide you with ~110 grams of protein.

In the post-ride phase, the resynthesis of protein within the body appears to peak with a protein intake of 20–30 grams. Dairy and whey protein appear to be the most effective forms of post-ride protein, but there is also evidence to suggest that protein resynthesis levels increase when protein is consumed alongside carbohydrate. This is really good news as you start to prepare for your next training session.

Post-ride carbohydrate intake

As well as using proteins to provide the raw materials to adapt to your training, you also need to refill the tank so that you are fully fuelled in readiness for the next training session. A carbohydrate-rich diet will help you achieve this, particularly when combined with two key strategies.

Start replenishing your carbohydrate stores within the 'golden hour', i.e. the hour immediately after completing your ride. Immediately post-exercise, metabolic pathways within your body are fully primed to take up and store carbohydrate. Over time these pathways begin to shut down, with the result that carbohydrate storage becomes less and less effective. The rate at which glycogen (the storage

>>All chemical reactions in the body take place in an aqueous environment, so without water you won't be pedalling anywhere.>>

form of carbohydrate) is replenished is 50 per cent lower if you wait two hours post-ride before consuming carbohydrate. Carbohydrate intake in the first 15 minutes post-exercise is most effective, but this can be challenging because of the need to stow gear and change. You may also have no appetite at this stage, which is where sports drinks and shakes can be really helpful. Just throw it down as if it's part of your training session. Aim for an intake of 1–1.2 grams of carbohydrate per kg of body mass per hour for the four hours post-ride, starting in the first 15 minutes if possible. An example of a meal along these lines is poached eggs on toast.

STAY HYDRATED

Approximately 60 per cent of your body is water. Nearly all of the major systems in your body depend on water. Water helps dissolve minerals and essential nutrients and, being the main component of blood, it carries these nutrients to your cells. Water lubricates joints, protects organs and tissues, helps eliminate waste and regulates body temperature. All chemical reactions in the body take place in an aqueous environment, so without water you won't be pedalling anywhere.

Water also plays a key role in body temperature regulation. When you exercise, you start to create excess heat that must be removed. Sweating provides the most effective way to do this; however, in doing so, it means that you lose water. Performance begins to decline with just a two per cent drop in body mass due to sweating. With fluid losses equating to a 5 per cent drop in body mass (4kg for an 80kg rider) you will be at risk of heat exhaustion and at a ten per cent drop, heat stroke and death become very real possibilities.

HOW HYDRATED ARE YOU?

As well as being helpful for weight management, daily weighing can help you to stay hydrated. Sudden drops in body mass (e.g. a 1kg drop in 24 hours) are often due to dehydration and so provide a quick indication of the need to increase your fluid intake. A simple estimate of hydration status can also be achieved regularly through observing urine colour at the start of the day. A pale light yellow colour indicates good hydration, whereas a darker yellow/light brown colour indicates dehydration.

STAY HYDRATED: PRE-RIDE

Regular monitoring of your hydration status should mean that pre-ride crash hydration courses are not necessary. On a daily basis, two to three litres of fluid intake should allow you to maintain adequate hydration levels.

In the pre-ride phase, aim to drink 500ml (approximately one bottle) of fluid two to three hours prior to the session. This will allow time for fluid to be absorbed into the body and for any excess to be expelled. Isotonic sport drinks, i.e. solutions with the same salt concentrations as your cells and blood, will allow you to ensure optimal hydration and to top up on fuel reserves. For very long distance rides, particularly on hot days, you might consume a hypertonic solution, i.e. a solution with higher levels of salt and carbohydrate than is found in the body. This will stimulate thirst and promote fluid retention, resulting in hyperhydration, which could come in handy when you really don't feel like drinking yet another bottle of sugary water in hour 14 of your ride.

STAY HYDRATED: IN-RIDE

Feelings of thirst start to kick in when your body weight drops by ~2 per cent, i.e. at the point where dehydration first starts to reduce your performance. It is vital, therefore, that you start drinking early in your ride, not waiting until you feel thirsty. Most riders lose in the range of 500–1,000ml fluid per hour, which can be replaced by consuming two or three mouthfuls of fluid every 10–15 minutes.

You can check exactly how much fluid replacement you need by completing a 60-minute sweat test. Weigh yourself in the nude immediately prior to riding for 60 minutes at ultra-race pace without consuming any food or drink. On completion, remove all clothes, towel yourself dry and reweigh yourself. The difference in grams between pre- and post-ride measurements will equate to your total fluid loss in millilitres. The result will of course be affected by a number of factors, not least the weather

conditions. Nevertheless, the sweat test will give you a good indication of how much fluid you need to take on during training and racing.

Your in-ride fluid intake strategy can deliver three things: water, electrolytes and energy. For short rides of an hour or less, plain water will be fine, though a bit of flavouring does aid palatability. For rides any longer than an hour you will need to add some electrolytes to your drinks. Electrolytes – the key ones being sodium and potassium – are salts essential for normal cellular function. Most sports drinks now contain an appropriate combination of electrolytes, but you can add electrolyte tablets to plain water if you are trying to reduce calorie intake. In most cases, however, taking on extra calories in fluid form is a helpful way to meet your in-ride calorie needs. A bottle of sports drink mixed at 6 per cent dilution will typically provide about half of your hourly energy requirement.

>> Hyponatraemia can cause changes in cognitive functioning which might reduce cycling performance, and, in serious cases, causes brain swelling and seizures. >>

LOW MAINTENANCE ULTRA-HYDRATION TIPS

Sports drinks suffer from the same problem as sports bars and gels; the sweet sickly taste can pall after a while. Purchasing pure electrolyte salts enables you to add them to any drink you like. For example, you can blend orange juice and water to the concentration you prefer and then add the right amount of salt. You can add the salts to cold tea, plain water, or to water with a dash of your favourite cordial. Because you are using pure salt, only a small amount is needed (roughly a quarter of a teaspoon per 500ml). Using a small pot and carrying an appropriate-sized measuring spoon can save having to weigh the salts each time. These can be carried on long rides, ready whenever you need to replenish your water bottles.

If you are really struggling to find the energy, pour some Coca-Cola or its equivalent into your water bottle, leaving the nipple open to allow the gas to escape. Ride with it on your bike for a short while to allow it to go flat. The huge amount of sugar and caffeine in Coca-Cola or its equivalent provides an energy kick. Ensure it has had a chance to go flat if adding salts, as these will react with the product, resulting in it bubbling up and out of the bottle, covering the bottle and your bike in a sticky residue. This should be a last resort as it can be messy, sticky and the sugar spike, while helpful, can create problems later.

TOO MUCH FLUID?

For many years sports scientists have recommended high levels of fluid intake to counteract the dangers of dehydration. It is, however, possible to consume too much fluid, resulting in a condition called exercise-associated hyponatraemia, an abnormally low level of sodium in the blood. By increasing blood volume, excessive water intake can dilute pre-existing levels of sodium. Hyponatraemia can cause changes in cognitive functioning, which might reduce cycling performance, and, in serious cases, causes brain swelling and seizures. The main sign to look out for is bloating, often manifesting as puffiness at the feet and ankles and under tight-fitting items like shorts and watches. Don't force yourself to 'overdrink'!

STAY HYDRATED: POST-RIDE

In order to replace lost fluids in the post-ride phase you need to consume more fluid than you have lost. Therefore, you should aim to consume 1.5 litres of fluid for every litre that you have lost. At this point the need for additional carbohydrate will be reduced, but you will still need to include electrolytes. As described above, at this point you might also look to include protein in your post-ride fluid strategy.

SUPPLEMENTS: THE MISSING INGREDIENTS?

A balanced diet will, for the most part, provide even the ultra-distance cyclist with all the ingredients needed for good health and high performance. Finding this balance is, of course, easier said than done, particularly if you have to significantly increase your calorie intake to provide sufficient energy to fuel the ultra-distance elements of your training programme. Of course, a diet can be balanced through a near-infinite combination of different food and drink options, with many opportunities for better ultra-distance-focused decisions! As well as balancing your macronutrient intake in the ways described in the pre-ride, in-ride and post-ride sections above, there are a number of micronutrient-related diet choices that may improve your training and racing performance.

A vast number of nutritional supplements are marketed with claims of ergogenic (i.e. performance enhancing) properties. In most cases, however, there is very little research evidence to support their use. Of the small number that have received scientific support, several popular nutritional supplements are unlikely to be useful for the ultra-distance cyclist. Creatine, for example, is likely to be most useful for athletes seeking to increase muscle mass and for those engaged in high-volume, high-intensity training. There is no evidence to support the use of creatine in ultra-distance sports. Other supplements, such as alanine and citrate, have also been shown to be beneficial for those engaged in high-intensity exercise. Although it is unlikely that such supplements will improve ultra-distance race performance, they may still have a role to play during training. As discussed in Chapter 5: Fitness, even the ultra-distance cyclist will benefit from some high-intensity training. While this section mainly focuses on 'endurance' supplements, one such 'high-intensity' supplement – sodium bicarbonate – is included.

>>Research has shown caffeine to be effective in improving performance over a wide range of durations.>>

CAFFEINE

As much as 90 per cent of the world's adult population consumes dietary caffeine on a daily basis. It has been a staple of the cyclist's supplement regimen for many years, with coffee being the number one beverage choice for many. Until 2003, the ergogenic effect of caffeine was confirmed by the fact that it was named on the World Anti-Doping Agency's prohibited substances list. That it has since been removed from the list reflects the challenge of regulating what is a normal dietary constituent, rather than suggesting that the effectiveness of caffeine has diminished.

Research has shown caffeine to be effective in improving performance over a wide range of durations, from very short, high-intensity efforts, up to and including long endurance rides. Caffeine also improves cognitive performance, for example by improving decision-making when fatigued.

The variety of effects means that there are likely to be a variety of mechanisms for caffeine's action. By increasing fat use, caffeine may spare stored carbohydrate; it may directly stimulate the contractile apparatus of the muscle and/or the central nervous system. Caffeine appears to prevent the interaction of adenosine with the brain, thus reducing feelings of fatigue and sleepiness. Taking caffeine alongside carbohydrate also appears to increase the absorption of carbohydrate: a double boost!

Recommended doses are usually in the range of 3–6mg per kg of body mass; however, performance benefits have occurred in doses as low as 1mg per kg of body mass. Studies have also shown the benefits of supplementation with caffeine-containing drinks such as cola, with endurance performance improving by more than 3 per cent.

SODIUM BICARBONATE AND CITRATE

Alongside caffeine, sodium bicarbonate boasts some of the strongest scientific support for its ability to improve endurance performance. The chemical process that converts the food that you eat into energy that can be used to fuel your muscle fibres produces hydrogen ions. Higher levels of hydrogen ions create more acidic conditions in the body. Alongside other mechanisms, this acidification causes fatigue.

Because of its key role as an extracellular buffer, increased levels of bicarbonate reduce blood acidity. This produces a hydrogen ion concentration gradient between the blood and body cells. As hydrogen ions move down this gradient and out of muscle cells, the acidic cellular environment is eliminated and fatigue is reduced. A dose of 24 grams for an 80kg rider (0.3g per kg of body mass), taken about two hours before a race, has been shown to be most effective. Do try it in training first though, as bicarbonate supplementation can cause nausea and diarrhoea in some riders. Taking it with carbohydrate can help and you should definitely avoid taking it on an empty stomach.

The research evidence suggests that sodium bicarbonate supplementation is most effective in short duration events, although Simon has worked with riders who have seen improvements in races of two hours and more. For true ultra-distance riders, sodium citrate may be a better alternative, particularly if riding in hot conditions. Ninety minutes before exercise, consuming 750ml of fluid with 5–10 grams of sodium citrate alongside sodium chloride (salt) in a 2:1 ratio will allow you to hyperhydrate. This will mean that you start your race or training session with added stores of water, helping you to minimise the health and performance risks of dehydration.

HERO FOOD: BEETROOT

Beetroot juice is one of the rare examples of a supplement that lives up to the hype. The critical ingredient, nitrate, is found in low doses in many foods, with beetroot being a high-dose exception.

During digestion, dietary nitrates are converted first into nitrite and then into nitric oxide. Circulating in the blood, an increased level of nitric oxide has a direct impact on blood vessels and on the mitochondria, the power-houses of the cell.

Beetroot juice in doses of ~0.5 litres has been shown to increase nitric oxide levels, leading to increased blood flow to the working muscles and a decrease in systemic blood pressure. Such supplementation has also been shown to decrease the oxygen cost of exercise and to lower the amount of energy needed for a given muscular contraction. Essentially, beetroot supplementation increases the body's efficiency, leading to a performance improvement similar to that seen following carbohydrate or caffeine ingestion.

A single dose of beetroot juice two to three hours before exercise appears to be just as beneficial as a two-week 'loading' regimen, although, as with any nutritional interventions, you should try this out during normal training to see whether this 'normal' response applies to you. Given that beetroot juice is an acquired taste, it might be very good news if you can benefit from a one-off drink before a key race.

A significant challenge when supplementing with beetroot itself is that the nitrate content is highly varied between vegetables, making it hard to determine how much beetroot you need to eat to get an ergogenic effect. Controlled doses are now available in a range of beetroot juices and even as a beetroot 'shot' if you really need to get the experience over with quickly!

AMINO ACIDS

Protein is an essential constituent of all body tissues. If, therefore, you need to repair or grow (e.g. increase the strength of) any of these tissues, you need protein. Protein is itself made up of a combination of some 20 amino acids. Non-essential amino acids can be synthesised in the body, while essential amino acids must be taken in the diet.

There has been considerable research into the supplementation of amino acids, with particular focus on the branched chain amino acids (BCAA): leucine, isoleucine and valine. Animal research suggests that BCAA supplementation helps to prevent central fatigue. It is believed that the BCAAs block the action of tryptophan, a neurotransmitter that, as its concentration increases, causes feelings of sleepiness and fatigue. The evidence is much less compelling in human studies, but BCAA supplementation could be worth a try during one of your more strenuous endurance training blocks.

Leucine also appears to play a key role in muscle growth. It has been shown to increase muscle growth when taken as a supplement during a resistance-training programme. It is, however, debateable whether this effect is any greater than when simply consuming additional general protein in the diet.

>> For optimal health and performance, the ideal ratio of omega 3 to omega 6 is about 1:1. >>

OMEGA 3 FATTY ACIDS

Omega 3 fatty acids are essential fatty acids; essential because they cannot be produced by the body and so must be consumed in the diet. These fatty acids are particularly important when considering their ratio with another essential fatty acid, omega 6. For optimal health and performance, the ideal ratio of omega 3 to omega 6 is about 1:1. Unfortunately, it is not unusual for many modern diets to result in a ratio of 1:20. We consume too little omega 3 and/ or too much omega 6.

You can increase your omega 3 intake by upping the amount of oily fish (e.g. mackerel, salmon, herring) that you eat or by adding omega 3 supplements to your daily regimen. Shifting the ratio back towards omega 3 results in a positive change in the structure of cell membranes, improved inflammatory signalling and, ultimately, a range of beneficial health responses such as reduced blood pressure and better control of blood glucose.

Although research into omega 3 supplementation is limited, there is evidence to suggest that it could be beneficial for ultra-distance cyclists. It may reduce the symptoms of, or even prevent, exercise-induced asthma and there is also evidence to suggest that omega 3 supplementation improves exercise efficiency by reducing oxygen demand. As with all of the supplements included in this chapter, omega 3 may be worth a try. The worst-case scenario is that it will only improve your health!

PROBIOTICS

Probiotics do not improve sport performance directly. They have, however, become increasingly popular due to their potential for improving health; and, of course, better health gives the opportunity for better performance, even if only by reducing the negative impact of ill health.

Probiotics are live microorganisms. Yoghurt is a great source, but they are also found in Kefir, miso and buttermilk. If consumed regularly (once or twice daily) they make a positive contribution to gut microflora. The many strains of probiotics have the potential to benefit many areas of health; however, the research focus to date has been on the impact on upper respiratory tract infections (URTI). It seems that by supporting the gut microflora, probiotics such as *Lactobacillus fermentum* are able to boost the body's immune system and reduce the incidence of URTI.

COLOSTRUM

As with probiotics, colostrum supplementation is unlikely to provide a direct boost to your ultra-distance cycling performance. Instead, by improving gastrointestinal health it may help your body to deal with periods of heavy ultra-distance training.

During periods of heavy training, blood flow to the gastrointestinal system is reduced as blood is directed to other areas, such as the working muscles. This reduces the system's ability to deal with normal dietary intake, let alone the increased intake that is associated with heavy training. The milk produced by cows in the one to two days after the birth of a calf (i.e. colostrum) contains higher than normal levels of immune factors and hormones associated with good health. Consumption of 10–20g of colostrum per day has been shown to prevent the increase in gut permeability that is associated with exercise-induced gastrointestinal damage.

RACE DAY SUPPLEMENTS

No nutritional supplement should be seen as a magic bullet. It is likely that you will respond more positively to some supplements than others. Indeed, you may benefit most from a combination of supplements at key times in and around key events.

In an ultra-distance event, maintenance of adequate carbohydrate availability becomes the critical nutritional issue. By combining robust pre-ride and in-ride carbohydrate intake strategies with some of the supplements highlighted above – for example, beetroot juice, BCAAs and caffeine – you will be able to maximise the impact of your nutrition strategy throughout your performance.

Having decided that eating normal food was non-negotiable, Dominic and his riding partner Charlie set about working out how to carry it on the bike. In the end it proved remarkably easy. Table 1 provides an indication of the type of things they ate and how they were carried. Everything was carried in a portion that would provide about 30 minutes of energy.

❯❯If there is one food that can always be eaten, it is watermelon.❯❯

Table 1: Food we ate/carried during the lejog successful record attempt

Sandwiches	Made from the small square individual sandwich flatbreads often referred to as 'thins', filled with things like cheese and pickle, peanut butter and jam, honey and banana, and Marmite. Wrapped in foil, these fit neatly into square top tube bags or into jersey pockets.
Fruit cake	Chopped into portion-size chunks, then individually wrapped in foil. These stack well in a top tube bag. Rich in dried fruits and nuts, this is a real winner.
Boiled sweets	A nice break from eating solid food. Popped into the corner of your mouth and allowed to dissolve. Mint flavour contrasts well with other foodstuffs. Buy them ready wrapped and put inside a small plastic bag.
Chocolate-covered brazils	Carried in a small plastic bag, these fit into corners of food bags in the gap left by sandwiches.
Chocolate-covered dates	Carried in a small plastic bag, these fit into corners of food bags in the gap left by sandwiches.
Homemade pizza	Individual slices wrapped in foil. A good savoury contrast to all the sweet stuff. Carried in the same way as sandwiches.
Crystallised ginger	Often put into the same bag as the chocolate brazils, this can help to settle the stomach when needed.
Ginger snaps	Portioned into bags of three biscuits. Carried either in a top tube bag or in jersey pockets.
Cocktail sausages	Meat for the meat eaters, Quorn (or its equivalent) for the vegetarians. A great source of easily eaten protein and a good contrast to all the sweet food. Carried in a small food bag wherever there was space.
Fig rolls	Portioned into bags of three biscuits. Carried either in a top tube bag or jersey pockets.
Liquorice Allsorts	Considered a treat, we had portions of our favourite brand in small bags. A real delight if you like this sort of thing. Because they are small items, they fill gaps left between other items.
Jelly Babies	About eight or 10 per bag. An instant energy boost, but too many could leave you feeling a bit queasy. Because they are small items they fill gaps left between others.
Watermelon	Served from the support car in skin-on wedges. If there is one food that can always be eaten, it is watermelon. Refreshing, light in flavour and easily eaten, it remains our go-to food when we are unable to eat anything else.
Apple	An apple is lovely and refreshing after all the other types of food. Given their bulk and weight, these are best eaten early as they are not the easiest things to carry.
Wedge of lemon	Excellent for refreshing the palate and can be helpful when feeling a bit tired to put a zing into your mouth!
Banana	Difficult to carry too many of these on a bike but if you have a support crew, these are a classic cycling food.
Porridge	If you have a support team, a pot of porridge is a real delight in the middle of the night. Add in raisins or banana for a touch of extra luxury.
Hot food	If the support team can purchase hot food during the ride, such as an omelette sandwich or similar, these can be an unexpected pleasure. Be sure that, whatever you eat, you have tested it before in training.

The thing you will notice about the list above is that almost all of these items are readily available from most food stores. Garages/gas stations are useful places to stop on long rides and will sell most of them. Over time, as you prepare more and more food for bike trips, you will be able to work out quickly the nutritional value of most combinations of foodstuffs, thus enabling you to replenish the bike with appropriate food from almost anywhere. Contrast this with a diet of sports-specific energy bars and gels that are not nearly so readily available.

HOW CAN YOU CARRY ENOUGH FOOD?

One of the things that bemused us in the early days of training for the Land's End to John o'Groats tandem record was that, while understanding the sense in eating normal food (i.e. not just sports bars and gels), the prospect of carrying around a pack of sandwiches in a back pocket seemed faintly ridiculous and impractical. The paradox was that an easily-carried diet of modern sports bars and gels can leave you unable to eat after seven or eight hours on the bike. You could put a piece of energy bar in your mouth, dutifully chew it and seconds later spit it out. The prospect of swallowing it was too much. Being unable to eat will severely constrain your ability to finish an event. If you manage your diet correctly, food will remain something to look forward to while riding. If it doesn't, then you have selected the wrong foods and/or you have an electrolyte imbalance.

TANDEM NUTRITION

One of the joys of riding a tandem is that the person on the back can prepare the food you need to eat. All you have to do is put your hand back when instructed and the food will be placed in your hand in the way you wanted it, in the hand that works best for you. The person at the back, freed from the need to have to navigate, think about gear selection or line on the road, can comfortably ride with one or no hands, enabling them to prepare food easily. They can also swap around water bottles, if required. The food can also be passed forward at just the right time, i.e. avoiding junctions, steep sections of hills (either going up or down), or waiting until a difficult piece of navigation has been completed.

When swapping places on the bike, the food always remains in the same place, i.e. whoever starts out as Captain stores their food at the front of the bike and whoever starts out as Stoker stores it at the back. This means that, after a position change, you will need to ask the other person to hand food to you. What doesn't change is who does the opening of wrappers and so on – a job always done by the person on the back. While there is nothing to stop the person on the front opening their own food, why would you when someone else, who is under less pressure, can do it for you?

»Training for a specific endurance event might not necessarily be the best time to try and lose weight.»

WEIGHT MANAGEMENT IN THE ENDURANCE CYCLIST

Many cyclists talk about their racing weight – the weight at which they feel they perform optimally. The general understanding is that the lighter you are, the quicker you will be. However, this is not entirely true and in some circumstances can prove the opposite. There is a fine line between being lighter to cycle faster and then taking things too far and becoming so light that you lose power and speed.

I always find it is helpful to look at body composition too. The human body is composed of a variety of different components:

- Lean tissues, such as muscle, bone and organs, which are metabolically active.
- Fat or adipose tissue, which is not metabolically active.

Together these components of fat mass and fat-free mass (lean tissue) make up an individual's total body weight. Being lean, i.e. less body fat, at a given weight is advantageous for performance, as it improves power-to-weight ratio; the more muscle you have, the more power you can generate. While being light can be beneficial to cycling performance, if you have a higher body fat percentage, you are unlikely to have as much power. For this reason, it is more useful to look at the body composition of an individual rather than weight alone. However, before you all rush off to try and decrease your body fat percentage, remember that some fat mass is essential for life; we all have fat surrounding our vital organs and it also makes up 60 per cent of our brain. In female cyclists, body fat should never drop below 12 per cent and in males this figure is 4 per cent.

So what is the best way then to go about improving power-to-weight ratio? The key is to not put your body under too much stress by over-restricting as this has negative consequences. Many individuals think that when they take up endurance cycling, they need to ramp up their intake of carbs, use energy drinks and sports products. What they don't put any thought to is the intensity at which they train.

In order to lose weight successfully, one of the fundamental messages is to increase protein intake, while restricting calorie intake. However, be realistic. If you try to drop your calories too low, your body will actually hold on to additional fat in order to preserve energy. Aim to spread your intake over three meals and one to three snacks, depending on appetite. This increase in protein prevents the loss of lean muscle mass. In addition, don't go completely carbohydrate-free, which will be detrimental to your training and increase the potential to depress your immune system. Aim to fuel up with carbs around your high-intensity, (Level 4 and above) sessions and stay fairly carb-free around the low-intensity (Level 2 to Level 3) sessions.

Another tip that can help those trying to lose weight is to delay your recovery. So, instead of feeling you need to recover immediately post-training, delay your recovery until your next meal. Make dairy products your friend as they help to build lean muscle mass as well as keeping you full for longer, preventing you from snacking on high-carb/fat snacks.

The bottom line though is that training for a specific endurance cycling event might not necessarily be the best time to try and lose weight.

»The evidence is clear – training fasted improves your ability to utilise fat.»

BALANCING TRAINING AND WEIGHT REQUIREMENTS

An aspect of sports nutrition that is gaining in popularity is training 'fasted', where the aim is to improve the ability of the body to utilise fat as a fuel. If your diet is high in carbohydrate, your ability to burn fat is, to an extent, supressed. The evidence is clear; training fasted improves your ability to utilise fat. A high-carbohydrate diet supresses it. Being able to burn fat more effectively at the low intensities required during ultra-distance events may be helpful as it reduces the reliance on carbohydrate utilisation.

To train fasted means to complete a training session without eating anything beforehand and with depleted levels of glycogen. Typically, these sessions are done first thing in the morning, i.e. after an overnight fast. Another method is to train in the morning to deplete glycogen stores, then train again later, avoiding carbohydrate before the second session.

Until you get used to it, fasted training is an unpleasant experience. The low levels of glycogen and blood sugar mean you will feel weak even before you start. If training fasted is just too difficult, consider consuming some protein pre-ride.

Do a fasted session for too long (more than a couple of hours) and the body will start to break down your body protein as a source of energy, i.e. the muscles that you have worked so hard to develop. It can also impair your immune function. Not all rides should be fasted. You will be unable to train at the high intensities that typify the polarised approach advocated in Chapter 5: Fitness unless you have sufficient energy on which to draw. High-intensity rides are best done having consumed carbohydrates beforehand.

Fasted riding does not imply restricting carbohydrate in your diet. In fact, a low-carbohydrate diet can reduce your effectiveness at utilising carbohydrate, which is unhelpful when it comes to performance. Reducing your overall energy intake too much can result in a decrease in your resting energy requirements. In other words, overdoing calorie restriction can actually reduce the calories your body needs. The illusion of weight loss from a low carb diet comes from the fact that water is stored with carbohydrate, so in reducing your levels of carbohydrate you lose water and hence are lighter.

STRUGGLING HOME ON EMPTY

Andy opened his top tube bag and, shuffling through the used wrappers, counted how many portions of food were left. A glance at the bike computer told him he still had 65km of off-road riding to go. It was 9 p.m. on a Sunday evening, approaching the final leg of the 325km out-and-back off-road route that is the 'South Downs Double'. The aim was to complete the challenge in under 24 hours and all had been going well. But the 'feeling flat' sensation had begun to wash over him and his heart rate was dropping, another indicator that energy stores were running low. At his current speed, it would take a shade over three-and-a-half hours to complete the ride, but based on his usual consumption of 60-90g of carbohydrates an hour, he had enough left for a little over two hours. Fortunately, he also knew from the many fasted rides done during training that, with careful pacing and by consuming the remaining food over a longer period of time, he could make it back. Carefully managing the pace on the ascents to stay towards the lower end of Level 2, he made it home. It took longer than planned and he was ravenous by the time he got there, but the ride was complete!

MEAT-FREE, PLEASE

Ultra-running legend Scott Jurek credited his win at the 2006 Badwater Ultramarathon – 220km through Death Valley in the heat of summer – to his vegan diet. Lizzie Armitstead, silver medallist at the 2012 Olympic Games and one of Great Britain's most successful female cyclists, has been vegetarian since the age of 10. And, in 2011, David Zabriskie became the first rider to attempt the Tour de France on a vegan diet; no small undertaking given the Tour's average daily energy requirement of more than 8,000 calories. As more and more athletes achieve success on a meat-free diet, it has never been easier to be a vegetarian or vegan cyclist.

WHAT ARE THE BENEFITS OF GOING MEAT-FREE?

Many athletes choose meat-free diets on ethical grounds. However, there may also be a number of health and performance benefits from choosing such a diet. Vegetarians and vegans typically have a lower body mass index and less body fat than those on 'normal' meat-eating diets. Similarly, lower rates of heart disease, stroke and type 2 diabetes are reported in vegetarians and vegans. The precise causes of these benefits are difficult to confirm, but they appear to be related to the fact that vegetarians/vegans eat more soluble and non-soluble fibre, more phytochemicals and antioxidants and less saturated fat. From a sports performance perspective many athletes have now shown that success is possible while on a meat-free diet. Indeed, upon making the transition, many athletes report higher energy levels and faster recovery rates.

Of course, it's one thing for a professional athlete with access to a dedicated sports nutritionist to be successful on a meat-free diet, and quite another for the amateur athlete with limited time. A balanced vegetarian or vegan diet is, however, possible as long as you make good decisions. Many such decisions are the same as for those on meat diets. For example, the increasing demand for meat-free food has led to an increase in the availability of ready-made (i.e. processed) food options. These convenience options often contain excessive amounts of sugar and bad fat, so you should choose whole unprocessed options wherever possible.

HOW MUCH SALAD DO YOU NEED TO EAT?

As mentioned above, one of the benefits of a meat-free diet is that it can help with weight loss. Of course, this is only helpful if and when you are trying to lose weight! Fibre-rich, calorie-light foods comprise a major part of meat-free diets. Such foods quickly sate your appetite but can leave you under-fuelled during long endurance rides and heavy training blocks. Many vegetarian athletes are left feeling that they cannot physically consume enough food to meet the caloric demands of their sport. Keeping a food and exercise diary can be helpful in showing whether or not you are actually consuming enough calories. The rapid development of food diary mobile phone apps makes this task easier than it has ever been before. Of course, if you find that you are under-fuelling you should consider alternative, more calorie-dense foods such as white rice and potatoes. While the emphasis should be on wholefoods, as an ultra-distance cyclist you will sometimes just need some easily and quickly digested calories, such as sweets, to keep you going.

NOT ENOUGH PROTEIN?

One of the first questions asked of the vegan athlete is, 'Do you get enough protein?' While it is true that plant-based foods typically contain less protein than does meat, the situation is not as bad as many believe. The first important point is that cyclists do not require huge amounts of protein. A male cyclist will typically require in the region of 95–105 grams of protein per day. While the 135 servings of carrot needed to meet this requirement is more than a little unrealistic, there are a variety of realistic plant-based options, for example, seven to eight servings of legumes (i.e. beans). In reality, you do not need to rely on only one foodstuff to fulfil all of your protein needs.

Another common protein-related misconception is that plant-based foods are not 'complete'; that they do not contain all of the essential amino acids that are vital for the muscle repair and development that takes place in response to training. In reality, many plant-based foods, such as legumes and vegetables, and specific foods such as quinoa and buckwheat, contain all of the essential amino acids. Even if you don't consume such foods, a balanced vegetarian or vegan diet, i.e. one that contains a wide variety of whole foods, will ensure that your protein intake is 'complete'. The key phrase for a successful vegetarian or vegan diet is 'variety, variety, variety!'

PUMPING IRON

The level of concern around iron deficiency is often inversely related to the number of animal products in your diet: the fewer animal products, the more likely those around you are to worry about you being iron-deficient. In reality, there is little need for vegetarians and vegans to be concerned about a lack of dietary iron as foods such as spinach and broccoli are iron-rich. Vegans may actually have higher iron intake than vegetarians, as they do not consume the dairy products that reduce iron absorption.

>>A busy working life can sometimes mean having to compromise on what you can consume.>>

VITAMIN B12

Vitamin B12 is the only vitamin not reliably supplied from a varied wholefood, plant-based diet with plenty of fruit and vegetables, together with exposure to sun. Although it is needed in only very small amounts, it has a key role in the normal functioning of the nervous system and in the creation of oxygen-carrying red blood cells. Vegetarians need not worry about vitamin B12 deficiency as many dairy products are B12-rich. Vegans, however, should eat B12-fortified foods (e.g. breakfast cereals) two or three times per day, or should take a regular B12 supplement.

VEGAN CYCLIST FOOD BOX ESSENTIALS

To help you get all the nutrients you need, keep the following in your food box.

Quinoa: An excellent source of minerals and B vitamins, this seed has twice as much protein as rice and contains all nine essential amino acids. It's easy to cook and can be used in place of rice, in salads or even as porridge.

Tofu: A great protein source combined with good levels of calcium and iron. Not the tastiest product on its own, but it absorbs flavours really well, making it a great option for homemade curries.

Flaxseed oil: Flaxseeds contain alpha-Linolenic acid, an important omega-3 source and a great alternative to oily fish. While it shouldn't be heated, it can be taken on its own, included in salads or added to fresh juices. Chia and hemp seeds are also great omega-3 options.

BE PRACTICAL

While everything in this chapter is good sense, a busy working life can sometimes mean having to compromise what you can consume. A day of

---

HERO FOOD: HERBS AND SPICES

Herbs and spices are a great way to make even the most basic dish a little more interesting and exciting; who wouldn't prefer rosemary-infused sweet potato wedges to plain old potato wedges? Or how about the warming properties of ginger when blended with butternut squash for a hearty soup? And you really can't beat the blend of lime, chilli and coriander to add zest and flavour to a stir fry. While palatability is essential for a sustainable diet choice, herbs and spices provide more than a taste uplift; they also make the hero foods list as they are potent antioxidants and a great way to give your immune system a boost.

---

meetings moving from one location to another may mean lunch is a sandwich from a coffee shop on your way to the next venue. As your knowledge of the content of food improves, you'll be able to look at a sandwich and make a reasonable guess as to what it contains, even if it's not covered by an app on your phone. An egg and salad sandwich can be understood as two slices of wholemeal bread at around 35-40g of carbohydrate, and if your guess is it contains about one-and-a-half eggs then they contribute around 10–11g of protein. The salad can be ignored for the purposes of the calculation.

Similarly, a business dinner can be assessed in the same way, and the appropriate amount of each course eaten. In this way you can keep a check on what you consume when you are out and about, without it needing to impact adversely on your training.

The same applies to restocking when on a long training ride. Knowing what your energy needs are and what different foods contain will help you make sensible choices.

≫Ask of every meal: how is it contributing to your ultra-distance goals?≫

SUMMARY

It is simply not possible to participate in ultra-distance training and competition without eating something at some point. There is, however, no need to make things complicated: eat real food and portion it into easily manageable packages that you can eat on the bike. Make sure it is a mix of low and high GI foodstuffs, mostly carbohydrate (60–90g per hour), with some protein from time to time. If you get your on-the-bike nutrition plan right, you will look forward to eating your next portion of food right the way through your ride. Don't worry if it doesn't always work out quite like that; at some point you may find yourself unable to eat, or indeed wanting to eat more.

Your ability to eat will be affected by variables such as the weather, fatigue and the palatability of the food you have with you. Whether it's sports drinks or pure electrolyte powder added to your favourite cordial, keep on top of your electrolytes intake. Without them you will be far less effective at absorbing the energy you are consuming. When you've finished exercising, try to eat within the first 15 minutes post-ride and certainly within the first hour. If the following day is a fasted session, stay off the carbs in the evening. If it is a session comprising some very high-intensity intervals, make sure you have eaten enough to restock your glycogen levels. In short, eat for what you are going to do, not just for what you have done.

When not exercising, eat a balanced diet. If you do this, there is little or no need for any form of supplements. Ask of every meal: how is it contributing to your ultra-distance cycling goals? Learn what different foods contain so that when faced with a choice in a restaurant or at a meeting, you can select those foodstuffs most suited to your needs. Food should be a pleasure and, given the amount of training you will be doing to be successful in ultra-distance events, you may as well enjoy it!

CHAPTER 4: EQUIPMENT

The right equipment can be the difference between untold misery and the pleasure of surviving through adversity.

Over the years, bike equipment has changed significantly and, no doubt, will continue to do so. To focus on a specific product is to go about equipment analysis in the wrong way. It is not the piece of equipment per se in which you are interested but what that piece of equipment will do for you. For example, you need something in which to carry tools. This could be achieved via an old water bottle, or a saddle bag. The starting point is the tools themselves. Will it keep them dry? Will they be easy to access? With these criteria in mind, you can then review the latest equipment options available on the market to see what satisfies your needs best. Rather than focus on specific products – information that would be out of date before publication! – this chapter will help you identify the key criteria that will always be relevant to your ultra-distance cycling.

THE TESTS

The test for any piece of equipment is:
- Is it fit for purpose?
- Is it reliable?
- Is it comfortable?
- Can it be used for more than one function?
- Can I find a lighter equivalent?

When thinking about the right equipment to carry, the following three questions are a useful frame of reference.
- Do I have the wherewithal to cope in the event of a mechanical failure that necessitates a rescue; specifically, to first be able to get that help and second, survive until that help arrives?
- Do I have sufficient skills and spares to be able to fix the commonly occurring basic mechanical problems that may occur during a ride, for example, things such as a puncture, a broken chain, snapped spoke, a loose bolt?
- Before I use this piece of equipment in a race, have I tested it in practice?

Satisfying yourself with these questions may mean you appear to carry more kit than fellow cyclists, but you're probably riding further and for longer than them too. A winter overnight off-road ride in the mountains will necessitate more survival kit than a daytime ride through towns and cities in the summer. While the average weekend rider will never be more than 50–80km away from where they started, you, as an ultra-distance rider, could be several hundred kilometres away from your starting point.

WHAT'S THE OUTCOME YOU WANT?

The key to any equipment discussion is to determine the outcome you need to achieve and then work back to find the right solution. It doesn't really matter whether you are talking about coats, frame material types, tyre choice or helmet choice. It begins with you working out what the equipment needs to deliver for you. For example, 'I need enough power to keep my GPS and phone working for 36 hours'. A dynamo provides a good source of power for electronic equipment on training rides and during unsupported races. If participating in a supported event, the crew can charge back-up devices such that, as one device runs out of power, the next is ready to go. One situation needs a dynamo, the other needs back-up devices. The correct solution depends on the outcome sought and the context in which it is used.

Take something as simple as spectacles. If your ride takes you from daylight to the darkness of the night, sunglasses won't work. Clear lenses will be great at night but do little for glare during the day. Lenses that react to light allow you to ride both during the day and night. Similarly, if you wear prescription lenses, changing the focal point to suit the fact that your head is tilted back when riding a bike can add a small amount of comfort. Whether you prefer Oakleys or an own brand label is up to you; just be certain that the glasses perform for the intended purpose.

The critical dimension for all kit intended for use in ultra-distance is comfort. If you are struggling to get comfortable then your ability to perform to the best of your ability is hampered. Whatever discomfort you experience at the start will be multiplied many times by the time you are five or six hours into the ride, and exponentially by the time 24 hours roll by.

Ultra-distance is still a niche sport and, as a result, most cycling magazines focus on activities that the average rider will be doing, which will, of course, be a lot shorter than you will/do ride. In the ultra-distance world, you need the comfort and reliability of *Audax* equipment and the speed considerations of a time trial rider or Ironman competitor. The result is a combination of equipment that would probably raise eyebrows from anyone who is not an ultra-distance athlete. It is not uncommon to find a heavy Brooks B17 saddle on a lightweight carbon bike. The saddle provides the all-day comfort and the bike the performance that is possible riding a lightweight machine.

PAY ATTENTION TO THE WEATHER

One of the most useful pieces of kit to have is a simple weather station. A quick glance before you head out on your session will tell you the actual temperature (which can often vary to that forecast). In addition, a weather app is useful for giving an indication of what the day holds in store for you. Generally speaking, most forecasts are very accurate up to a period of around 24 hours; greater than this, depending on the incoming weather systems, they can be less accurate.

COLD REFLECTIONS

It was Sunday morning. Alfonso left home at 5 a.m. on a 200-mile ride. It was pouring with rain and just above freezing. Two-and-a-half hours into the ride and after three punctures, Alfonso had run out of spares. Did he carry on or abandon the ride? He chose to carry on. A few kilometres later, yet another flat brought the ride to an end. Where he lives, the rain washes tiny flints out of the ground, as sharp as razors. These make mincemeat of any tyre and the bigger ones can destroy a tyre in one go, such is the deep cut they can make. Wanting to ride with as little kit as possible, Alfonso had a phone, cash and credit cards and had assumed this was enough. It took his wife over an hour to reach him, at which point he was numb with cold and couldn't speak properly. It took hours before he thawed out. Alfonso and his wife realised that a simple incident had become dangerous.

He was grateful for learning this lesson when, at 3 a.m. one morning, he had a flat in the back of beyond on some country lanes. This time the temperature was well below freezing and the road surface had at times resembled an ice rink. He put his head torch on, found a tree stump to sit on and, before repairing the tyre, popped on the lightweight and small duvet pullover he had stuffed into his saddle bag. It was only for a few moments, but he knew his damp sweaty body would chill rapidly in the icy blast blowing across the fields. A few minutes later he returned the jacket to his bag and was on his way, his core temperature retained.

>> Pay attention to the clothes you wear and how comfortable you feel in relation to the weather conditions. >>

Temperature can vary significantly depending on the specific local topography. Cold air is denser than warm air, and tends to flow downhill, where it can become trapped by warmer air above it. Thus, in winter, a ride along a valley floor may well be several degrees colder than a ride just a few hundred metres higher. The accumulation of local knowledge means you can avoid those places where such frost pockets occur.

Pay attention to the clothes you wear and how comfortable you feel in relation to the weather conditions. Over time you will build up an understanding of what combination of kit works best, and in which conditions. The knowledge gained from experience, combined with the actual temperature and the forecast, means you can often avoid the need to carry lots of kit 'just in case'. More importantly, it means you will be comfortable and able to focus on your training session, rather than either trying to stay warm or having to cope with too many layers.

THE IMPACT OF ALTITUDE

While localised conditions can lead to temperature inversions, as a crude rule of thumb it gets colder the higher up you go. This is because the air pressure drops and, as a result, the air cools. For every 1,000m above sea level, the temperature falls by just under 10 degrees, assuming the sky is clear and it is not raining. If it's wet, the rate of temperature loss is less, at about six degrees per 1,000m of ascent. This is known as the lapse rate.

Some of the highest passes in the Alps exceed 2,500m. The difference between the valley floor and the col can be as much as 20–25°C. A lovely warm summer's day in the valley at 500m somewhere in the Dolomites could be 25°C. Ride to the top of the Passo Fedaia, for example, and, at 2,057m, it will be approximately 15 degrees colder, and nearer 10°C. You will be hot and sweaty from the long climb up, and the rapid descent in the much cooler temperature, combined with wind chill, means that it will become an unpleasant, bitterly cold affair. Add into the mix rain or strong winds and it is very easy to become hypothermic, even if, only moments before, you had been sweating profusely with the effort of the climb. You need the right combination of equipment and clothing to cope with both the heat and the cold.

Figure 3 shows the approximate lapse rates, assuming it is 20°C on the valley floor and the

>> Your selection of clothing needs to to take into account not only the weather forecast at sea level, but the impact of altitude as well. >>

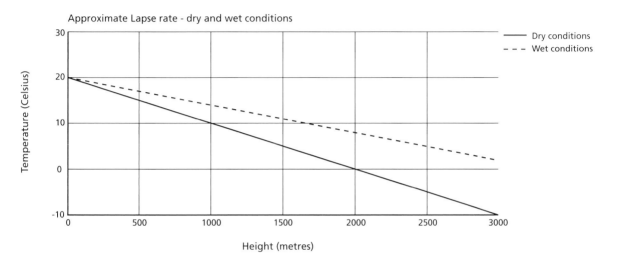

Approximate Lapse rate - dry and wet conditions

*Figure 3: Lapse rate –
dry and wet conditions*

valley floor is at sea level. The climb up to the Cime de la Bonette in the French Alps reaches an altitude of 2,830m. The Stelvio Pass in Italy, much beloved of cyclists, tops out at 2,757m. As the graph shows, by the time you reach the top of these passes the temperature will be below freezing. It will, however, be even colder should you have chosen to ride over Cottonwood Pass or Independence Pass in the United States of America as these reach heights of almost 3,700m. Lapse rate, however, is affected by a number of variables that mean it may not be quite as cold as this diagram implies. For example, in wet conditions, the lapse rate is less. The key point to know is that height affects temperature, and time

spent checking out the forecast at the highest points on your ride is a useful way of working out what equipment you will need.

Mountains can also produce a range of severe weather conditions such as strong winds, heavy rain and/or snow and fog, when those in the valley below are experiencing little more than a cloudy day. Therefore, your selection of clothing needs to take into account not only the weather forecast at sea level, but the impact of altitude as well. A very demanding hilly route can require regular pit-stops to either add or remove layers of clothing. If you choose to ride self-supported in these conditions, your choice of equipment can be critical, even life-saving.

COFFEE AND SHAKES – A STORY FROM THE RACE ACROSS THE ALPS

Dom learned the hard way the impact of altitude on temperature, combined with the impact of wind chill. He was already cold before he started the descent off an Alpine Col in the early hours of the morning. His inadequate windproof jacket worn over his short-sleeved cycling jersey and his legs clad only in shorts was simply far too little clothing. At first the descent was little more than uncomfortable – and then the shivering started. It became so violent that the front of the bike wobbled, becoming very unstable. His hands seized, he was unable to either squeeze the brakes more or release his grip. His eyes were struggling to stay open as waves of fatigue washed over him.

Finally, as the gradient eased, he ground to a halt, just managing to unclip in time. The support team rushed over to him and all three of them wrapped themselves around Dom to provide some instant warmth. He could no longer stand nor think properly. It took 30 minutes inside the car with the heater on full blast and several mugs of lukewarm coffee before Dom began to stop shaking. Getting out of the car to recommence the race was one of the hardest things he has done on a bike.

THE SPARE KIT PEOPLE CARRY

Table 2 on page 108 details the kit that Dominic carries on training rides and in solo, unsupported, races. The kit required for supported rides is dealt with later in Chapter 8: Teamwork.

BAGGING IT

There are those that heap scorn on saddle bags, top tube bags and the like, insisting that if it cannot be carried in the jersey pocket, it isn't needed. These people are not ultra-distance cyclists. They know not, nor have thought about, the consequences of problems hundreds of kilometres into a ride with little or no immediate support available – problems that can occur any time, day or night. The paradox is that the longer you cycle, the better it would be to travel light, but the more stuff you need to carry. As a result, it is useful to have a box full of different bags for packing stuff when on the bike. These include:

- different sizes of top tube bags for food;
- frame bags (bags that go on the inside of the main triangle);
- saddle bags;
- rack-top bags that sit on top of a pannier rack;
- pannier bags; and
- waterproof pouches.

It can become an obsession to find the right quality, lightweight, fit-for-purpose bags. You will want to carry as much as you need but no more. To paraphrase Einstein again, keep it as simple and light as possible, but no simpler or lighter.

TOP TUBE BAGS

Useful for:

- food;
- phone;
- stashing used wrappers; and
- carrying a hex key or similar if you have changed your set-up and think you might need to tweak it during the ride.

Carry as much food as you are likely to consume in the time it takes your water bottles to run out. For example, two x 1-litre water bottles in moderate weather could last up to about 150km before needing to be refilled.

Therefore, you should carry enough food to last about 150km. Your fluid consumption will increase after this and so the next two bottles will probably last only about 115km. You then, therefore, need only enough food for 115km as there is no point in carrying excess food; it is just unnecessary weight that will slow you down.

FRAME BAG

A frame bag is very useful as an alternative place to store bike spares or food. It is probably one of the most versatile bags you can have as it is easy to reach while you are riding and can hold a decent amount of kit. The bigger the frame bag, the more it fills the space in the frame and the less space there is for water bottles. You could use a hydration pack instead and fill the whole frame, but the difficulty with hydration packs is that it is difficult to work out the precise volume of fluid you are replacing when you fill it up, and this in turn makes judging the amount of electrolyte to add somewhat difficult. Bottles, on the other hand, are much easier to judge because of their rigid shape and they often have markings on the side. Using a bag that fills the whole of the frame also creates problems as it can make the bike very unstable in cross winds.

SADDLE BAG

A saddle bag is the traditional place for bike spares, jackets, gloves and so on. Ideally waterproof, they are also far more versatile if they have side pockets you can open on the move. If every time you want something you have to stop to open the bag, you can waste a lot of time. Saddle bags provide an additional place for food, instructions, sun tan cream, etc.

RACK-TOP BAGS

Rack-top bags sit on top of a pannier frame. They are incredibly versatile and easy to use. They also lower the centre of gravity more compared to saddle bags. They are excellent for superlight touring trips or self-supported rides where the conditions are likely to be inclement and you need to carry more layers with you. The downside is they require a pannier frame, which adds weight.

Table 2: Kit carried on solo training rides/unsupported races

What	When	Reason
Identity bracelet	All year	Allows others to identify you and your emergency contact, should you become unconscious in the event of an accident
Credit card/cash	All year	In case of having to purchase bike spares, food or drink.
Rescue service details	All year	A rescue service that will pick you up and drop you within a 40 km radius or a train station
Phone	All year	To call for help/back-up/navigation/music
Tyre levers x 2	All year	To remove stubborn tyres
Inner tubes x 2	All year	It is not uncommon to have two punctures in a ride
Tyre patches	All year	In case a tyre gets gashed. The patch can be used as a temporary measure to block a hole.
Inner tube patches	All year	In case the number of punctures exceeds the number of spare inner tubes you are carrying
Chain tool	All year	Chains can snap or get twisted
Spare chain links	All year	To connect two good bits of chain together
Multi-tool	All year	To tighten bolts
Three zip ties	All year	In case a strap or bracket breaks. Zip ties can be an effective temporary fix
Spoke key	All year	A snapped spoke can mean the wheel is buckled. A spoke key allows you to crudely realign the rim
Mini pump	All year	To pump up tyres after flats. Better than CO_2 canisters as these can only be used once
Small tub Vaseline	All year – long rides only	In case of sore spots due to friction
Electrolyte powder	All year – long rides only	To add to whatever drink is available to make into a 'sports drink'
Battery back-up	All year – long rides only	To keep the GPS and phone powered. Essential on rides over 10 hours
Appropriate leads	All year – long rides only	To connect the battery back-up to the phone and GPS
Food	All year – over two hours	Enough to keep you going as long as your water bottles will allow before you need to get them refilled
Water bottles	All year – long rides only	2 x 1 litre, generally enough for up to 150km, depending on the weather
GPS transmitter	All year	Allows people to see your location in case of a problem and also has an SOS button for calling for help
GPS navigation device	All year	Contains route to be ridden; saves having to carry a map
Waterproofs	Depends on the forecast	Type of jacket will depend on the weather forecast and temperature
Buff	Spring/winter autumn/winter	Very useful when the temperature drops to cover head, ears and neck
Gloves	Winter – long rides only	Thin gloves for layering under outer gloves for additional warmth
Hat	Winter – long rides only	Taken only when conditions are likely to be sub-zero
Sun tan cream	Summer – long rides only	Taken in summer to reapply later on in rides
Emergency blanket	Winter – long rides only	Taken in winter in case of a breakdown in the middle of nowhere
First aid kit	All year	Particularly useful if riding off-road or kilometres from anywhere
Sleeping bag	Extreme winter cold	Taken on long mountain bike rides in winter in case of ending up injured off the beaten track. Used in conjunction with the emergency shelter
Emergency shelter	Extreme winter cold	Taken on long mountain bike rides in winter in case of injury when off the beaten track. Used in conjunction with the sleeping bag.

>> A small waterproof pouch serves two functions: it keeps your phone dry and it cuts out wind noise when placing or receiving a call. >>

PANNIER BAGS

These are great for touring, but the minimalist approach required for self-supported racing means you need only a large saddle bag or top-rack bag. However, the main advantage of pannier bags is they sit low on the bike, keeping the centre of gravity down. A lower centre of gravity helps the bike feel more stable – useful when you are tired.

WATERPROOF POUCHES

Not all phones are waterproof. A small waterproof pouch serves two functions: it keeps your phone dry and it cuts out wind noise when placing or receiving a call. This is very useful as it only takes a small amount of wind noise to make a phone call impossible. The authors do not advocate the use of a phone while riding.

Larger waterproof/dry bags are great for keeping kit dry inside a bike bag. Some bike bags are designed to be simply holders for a dry bag, recognising that if all your stuff is inside a dry bag you do not really need another bag outside of that. On a wet and cold winter's day, having a dry jacket to put on if you have to stop can mean the difference between surviving comfortably and becoming hypothermic.

MATERIAL CHOICE

Bags come in a wide range of materials, incorporating everything from duck cotton to rip-stop nylon and waterproofed welded plastic. The weight and volume can vary enormously. For example, a duck cotton 10-litre saddle bag can weigh 600g, whereas a 14-litre rip-stop nylon bag can weigh as little as 250g. While lighter may be better for speed, accessibility to the kit inside may be more useful (and possibly saves time).

WATERPROOFS

If you have ever shopped for a waterproof shell, you will know there are a bewildering number of options available, with an array of prices to match. You sweat to cool yourself down: the evaporation of moisture on your skin is a very effective way of lowering your temperature. While sweat achieves this effect when you are hot, rain also has this effect and can make you cold, in fact, very cold when combined with a stiff breeze. This is the reason you wear a coat.

The waterproofness of a jacket is measured using a 'Hydrostatic Head Rating'. In essence, this means placing a piece of fabric over the base of a long tube and then filling that tube with water and seeing how much water can be poured in before the fabric lets water through. The water is measured in terms of the height of the column of water achieved. As you can imagine, driving rain demands a certain level of resistance to pressure in order to be waterproof. The higher the column, the more waterproof. For something to be called waterproof, the hydrostatic head needs to be at least 1,000mm. It could be assumed that the higher the hydrostatic head, the more waterproof and therefore the better the jacket; however, it is more complex than this.

A jacket that is 100 per cent waterproof and not breathable is an unpleasant thing. While it will keep the rain off, it will also stop sweat escaping. You will be wet on the outside and inside, but for different reasons. That damp, 'clothes stuck to you' feeling is deeply unpleasant. Breathable jackets keep the rain out and allow some water vapour to escape. Breathability of fabrics is therefore an important factor. Waterproof breathable jackets tend to have a membrane and taped seams, whereas water-resistant jackets have some form of coating often referred to as DWR (Durable Water Repellence). Take a jacket properly coated with DWR treatment, hold it under the tap and the water runs off. There are a number of variations on a theme in terms of the specific chemicals used to create the DWR layer. Waterproof jackets with membranes in principle allow hot air and sweat to escape, hence the label 'breathable'. This is because the pores at 0.1–10 microns in size in the material are large enough to allow water vapour molecules, with a diameter of 0.0004 microns, to escape, but are too small for water droplets to get in.

When riding a bike, the levels of effort may

> **>>Membrane jackets are in effect like wearing a bin bag with tiny holes in the polythene.>>**

produce enough sweat to overwhelm the breathability of a membrane system found in a waterproof jacket. Membrane jackets are in effect like wearing a bin bag with tiny holes in the polythene. As a result, when expending reasonable effort, you end up wet inside the jacket from sweat rather than the rain pouring on you. A water-resistant jacket may be far more breathable, allowing you to stay dryer, but in turn may become overwhelmed by the quantity of rain, in which case you will get wet anyway. In both situations, the jackets will have helped protect you from some wind chill. When the wind hits wet cycle clothing that doesn't have the protection of an outer shell it can lead you to feel bitterly cold very quickly. This is less of an issue when the temperature is warmer but can become extremely serious as the temperature drops, leading to hypothermia and loss of bike control because of cold, numb hands.

There are other waterproof systems. For example, Páramo uses a two-layer system that supposedly replicates the way animal fur behaves – an outer layer with a DWR treatment sheds most of the water and an inner liner has the effect of pumping water away from the body using capillary action. The result is a jacket that is heavy and requires regular re-proofing but is superbly comfortable. The frustration is how heavy it is.

Whatever brand or method used to keep you dry, they all require some form of maintenance, even if just washing, and they all wear out. What matters more is the functionality and the circumstances in which you will be riding. In an ideal world, a jacket would be so well-designed that, whatever the weather, you could adjust it such that you maintain the ideal level of warmth/coolness. In the early morning the sun's rays are

so shallow the atmosphere absorbs most of the energy, hence daybreak is often the coldest time of day.

Some jackets go a long way to help you by having a range of different vents in them to allow you to moderate your temperature. These can include vents under the arms, down the sides or on the back. They can be very effective. A ride can start off in the early morning when temperatures are lowest. All the vents are zipped up, wrist closures done up tight and, if it is raining, you even have your hood up under or over your helmet (under is warmer; over allows more air to get around your head). As the sun rises and the temperature increases, it is time to start opening a vent or two until eventually it warms up enough to ditch the jacket altogether. As the ride continues into the evening, it is time to put the jacket back on and reverse the process, gradually closing the vents as the temperature drops.

So, is there a perfect jacket? Once again, it is 'horses for courses'. When the winter is at its coldest and wettest here in the UK, the one jacket that gets used more than any other by the authors is the Pàramo jacket. On training rides where weight is not a concern, the incredible breathability of this jacket, combined with being waterproof, means you stay far warmer and more comfortable throughout long rides. With vents on the sides and on the sleeves, a two-way front zip and hood mean that it is possible to stay comfortable across a significant temperature range from well below zero up to about 10°C. After this they are simply too hot. Every few months it also needs to be re-proofed (for which there are a variety of products available). It is also heavy when compared to other jackets, at almost 700g. If there is any chance the weather

>> **Research suggests that the best way to be seen is to place reflectors on your knees and ankles.** >>

will improve such that the jacket is not necessary, it is too bulky to carry in a pocket, requiring instead a large saddle bag.

In contrast, a Montane feather light Smock has no vents, pockets, hood and only a small zip at the neck. If it has been treated with a DWR (the same as you use to reproof a Páramo), it holds off the rain very effectively and is very breathable. It packs down to the size of an apple and weighs just 100g. But, while it keeps the wind and rain off, it offers almost no warmth and has no flexibility in being able to moderate temperature. It is either on or off. In prolonged rain, the lack of taped seams means the water does eventually penetrate through, and if the temperature drops you can end up cold and wet. For occasional showers, however, or riding in the early morning where a windproof shell is just enough to hold the cold at bay, it is a brilliant jacket. It can be stuffed in a pocket when not in use, taking up very little space. In warmer, wet weather you could use a membrane-based waterproof jacket, accepting that you will still be damp underneath from sweat, but it does effectively keep the rain at bay.

REFLECTIVE CLOTHING

There is a common perception that High Visibility (Hi-Viz) clothing is the key to safety on a bike on the principle of 'be safe, be seen', with the bright colour of a fluorescent jacket being the best way to 'be seen'. Interestingly, research actually suggests that the best way to be seen is to place reflectors on your knees and ankles. The movement helps drivers work out that you are a cyclist and makes them more likely to respond quickly than if the cyclist was wearing a reflective vest or black clothing. A back light, whether flashing or not, does not seem to enhance the conspicuousness of the rider. Perhaps the main reason why reflectors on ankles and knees work so well is because we have evolved to detect changes in our environment, either to spot prey or approaching danger.

In the day, fluorescent colours of orange or yellow can help, but it is incorrect to assume that they are always the best option. What is more important is the level of contrast between you and the background. Thus, you may stand out better in black if the background is brightly

coloured, whereas a damp grey, foggy morning is ideal for Hi-Viz clothing. At night, fluorescent clothing is just as invisible as black clothing, but reflective stickers work very well, especially if they are on moving parts of the body and bike. Using lights that help to mark you as a cyclist by their positioning, in addition to unusual flashing sequences, will also help.

As an ultra-distance cyclist you will want to keep weight down. Wearing additional items of reflective clothing may help you to be seen, but it also slows you down, because of the extra weight and the time it takes to change clothing. A solution is to use reflective tape down the seat stays. The tape wraps around the whole length of the stay and is thus visible from any angle. Reflective stickers on the heel of cycling shoes also help. If you use overshoes, buy some with reflective portions at the back and sides.

The most important thing to remember is that being smothered in reflective clothing does not guarantee you will be seen. If you stand on the side of a road and hold your hand stretched out, palm facing forward and away from you and close one eye, you can see as you move it across the horizon how much disappears from behind it. Houses in the distance will disappear. In just the same way, they disappear behind the windscreen pillar or GPS/phone mounted on the windscreen. Sometimes, no matter what you are wearing or what lights you have on your bike, a driver will not see you, and as the authors know to their cost, this can sometimes mean they drive straight into you.

Power One of the problems with the majority of electronics used on bikes is battery life. At the time of writing, GPS bike computers typically last no longer than 12–16 hours depending on their complexity (mapping, ANT+, links to phones, etc.). Bike lights last even less time. Given that an ultra-distance training ride can last longer than this, you have the challenge of powering all of this 'stuff'. There are two options: battery-powered and dynamo-powered.

DYNAMOS

Dynamos allow you to run whatever you wish, for as long as you wish, without fear of loss of battery life. Riding through deep shaded areas, having ridden from bright sunshine, can mean that the bike 'disappears' in the gloom and, therefore, motorists cannot see you. Switching on a light increases your visibility and safety. You can use the light in this way as often or as little as you wish without fear of batteries going flat.

A dynamo light typically has a standby of around 10 minutes. If you need light for longer than it takes to carry out a short repair, it is better to carry a head torch with you. This is because dynamo lights are hard-wired into the bike and are generally bolted to the bike. It is therefore not easy to remove them to shine the light on any other part of the bike to be able to deal with a repair.

Dynamos do create drag – as much as six or seven watts when the dynamo is running. This is about 2 per cent of total power output for very fit, strong riders and 4 per cent for smaller and less fit riders at endurance levels of effort. It may not be much, but over the many hours of a race it mounts up.

One of the limitations of dynamo lights is their output. German regulations on bike lights constrain their power output and beam shape. In Germany, dynamo lights were compulsory on bikes weighing over 11kg until 2011, which resulted in most lighting systems being designed to meet these restrictions. The best dynamo lights at the time of writing are made in Germany; however, when compared to battery-powered lights, unconstrained by such rules, dynamo lights are good but fall a long way short of the brightness delivered by top-end battery-powered lights. Even including back-up batteries, a non-dynamo system will be the lower weight option. The choice is lighter and brighter versus versatility and 'always available'. Which system to use depends on the duration of your ride and the opportunity to get equipment charged.

DYNAMO SET-UP

On Charlie's bicycle the dynamo powers the front and rear light. Connected via a piggyback connector is a lead that runs to a device that enables him to vary the voltage and current to suit whatever he wishes to charge. This in turn can feed a cache battery that evens out the supply, necessary for some devices. The different types of connector necessitate carrying a couple of cable options, these being housed in a small dry bag in the saddle bag.

On a long ride Charlie runs his mobile phone and GPS on their internal batteries and uses the lights powered by the dynamo as and when needed. When the GPS battery needs charging he will plug it directly into the battery cache mounted on the bike, which in turn is plugged into the dynamo. After a few hours this will be fully charged and he can then charge his phone. He can vary when he charges each device if there is a likelihood of rain, in which case he will keep both phone and GPS topped up from the dynamo until such time as it starts raining and then he will disconnect both and replace the waterproof seals to protect the devices from water ingress. *In extremis*, in the event of rain throughout the ride, use a GPS powered by AA batteries. The downside of this is that such devices are mostly not ANT+ (ANT+ is an ultra-low power wireless protocol used for sending information from one device to another device, e.g. from a power meter to a computer head unit) and so do not collect power output data. In the rain, the phone is charged inside a waterproof case.

>> Shoe choice should allow enough space for the feet to expand after many hours of cycling. >>

SHOES

You may be one of the unlucky people who suffers from 'hot foot' when cycling. Commonly misunderstood to be due to shoes being too tight or not wide enough, more often than not the problem has nothing to do with the fit of the shoe. Rather, it is the repeated pressure of pushing on a pedal that causes what can be severe discomfort, specifically the sensation of a 'hot foot', or a pain like a hot poker being pushed through the sole of your foot. This is due to the repeated compression of the nerves in the foot. The pain eventually fades with the onset of numbness. After a particularly long and hard ride, this numbness can take weeks and sometimes months to disappear. While you wait for your foot to go numb it can be agonising, severely reducing performance. This problem is addressed in detail in Chapter 1: Riding technique, pages 33–55.

Shoe choice should allow enough space for the feet to expand after many hours of cycling. If riding in hot weather, choose a pair with plenty of ventilation. In cold weather, choose shoes with little ventilation. Often there are holes where the cleats fix into the shoes. If necessary, a small amount of wax can be melted into the hole to fill it up, or you can use a small piece of duct tape.

> **»Unless you are comfortable on the bike you are unlikely to be able to ride it any distance, let alone ultra-distance.»**

BIKES

You might expect a chapter on equipment to focus heavily on the bike. However, a rider should be much more interested in what the bike will do for them, rather than the bike itself. As with all equipment, what constitutes the right bike depends on what you plan to do with it. As with all kit, there are trade-offs that have to be made; getting the right balance is very much a personal decision.

The first and foremost requirement is comfort. Unless you are comfortable on the bike you are unlikely to be able to ride it any distance, let alone ultra-distance. Signs that your bike is not quite right include neck pain, wrist pain/numb fingers/numb hands, backache and knee pain.

In extremis, pain will bring your ride to a premature end. However, with your bike set up properly, it is possible to ride for days at a time without significant discomfort beyond a general sense of fatigue. There are a great many people offering bike fit services. These provide a good starting point. Once set up, the next thing is to learn from the lived experience of riding your bike for hours and hours. This will provide a rich source of feedback. See Chapter 1: Riding technique.

PRICE VERSUS WEIGHT

If weight is something that matters to you, then roughly speaking, the more you pay the lighter the bike. Superlight bikes are not necessarily the most aerodynamic. One of the most aerodynamic bikes, the Cervelo S5, is 3kg heavier than the lightest bike currently available. You could buy a bike of the same weight for one-fifth of the price. The cheaper bike is probably more suited to self-supported ultra-distance rides as it allows bags to be more easily attached, whereas the more expensive Cervélo would suit a flat course with a support crew. It comes down to the type of riding you intend to do.

What is clear is that to buy a superlight bike weighing under 7kg requires two to four times the investment of a bike weighing 2kg more. That same weight loss can be achieved through diet, which will benefit you in many ways more than the equivalent reduction in bicycle weight.

If you have got yourself down to race weight and can afford it, then saving 2–3kg with your choice of bike is a good way of aiding speed, provided that the bike is capable of performing in the way you need.

>> The difference between time trial bikes and road bikes essentially comes down to one major difference: the angle of the seat post. >>

BIKE PERFORMANCE

Bikes are like cars. A super lightweight sports car requires constant driver inputs, such is the level of responsiveness of the set-up and engine. They are great fun to drive, but the firm suspension, low-profile tyres, low seating position and lack of storage space make them unsuited to long journeys. In contrast, a family saloon is spacious, set up for comfort and, while a bit dull to drive, long journeys pass with ease. In the same way, short wheel base, steep-angled ultralight race bikes are exciting to ride, but after a few hours you can feel like you have been hammered by the road. More relaxed geometry, a longer wheel base and larger tyres, and the appropriate fittings that allow mudguards or pannier racks to be attached, makes for a much more comfortable, if a little slower, ride.

For four or five hours in the saddle the sportier bike is always likely to be the first choice, but for longer 12-, 24-, or 48-hour rides, comfort is more of a priority. If you are able to ride in an aerodynamic position on an aerodynamic bike, then you should, as the gains in speed will be significant. However, be very certain that you can maintain the position, because if you are going to have to sit up to be comfortable you will be better off with a bike that is designed for that position, i.e. has a more relaxed seat post angle (72–4 degrees).

Longer wheelbases are more stable at speed and more comfortable, but slower to turn. The length of the chain stays also affects comfort.

The shorter they are, the more the wheel is under the saddle and the more road shock is transferred directly to the rider. It's like sitting over the axle on the rear of the school bus – bouncy. Traditionally, shorter stays were seen as 'better' as less energy was lost due to flexing of the frame. This was true when steel dominated frame building; however, modern steels, titanium, aluminium and carbon fibre are now all manufactured in a way that means this is no longer an issue.

The difference between time trial bikes and road bikes essentially comes down to one major difference: the angle of the seat post. All other variables centre around aerodynamics and general geometry adjustments that allow the chosen seat post angle to work. On normal road bikes with seat post angles of 72–4 degrees, it is very comfortable to ride with the hands on the hoods. The angle of the hips and body, approximately 90 degrees (when the leg is extended), is maintained in a time trial position, even though it might look like the rider is bent over more than on a road bike. This is achieved by increasing the angle of the seat post (77–85 degrees). The effect of this steeper angle is to rotate the rider over the bike. Thus, while the hip/body angle remains the same, the net effect is that the rider is lower at the front of the bike: a more efficient aerodynamic position. This more aggressive position comes at a price as it can lead to neck pain and makes seeing forward more difficult.

>>Cold water spraying up your back and over your feet is a sure-fire way to misery.>>

FIT FOR PURPOSE

Whatever bike you choose, whatever the frame material, braking system or gear mechanism, it needs to be fit for purpose for the type of ultra-distance cycling you intend to do. If you are planning to complete supported rides, a super-lightweight bike may be the best choice as you have no need to carry anything. If, on the other hand, you intend to go solo unsupported, your bike needs to be capable of carrying whatever kit you intend to take, and your wheels must be strong enough to cope with the combined weight of bike, rider and kit.

In addition to whether the bike is fit for purpose in terms of strength and resilience, it is worth considering how versatile the bike is for different conditions. Training for ultra-distance involves a lot of cycling. Depending on where you live, this could mean putting in the kilometres in the thick of winter when it is often raining and frequently cold. Cold water spraying up your back and over your feet is a sure-fire way to misery. For some reason beyond our comprehension, most high-end bikes sold today do not come with eyelets for proper mudguards. While there are a range of mudguards for bikes with no eyelets, they tend to be flimsy, are fiddly to fit and difficult to stop rubbing when compared to mudguards designed to bolt onto the frame using proper eyelets. However you get them onto your bike, use mudguards to keep warmer and drier when training in wet conditions.

Another factor you may wish to consider when selecting your bike is the ability to take a pannier rack. This gives you the option of using top-rack bags and pannier bags. It is possible to buy a pannier rack that mounts to the seat post, but these have limitations; notably, they cannot always be used with carbon seat posts and, with just one point of attachment, they are prone to move sideways. The maximum amount of weight they can carry is less than a frame-mounted pannier rack and the centre of gravity is higher than a frame-mounted pannier rack. There are designs that have three points of attachment – the seat rails and the seat post. These are more stable, expensive and can be heavier than traditional racks that mount on the seat stays. Having the facility to use panniers enables you to build training into your non-cycling life, carrying around the kit you need.

GEARS

Choose gears suited to the terrain over which you will be riding. Lots of climbing will require much lower gearing than riding along valley floors. Your choice of gear will enable you to maintain your ideal cadence over whatever terrain you face (this is explored more in Chapter 1 on Riding technique). A 'compact' chain set comprising two front rings of 50 teeth and 34 teeth (50:34) and a rear cassette with a maximum sprocket size of 32 teeth and the smallest with 11 teeth (11:32) makes riding Alpine climbs after many hours of riding more comfortable and achievable than the more speed-oriented 53:39 front rings and 11:25 rear cassette range suited to flatter routes. Experiment with different gear options to find the ratios that suit you best.

TYRE CHOICE

Tyres are a series of compromises. Lightweight tubular racing tyres, beloved of professional riders, are almost impossible to change mid-ride without seriously compromising safety

>> Too-high tyre pressures cause the wheel to bounce, wasting energy and providing a very harsh ride. >>

and without a significant time penalty. Very lightweight 'clincher' tyres paired with similarly svelte inner tubes may reduce rotational weight substantially, but if you have to stop continually to repair punctures, any gain in speed is lost.

Tyres provide much of the cushioning that a bike has. The design of the bike frame can contribute some comfort, but the 'give' in the tyre enables your power output to be transferred to the road, while at the same time cushioning you from the road. Tyre pressures that are too high cause the wheel to bounce, wasting energy and providing a very harsh ride. A badly-scarred road surface is covered more easily using larger diameter tyres (as measured by the tyre profile) as the imperfections are absorbed by the tyre reducing the vibration experienced by the rider. The larger the diameter of the tyre, the lower the pressure that can be run and the more comfort experienced.

Of course, the larger the diameter of the tyre, the greater the rotational weight, and the more effort is required to turn the wheel. Much research has been carried out into the impact that tyre size has on rolling resistance. Narrower, smaller-volume tyres have long thin contact patches, whereas larger volume tyres, at the same pressure, have wider, shorter contact patches and less rolling resistance. Thus, a larger diameter tyre may roll better.

Larger riders (>80kg), or those required to carry a load, will benefit from the comfort of larger tyres and will also be less likely to suffer from 'pinch flats'. This is where the sudden compression of the tyre caused by riding over a stone or through a pothole squeezes the inner tube onto the rim and literally pinches it, typically resulting in two small parallel tears in the inner tube.

The consensus seems to be that 25mm tyres are a good compromise of aerodynamics, comfort and weight. If you're racing with a support team and have access to multiple wheelsets, tubular tyres are the way to go as they are lighter than clinchers. This is because the structure of a clincher rim has to be able to hold the tyre bead in place under high pressure, whereas a tubular tyre is held on by glue and compression. If you have only one or two sets of wheels, clinchers are the more user-friendly. Different choices of tyres and inner tubes can be selected to suit the road conditions over which you will be riding: lighter weight for good-quality roads and more substantial tyres for rough pothole-strewn roads covered in debris.

IN PRACTICE

The picture on page 124 illustrates a common bike set-up for winter training for ultra-distance events, and Table 3 explains the purpose and function of key elements of the set-up. This is not an expensive set-up; it is a bike designed for training and for being comfortable for very long periods of time.

Table 3: Facets of a winter training bike

No	What and why?
1	25c or 28c puncture-resistant tyres suitable for coping with thorns and flints on the road during winter, on high spoke count wheels. These are strong and robust and can cope with unseen potholes
2	A comfortable saddle: essential for the long distance rider. A leather saddle will mould to the shape of your bottom through use.
3	Consider using a front wheel with a dynamo that powers the lights on the bike and also provides power to re-charge the bike computer/mobile phone
4	Full-length mudguards to protect the rider and the water bottles from road grime
5	Consider using a large saddle bag attached to the seat post. On an autumn and spring day the temperatures can be below freezing early in the morning and rise to double digits in the middle of the day. Being able to remove and comfortably carry layers of clothes as well as spare food and bike parts is a necessity.
6	This is a beautifully made custom built steel PaulusQuiros bike. The geometry is relatively relaxed and makes for a very comfortable riding position. If you can sustain a more aggressive seating position, it is worth doing so to gain from being more aerodynamically efficient
7	Double wrapping the handlebars with two layers of bar tape, and or use gel pads underneath the tape to provide additional comfort and insulation
8	Choose your gears to suit the terrain over which you will be riding and the amount of food and spare clothing you will be carrying in order to enable the rider to spin comfortably up the steepest slopes
	Whether you opt for a pedal mounted power meter or a Crank arm power meter - use one. A power meter feeds data on effort to the bike computer and helps the rider pace the ride very accurately and to ensure interval training sets are completed at the right intensity
	A bike computer. displays and records power output data. It also provides details of the route, how far has been ridden and how far there is to go. The timer function helps when doing intervals and ensuring you eat regularly.

❯❯Cold feet are one of the more unpleasant aspects of winter riding.❯❯

COLD FEET

Like cold hands, cold feet are one of the more unpleasant aspects of winter riding. They can turn an otherwise delightful ride into a living hell. Unless the weather is dry and warm, you will end up with wet feet, either from spray off the road, from rain running down your legs and into your shoes, or because of the build-up of sweat underneath overshoes. Dry is best. Warm and wet is tolerable. Wet and cold is miserable. Over the years the authors have experimented with a great many options and sought advice from many other riders, finally identifying some solutions that work.

LAYERING

It is widely recognised that wearing multiple layers is more effective than wearing a single thick layer, because of the air trapped between the layers, which acts as thermal insulation. Heat flows from hotter objects to colder ones, so warm feet moving at speed through the air lose their heat to that air. The speed of that heat loss directly relates to the difference in temperature between your feet and the outside air – the colder the air, the faster you lose the heat. The air trapped between layers of clothing acts as a barrier, reducing the speed of heat loss. However, there needs to be sufficient space in your shoes to allow the layering effect to work. Squashing your feet into your cycling shoes with many layers of socks may actually make things worse because the air trapped between the layers is compressed. Part of the solution then is to wear two pairs of socks – one thin pair and one thicker pair over the top – as long as there is space in the shoe to do this.

Wool is typically highly resistant to odours, in contrast to artificial fabrics like nylon, polyester and microfibres, which, unless treated with an anti-odour product, can end up becoming very smelly because the fibres are hydrophobic. As a consequence, they do not absorb water but readily absorb short-chain fatty acids excreted by the body. It is these fatty acids that are responsible for malodour.

OVERSHOES

Waterproof overshoes work in the same way as waterproof coats. Breathable fabrics work because water vapour can escape through the pores. When it rains, shoes fill with water running down the sides of your legs. As a result, the breathability of the overshoe is ineffective. Breathable overshoes work well on dry, cool days where your feet are at a moderate temperature.

You can also layer overshoes. A thin overshoe underneath a warmer outer overshoe can help with warmth. Many overshoes are made of neoprene. These work like wetsuits and need to be tight-fitting, trapping a layer of water beneath the surface. This layer of water is warmed up by your feet and, provided the neoprene is snug, stays warm. Neoprene has a cell structure made up of foam rubber, often sandwiched between two layers of nylon to provide some abrasion resistance. Each cell of the foam rubber is filled with nitrogen and, in exactly the same way as a layer of material traps air, the cell structure provides an insulating layer. If the overshoes are too loose, the air can get underneath the neoprene and heat is lost quickly as wet feet lose heat much more quickly than dry feet. The challenge is to ensure that the overshoe is tight to the shoe and not the foot.

>> A shoe lined with an active foot warmer, combined with two pairs of socks inside a loose-fitting shoe capped with one or two sets of overshoes, is about as good as it gets. >>

ACTIVE FOOT WARMERS

There are a few options to actively heat your feet, one being a battery-powered shoe warmer, although these have limited battery life, so are often unsuited to ultra-distance. Another option is a chemical foot warmer, where chemicals activated by air react to produce heat. These last about six hours, which may be long enough to get from the freezing cold start of the day to milder temperatures. They are reasonably small and light, allowing a second pair to be carried for later in the day. They can be positioned under and over the foot, provided there is enough space in the shoe.

It is generally a combination of all of these solutions that provides some comfort against the cold. A shoe lined with an active foot warmer, combined with two pairs of socks inside a loose-fitting shoe capped with one or two sets of overshoes, is about as good as it gets.

JACKETS AND JERSEYS

Jackets and jerseys are mostly similar in style, consisting of a zip either part-way or full-length at the front, with either no sleeves or short- or full-length sleeves and anything from one to three pockets at the rear. The weight of the fabric will vary depending on whether they are meant for summer or winter use. While broadly similar in design, execution varies enormously. Some pockets are mounted so high as to require the ability of a contortionist to access them while riding. Other materials are so stretchy that anything put in the pockets causes the jacket to sag over your backside and sway about uncomfortably. Sometimes just one large rear pocket is provided. This has limited value as everything moves around inside the pocket and it is difficult to get items comfortably positioned.

Jackets can be a perfect fit in the body but with arms so voluminous that the material flaps about in the breeze. The fit can vary enormously, from feeling like a trussed chicken to your first day at junior school in your slightly-too-large school uniform. On some jackets, the elastic at the bottom is so tight it compresses the stomach/bladder leading to the sensation of needing to urinate. To avoid frustration, try before you buy.

Ideally, your clothing will be close-fitting as this is both aerodynamically more efficient and more comfortable (flapping fabric is irritating). Pockets should be reached easily and capable of holding whatever you wish to carry. Ideally, get the bike to carry everything rather than you. Buy a selection of jackets commensurate with the conditions in which you will be riding. On cold days, it is better to use a layering system to keep warm rather than one super-warm jacket. Changes in temperature, riding into or with the wind, and your level of effort can all affect how warm you will feel. Being able to add or remove a layer enables you to moderate your temperature effectively.

Gilets are a very useful piece of kit. Having sweated your way to the top of an alpine climb, the descent can be a miserable experience as the combined effect of little or no effort and the cooling effect of the air rushing by leave you bitterly cold long before the descent is over. Putting on a lightweight windproof gilet at the top of the climb can help slow the rapid cooling that takes place.

SHORTS AND BIB TIGHTS

Shorts without shoulder straps may be easier to remove. The downside is that the combination of the waist elastic in the shorts and the elastic in the hem of the jacket can create undue and unwanted pressure on your midriff. This is worse when riding in a more aggressive aerodynamic position, where the rider is doubled over. The downside of using shorts with shoulder straps is that you have to remove whatever layers you have over them in order to change kit or go to the toilet; however, the lack of an elastic waistband means they are more comfortable.

As with jackets, bib shorts and tights come in a variety of lengths and weights, some with pads and some without. Unpadded shorts and tights are great for layering over shorts or tights with pads. Layering up two sets of padded shorts or tights can impact your riding height and therefore efficiency on the bike, as well as being uncomfortable. Ankle zips on bib tights mean they can be removed without having to remove your cycle shoes, although some people find the zip an irritation. Bib tights can be treated with a water-repellent coating for those showery days that do not necessitate full waterproofs; however, this coating doesn't last long once the tights have been washed a few times.

BIKE PADS

While originally made from chamois leather, the bike pads in cycling shorts and bib tights have long since been made of foam. Nevertheless, the term 'chamois' is often still used to refer to the pad. More expensive shorts use a combination of foam densities to provide comfort. Where there is more weight on the chamois the density is greater; for example, under the sit bones. Cheaper shorts often have just one density of foam. More expensive pads are often treated with antibacterial agents to reduce the chance of saddle sores developing. A good pair of shorts can help you remain comfortable for longer. Loose shorts are disadvantageous as they create more friction, increasing the likelihood of saddle sores as well as being less aerodynamically efficient.

LEG AND ARM WARMERS

While offering a great deal of versatility for the ultra-distance cyclist, the fit of leg and arm warmers is critical. Too tight and they are uncomfortable to wear and may cause irritation; too loose and they will slump down your legs and arms, requiring frequent 'on the move' adjustment. Arm warmers leave a cold spot at the top of the arm and shoulder, while leg warmers leave a cold spot between the top of the leg and the cycling pad. If the temperature drops, these gaps can be uncomfortable. Their major advantage is size. They pack down small and are carried easily.

HELMETS

Helmet design has improved dramatically in recent years, with a much greater variety of designs for aerodynamics and/or improved airflow. Given that you may be wearing the helmet for days at a time, comfort is once again key. Once comfort is sorted, the nature of your ride will dictate the right choice. On long hilly rides in hot climates where aerodynamics is less of an issue because the average speed of the ride is slower, a helmet that allows lots of air to flow through may be best. For a fast long-distance ride where aerodynamics can play a significant part, an aerodynamic or semi-aerodynamic design will be better – provided, of course, that it is comfortable.

Keeping a helmet clean is a challenge. The helmet pads need to be washed regularly to avoid skin infections on the forehead. Another solution is to dispense with the pads altogether and instead use some sort of helmet liner. These vary in design, from a close-fitting skull-cap to a bandana. The advantage is that they can withstand far more washing and you are less likely to lose it compared to helmet pads, which are often in many small parts.

>> Sweat does not smell. The unpleasant odour is a result of bacteria on the skin breaking down the sweat into acids. >>

BODY ODOUR

If riding your bike for a long time, it is inevitable that you will begin to smell, due to sustained exertion and the resultant sweating. While of superficial importance, it's more pleasant for you and your support crew if you are not malodorous. Sweat does not smell. The unpleasant odour is a result of bacteria on the skin breaking down the sweat into acids. Food rich in garlic or spices may contribute to the odour.

The key to not smelling is washing yourself and your kit. On a sustained ultra-distance ride, this is not possible. Material choice can help. Unlike the microfibres in manmade materials, which are hydrophobic, natural wool products (such as merino wool) absorb water vapour, assisting the process of evaporation. Unlike cotton, merino wool remains warm when wet.

The ability to absorb the water vapour reduces the speed at which you begin to smell as the sweat is drawn away from you. It is therefore an excellent base layer when worn next to the skin.

When purchasing merino wool products, reference is made to the weight per metre squared. The greater the number, the warmer the garment. Approximately $170g/m^2$ is suitable as a lightweight base layer. A weight of $230g/m^2$ is better suited as a mid-layer, and any more than this is probably too warm and heavy for all but the very coldest of days. Merino wool is very breathable and when riding into a wind it will easily pass through the fabric. This necessitates some form of windproof layer over the top. Merino wool is also expensive when compared to manmade products. Its supple nature makes it unsuitable for cycling shorts or tights as the material tends to sag when compared to tight-fitting Lycra.

>> A saddlesore is caused by abrasion, which can lead to an abscess. They are very uncomfortable and can severely impact performance. >>

CHAMOIS CREAM

Chamois cream is an anti-friction product that is smeared over the pad in your cycling shorts and/or onto your perineum and your sit bones. Its job is to stop the chafing that can occur over long periods of time as the fabric of your shorts rubs against your skin. Some products contain anti-bacterial and moisturising agents to help prevent saddle sores. A saddle sore is caused by abrasion, which can lead to an abscess. They are very uncomfortable and can severely impact performance. In addition to the use of chamois cream, good personal hygiene is essential to help avoid the sores occurring.

There are a great many brands and varieties on the market. Experiment with different types until you find one that works best for you. You may even want to consider manufacturing your own (which is what the authors do). On long rides, it is useful to decant a small portion of chamois cream to a travel pot, carrying this in your saddle bag. It should be re-applied before you start to feel discomfort as, by this point, the damage will have been done. As you train more, you can cope with longer distances before you need to reapply. Wet weather can exacerbate the problem and may necessitate more frequent application.

If you are riding with a support team, at suitable intervals (e.g. every four to six hours) reapply the cream as part of any stop you make.

It is useful to have a planned sequence of activity for this, for example:

- When you stop, a member of the support team hands you a disposable glove.
- Wearing this glove, help yourself to a handful of chamois cream from a pot held open by the support team.
- Apply liberally to the appropriate areas.
- Remove and discard the glove.

The reason for the glove is to avoid becoming plastered in chamois cream. It would otherwise end up on your bar tape, making it slippery, and on your food. Its sticky nature is also a magnet for dirt, which in turn increases the risk of ill health. If riding on your own, a small travel pack of wet wipes enables you to maintain hand hygiene, as well as being useful as toilet paper in the event you are caught short kilometres from the nearest public convenience. A common line of thinking is that petroleum jelly (e.g. Vaseline) is a cheap and suitable alternative. It does work very well; however, it is also absorbed into the pad in your shorts and is difficult to clean and remove. Nappy rash cream is another oft-used alternative, although its anti-friction properties are not as good as those made specifically for cycling. Whatever your choice of product, apply it before you experience any discomfort and keep applying it throughout your longer rides.

SUMMARY

The key to choosing the right equipment is to first identify what you need to be able to do, before then working out the best tools to help you do it. The nature of ultra-distance means that reliability is perhaps the foremost factor influencing your choice of equipment, followed by weight. You need enough equipment to get you through the event. Any more is just dead weight that you have to lug over the hills. While you should aim to reduce weight to a minimum, do ensure you carry enough to survive in the event that things go wrong and you need to be rescued. On a warm summer's day you will need relatively little, but on a sub-zero winter's night you may need a rucksack full of equipment. It's all about the context. Whatever kit you end up using, test it in training.

CHAPTER 5:
FITNESS

A well-thought-through training plan for making the most of the limited time you have available is essential. While more hours are better than fewer, much can be achieved in just a few carefully planned hours per week.

HOW DOMINIC'S TRAINING CHANGED

The thing that struck me about training with Charlie (my tandem partner), long before he became my training partner, was just how fast he was, given how little training he did compared to me. A love of single-speed riding and of being outside meant almost all of my rides were steady drifts around the countryside. If riding time equalled performance, I should have had a place on the GB cycling team. But it doesn't. Charlie used to rib me about not taking enough rest. Weeks could go by before a day would pass when I wasn't riding. I tried riding with a heart rate monitor to make sure I was training hard enough, but I could never achieve the numbers the books suggested I ought to be able to achieve. I was later to find out that I have a very slow beating heart; the high heart-rate targets set by a former coach were hopelessly out of reach.

Based on the knowledge I gleaned from completing a number of Ironman distance races, I set out a training plan for my then riding partner and myself with a view to breaking the tandem 'Lejog' record. It was, with hindsight, hopelessly inadequate. I simply was not scientific enough in my approach. I had become extremely good at riding slowly. I learned how to ride a very long way on insufficient food and often ended up feeling sick. This was no way to break a record and so it proved. Building up to my second record attempt, I sought help from Simon and my performance was transformed in just a few weeks. Sadly, my riding partner at the time didn't share the same philosophy about training. This, among other factors, regrettably meant my second attempt at the tandem record also failed.

It was only when Charlie and I decided to have a go at the tandem record and took the decision to take a disciplined, scientific, evidence-based approach to performance improvement that we were able to achieve the almost impossible – smashing the record by over five hours. The change in what we were able to achieve was, quite simply, staggering.

Dominic

>>The best advice for improving your genetics is to choose your parents wisely.>>

GOING THE DISTANCE

There are many things that influence sports performance: sleep; nutrition; equipment; whether or not your significant other 'understands' what you're doing! The two most important factors, however, are genetics and training. Different scientific studies have suggested different relative contributions of these factors, but it is helpful to think of an approximate 50:50 split; about 50 per cent of your sports performance is determined by your genes and about 50 per cent by training.

Genetic engineering and a growing knowledge of epigenetics may mean that humans are able to modify their genetic endowment in the future. For now, however, the best advice for improving your genetics is to choose your parents wisely. For those of us that have not done this, there is still hope because of the major potential impact of training.

A helpful way to think about genetics and training is to realise that your genetics set the upper limit for how fit you can possibly be; they determine the size of your fitness endowment. In contrast, your training determines how much of your fitness endowment you can draw upon; you train in order to be able to express more of your fitness potential. You train to get fitter, and by getting fitter your performance potential goes up and up.

Of course, not all training is created equal. Daily five-hour endurance rides will not help you to win a track sprint, while daily squats will not help you to beat the 24-hour record. Specificity is the key. Thus, strength training will be vital for sprint events and, when it comes to cycling a very long way, Eddy Merckx was at least part right when he recommended that aspiring cyclists 'ride lots'. But, of course, there is a little bit more to it than that.

WHAT IS FITNESS?

You could be 'fit' enough to run 100 metres in 10 seconds, but not 'fit' enough to run a marathon in two hours and three minutes, or vice versa. 'Fitness' is context-dependent: being fit for the 100 metres is different to being fit for the marathon. Fitness then is about being suitable to fulfil a particular role or task. While in one sense this whole book is about how you can improve your fitness for ultra-distance cycling, this chapter is about how you can improve your physiological fitness for ultra-distance cycling.

Physiological fitness relates to those elements of your body that impact on your ability to apply power to the pedals for a long period of time. At a cellular level, this relates to variables such as the number of mitochondria (the sites of aerobic energy production in muscle cells), and the efficiency of energy production within the mitochondria. At a tissue level this relates to, for example, the number, size and type of your muscle fibres. At the level of the whole organism, physiological fitness relates to factors such as your ability to deliver oxygen to the cells, an ability provided by a vast array of underpinning variables, such as lung structure and blood vessel density.

All of these systems function at a baseline level, but are capable of operating at a higher level should sufficient stress be placed upon them. Your cycling training provides this stress, stimulating physiological adaptations that allow you to apply more power to the pedals and for longer.

GET 'IN THE ZONE'

For the ultra-distance cyclist, it goes without saying that at some point you will be riding lots, but is it necessary to 'ride lots' every day? Should every ride be a long, hard slog or should you also be doing some short, sharp bursts? The answer is somewhere in between, with this 'somewhere' depending on, for example, where you are in your training cycle. Ultimately, however, you have to work on (i.e. train for) the things that may hinder your performance. These 'things' may include your bike-handling skills, your ability to ride hard through the night, your capacity to stay in the saddle or to ride in an aerodynamic position. From a physiological point of view, you may have a strong endurance capability but a need to improve your relatively weak threshold power output. Your training, therefore, needs to be targeted, both over time and at each session. If you're not a full-time cyclist you will want to get the most 'bang for your training buck'!

To develop your threshold power output, many of your training sessions will be at threshold exercise intensities. If you need to develop your endurance, many of your training sessions will be completed at endurance intensities. Sounds simple, but there are two important challenges:

- The areas that we need to develop are usually those we least enjoy.
- What on earth is 'threshold' intensity?

Exercise physiologists have identified a range of exercise intensity domains: moderate, heavy, very heavy, severe, and supra-maximal. Each domain possesses a unique physiological characteristic, based on standard laboratory measures of heart rate, oxygen uptake and blood lactate. The exercise training zones presented in Table 4 are the conceptual equivalent of these domains, translated from the laboratory into the real world of the athlete.

Table 4: Training zones

Zones	Name	Training session type	Perceived exertion	Average power output*	Average heart rate$
Level 1	Active Recovery	Easy spinning. Typically used for active recovery after strenuous training days, races or between interval efforts.	<2	<55%	<68%
Level 2	Endurance	Classic long steady distance. Daily workouts of moderate duration (e.g. two hours) possible.	2–3	56–75%	69–83%
Level 3	Tempo	Typical intensity of fartlek workout. Greater sensation of leg effort and fatigue than Level 2. Conversation must be somewhat halting.	3–4	76–90%	84–94%
Level 4	Lactate Threshold	Just either side of Time Trial effort. Continuous sensation of moderate or greater leg effort and fatigue. Usually performed as multiple 'intervals' of 10–30 minutes.	4–5	91–105%	95–105%
Level 5	$\dot{V}O_2$max	Strong to severe sensations of leg effort and fatigue. Consecutive days of Level 5 not desirable. Typically intervals of three to eight minutes.	6–7	106–120%	>106%
Level 6	Anaerobic Capacity	Severe sensation of leg effort and fatigue. Heart rate generally not useful as a guide to intensity. Typically short intervals of 30 seconds to three minutes.	>7	>121%	N/A
Level 7	Neuromuscular Power	Very short (seconds), very high-intensity efforts (i.e. short sprints). Power useful as a guide when compared to previous Level 7 sessions	Maximal	N/A	N/A

* = % of Functional Threshold Power. $ = % of heart rate at Functional Threshold Power.
Adapted from Allen & Coggan, *Training and Racing with a Power Meter*, Velopress (2006)

>> It is the not the numbers that are important but the different elements of your physiology that the numbers allow you to target. >>

Other training zones systems are in use, many having fewer than the seven zones shown here. In the authors' experience, however, the seven-zone system provides the best balance of usability and applicability to the underlying physiology. This last point is particularly important. From a training perspective, it is not the numbers that are important but the different elements of your physiology that the numbers allow you to target.

Training zones provide a vital means of making your training sessions more targeted. If you knew that your 'threshold' was in need of some development, you now also know exactly how hard you should be training, in any given 'threshold' training session, to achieve this. You also know how hard you *shouldn't* be training! If a given training session is targeting threshold development, there is no need to ride above Level 4 (as defined in Table 4 on page 135). This sounds obvious, but think about those sessions where you're on a good day and you know that you can take the power up a notch. This seems like a good thing, but it could actually take you into the next training zone. Your coach will be pleased that you were feeling good, but disappointed that you've completed neither a Level 4 threshold session nor a Level 5 $\dot{V}O_2$max.

Your training zones also provide an invaluable *lingua franca* with fellow cyclists and your coach. 'I'm on an L2 day today,' 'We're focusing on L4 for the next two weeks,' and 'Recover at L1 between intervals' is all useful shorthand for the physiology that you are training to develop. 'L' refers to 'Level'.

WHERE ARE YOU NOW AND WHERE DO YOU NEED TO BE?

A wealth of online and hard copy resources means that it is possible to purchase training programmes that prescribe training from one month to one year and everything in between. Such generic programmes may result in improved performance simply as a stimulus to increased training structure; however, an individualised approach to training will always be most effective as it will take account of your specific fitness-related strengths and weaknesses. It is important, therefore, that you identify where these strengths and weaknesses lie. The chances are that you will have a good idea of this already (if you hate threshold intervals, this is probably an area of weakness!), but some dedicated testing will allow you to be completely objective.

VISIT THE LAB

The most accurate measurement of your fitness-related strengths and weaknesses will be provided by a trip to your local sports science laboratory. Here you will be able to use the latest technology to measure key determinants of endurance cycling performance such as peak power output, $\dot{V}O_2$max, lactate threshold, efficiency and haemoglobin mass. The results of such testing will allow you to target those aspects of your physiology that require development. Testing is usually conducted at the beginning of the training year to inform early season training targets, shortly before the beginning of the competition phase, and midway through the competition phase to aid the evaluation of training effectiveness and to give an opportunity for fine-tuning training.

≫The rate at which you consume oxygen is one of the primary physiological determinants of your performance.≫

WHAT IS YOUR $\dot{V}O_2$MAX?

Most cycling disciplines are heavily dependent on metabolic processes that require oxygen. The energy that is provided by these aerobic processes is supplemented by anaerobic (i.e. without oxygen) processes for very high-intensity situations, such as sprints. As an ultra-distance cyclist, the rate at which you consume oxygen is one of the primary physiological determinants of your performance. The higher your upper limit for oxygen consumption, i.e. your $\dot{V}O_2$max, where $\dot{V}$ = volume, O_2 = oxygen and max = maximum, the bigger your aerobic engine and, at least in theory, the better your performance.

A $\dot{V}O_2$max test is usually completed on a cycle ergometer, set up to match the dimensions of your main bike. You will usually wear a heart rate monitor and a mask or mouthpiece that allows the measurement of oxygen and carbon dioxide in the air that you breathe out. Typically, after a light warm-up the test will start at a relatively low power output (measured in Watts 'W' and usually between 100 and 200W), increasing incrementally until you can no longer continue. The rate at which power output is 'ramped' up varies between laboratories. A common protocol increases power output by 20W every 60 seconds. The incremental phase of the test usually lasts between seven and 15 minutes.

The main results of the test will be your $\dot{V}O_2$max, expressed in litres per minute (L·min-1) or in millilitres per kilogram of body weight per minute (ml·kg-1·min-1); maximal aerobic power (the highest power output that you can sustain with energy generated through aerobic energy pathways); and maximum heart rate.

FINDING YOUR THRESHOLD

While your $\dot{V}O_2$max is important, the percentage of this value that you can sustain for a long period of time is even more important. This is true in ultra-distance cycling more than it is in other disciplines. The percentage in question is usually a 'threshold' as it represents a point beyond which body systems lose the ability to balance the production of energy with the removal of metabolic waste products.

The most commonly measured 'threshold' is the lactate threshold. Research has identified a strong correlation between lactate threshold and race performance. Therefore, the higher your threshold is as a percentage of your aerobic capacity (i.e. your $\dot{V}O_2$max), the faster you will race.

WHICH 'THRESHOLD'?

Threshold can be measured in a number of ways, which results in a variety of threshold types. While there are physiological differences between lactate threshold, anaerobic threshold and ventilatory threshold, for most cyclists they can be considered to be relatively synonymous. From a testing point of view, the key thing is to be consistent in the type of threshold test that you complete to ensure that you have comparable results each time.

Recognition of the similarity between different thresholds may also be helpful in a training setting. For example, ventilatory threshold closely correlates with lactate threshold; you reach both at about the same time. You can't feel your lactate threshold but you will often notice when you reach ventilatory threshold. As your power output increases, your breathing frequency and depth rises along with it, until suddenly it feels as though a switch has flipped,

>> With adequate nutrition, you can ride for hours, even days below threshold. As soon as you go past threshold, you're riding on borrowed time. >>

with a particularly deep breath or sigh marking the start of breathing much deeper and faster. This switch happens at ventilatory threshold, telling you that you are also close to lactate threshold. Therefore, paying attention to your breathing is a really helpful intensity check when both training and racing. This is of particular benefit if your power meter has failed as it tells you that you have moved to an intensity beyond your threshold. With adequate nutrition, you can ride for hours, even days, below threshold. As soon as you go past threshold, you're riding on borrowed time.

A lactate threshold test can be quite similar to a $\dot{V}O_2$max test. Indeed, it is possible to carry out a combined lactate threshold/$\dot{V}O_2$max test. After a light warm-up, the test begins at a low

>>The rider who has to put the least amount of energy to produce a given power output will be the most efficient rider.>>

power output (e.g. 100W). With stages lasting four to five minutes, the required power output is increased by 25–50W for each new stage until an obvious spike in lactate concentration is observed. The lactate level is measured from a finger prick blood sample taken during the final seconds of each test stage.

With concomitant power output and heart rate recording, the key information from the lactate threshold test will consist of power output at lactate threshold, heart rate at lactate threshold and the percentage of $\dot{V}O_2$max at which the lactate threshold occurs. Elite male cyclists would expect to be able to maintain a power output of 5–6W per kg of body mass at lactate threshold.

JUST HOW EFFICIENT ARE YOU?

Cycling is all about producing 'work', which we usually measure as power output. When all other things are equal, more power means more speed; however, individuals differ in how much energy they have to put into producing this power. The rider that has to put in the least amount of energy to produce a given power output will be the most efficient rider. It is, therefore, possible to compensate for not having the highest $\dot{V}O_2$max in the peloton by having a high efficiency. The fact that your fitness 'tank' is smaller than that of your competitor doesn't matter if you are able to extract just as much or more from your tank than they are.

To measure your efficiency, the two sides of the efficiency equation are measured; the amount of energy that goes in and the amount of energy that comes out. Energy in is calculated by measuring the amount of oxygen that is consumed. Energy out is simply measured as power output.

An efficiency test is completed at submaximal power outputs, making this an easier test than the lactate threshold test, and certainly the $\dot{V}O_2$max test described earlier. The test will typically comprise three or four six-minute stages, at power outputs of, for example, 150W, 180W and 210W. You will wear a mask or a mouthpiece that allows the collection of expired air during the final minute of each stage.

The main result of your efficiency test will be a value in the range of 15–28 per cent. Untrained individuals tend to have values at the lower end of this range, with professional road cyclists at the upper end.

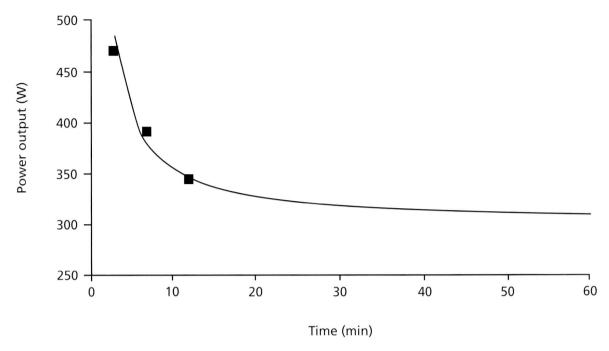

Figure 4: A power–time curve plotter through application of the Critical Power Model to three maximal all-out efforts (black squares)

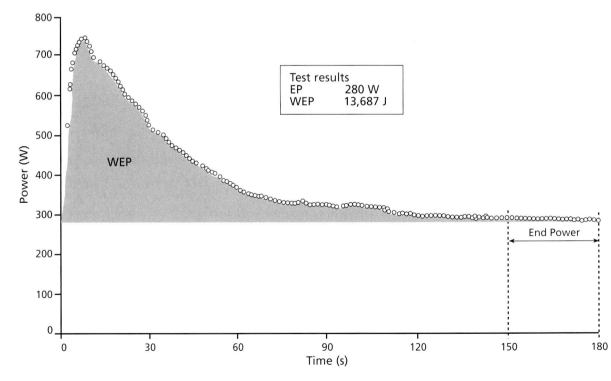

Test results
EP   280 W
WEP   13,687 J

Figure 5: A typical power trace from the three-minute all-out critical power text (EP = end power; WEP = work above end power)

>> **To get an accurate measure of their strengths and weaknesses it is sometimes necessary to complete testing in the field.** >>

REAL-WORLD TESTING

While laboratory equipment is very accurate, for some riders the lab environment is so different that they are unable to complete the tests to their maximal capability. To get a true, i.e. accurate, measure of their strengths and weaknesses it is sometimes necessary to complete testing in the field.

The abundance of testing technology (e.g. heart rate monitors and power meters) now available means that it is possible to complete regular self-tests at a time and place convenient to you. Field testing removes some of the time constraints of lab testing, and so the loss of a little accuracy is compensated by the opportunity to test over a wide range of intensities in order to get a broader picture of your physiological condition. As long as you adhere to several key principles (see Box on page 139) you will be able to maximise the reliability of your testing.

PROFILE YOUR POWER

Your 'Power Profile' consists of your highest power outputs over durations of 5 seconds, 1 minute, 5 minutes and 60 minutes. Hunter Allen and Andrew Coggan's 'Power Profile Test' starts with a 45-minute warm-up (including a 5 minute effort at threshold power output and three 1 minute fast pedalling efforts). This is followed by a 5 minute all-out (i.e. maximal) effort, 10 minutes' recovery at endurance pace, 1 minute all-out, 5 minutes' recovery, 1 minute all-out, 5 minutes' recovery, 15 seconds all-out, 2 minutes' recovery, and 15 seconds all-out. The test is completed with an easy warm-down. The 60 minute value is established during the functional threshold power test (page 142).

MEASURE EVERYTHING IN THREE MINUTES!

Although critical power testing is well-established, the time needed to complete multiple trials to exhaustion is disruptive for many athletes and coaches. The three-minute test resolves this problem by estimating critical power and anaerobic capacity from a single short test session.

The theory behind this test comes from the assumption that the anaerobic system can only sustain exercise for a short time, and that it can be fully exhausted in fewer than three minutes of maximal effort cycling. If this is true, the power observed at the end of the three-minute test must be maintained using aerobic energy production systems and, therefore, Critical Power.

During the three-minute test, the estimation of Critical Power is termed *End Power* and anaerobic capacity is termed *Work above End Power*. Following a suitable warm-up, the athlete is required to cycle 'all-out' for three minutes. This is not a paced effort and maximal cadence and power should be attained within the first few seconds of the test. After downloading the power output data from the test, End Power can be calculated as the average power output achieved during the final 30 seconds, with Work above End Power calculated as the area under the power curve but above End Power (see Figure 5).

These results can be used by coaches to set rider-specific training zones, basing the zones around Critical Power/End Power in the same way that the training zones described above are based on Functional Threshold Power.

James Wright, postgraduate researcher

>>The power output that can be maintained for one hour closely correlates with various 'scientific' thresholds.>>

By comparing your results to Allen and Coggan's Power Profile table, you can see where your relative strengths and weaknesses lie. For example, within your road race category you might have high 5-second, 1-minute and 60-minute values, but a low 5-minute value. In this instance, focused Level 5 $\dot{V}O_2$max training would likely lead to a much bigger improvement in road race performance than would a continued focus on 'endurance' training.

CRITICAL POWER

As shown by the Power Profile, as the duration of effort increases the power output that you can sustain will decrease. This relation between power output and time can be described by the Critical Power mathematical model, and you can use this model to predict the power outputs that you should be able to sustain for any duration (see Figure 4).

To establish your Critical Power you will need to measure your power output during three (or more) maximal all-out efforts. Traditional Critical Power testing requires 24–48 hours' recovery between efforts; however, the authors have recently found that only a 30-minute recovery is required, meaning all efforts can be completed in one session.

Following a good warm-up, complete three to five all-out efforts, interspersed with 30-minute recovery spins. The duration of each all-out effort should be different – typically between three and 12 minutes – in order to provide a good power–time range. The mean power output for each all-out effort can then be used to calculate your Critical Power and, more importantly, to plot your power–time curve (see Figure 4). This curve can be used to guide power output targets for individual race efforts and/or training

sessions. When designing your interval training sessions, for example, you could use the curve to identify the power output that you could sustain for the desired duration of each interval. In this way you would maximise your training gains by maximising the impact of each interval.

FUNCTIONAL THRESHOLD POWER

Your body is constantly producing and removing metabolic by-products. At low intensities, removal outweighs production but, as intensity increases, there comes a point at which by-products start to accumulate as removal begins to lag behind production. At this point you have passed a 'threshold', beyond which metabolic by-products cause fatigue and reduce performance.

The power output that can be maintained for one hour closely correlates with various 'scientific' thresholds. The highest power output that a cyclist can maintain in a quasi-steady state, without fatiguing, for approximately one hour, or 'Functional Threshold Power' (FTP), is therefore a valid field-based measure of 'threshold'.

The 'Threshold Test' described by Hunter Allen and Andrew Coggan is great for regular self-administered testing. The test begins with a 30-minute moderate pace (i.e. 65 per cent maximum heart rate) warm-up that includes three 1-minute fast pedalling (i.e. 100rpm) efforts between minutes 20 and 25. This is followed by a five-minute all-out effort, 10 minutes at moderate pace and the main part of the test, an all-out 20-minute time-trial. The test is completed with 15 minutes at moderate pace and a further 15 minutes easy warm-down. FTP is calculated as 95 per cent of average power output during the 20-minute time-trial phase of the test.

>>No matter the disipline, all cyclists will benefit from sessions of long duration because cycling is, at it's core, an endurance sport.>>

TRAINING: HOW LONG, HOW HARD, HOW OFTEN?

Effective exercise training is a systematic preparation for a specific physical goal: a race, a tour, a record attempt! Training is predicated on the assumption of biological adaptation to a disturbance caused by an exercise session or series of sessions. This disturbance causes the body to 'overcompensate'; to adapt in such a way that the next time the same exercise stimulus comes along, it causes no disturbance. This overcompensation may be provided by an array of adaptations, such as growth of muscle fibres, deposition of stronger connective tissues (tendons and ligaments), and increased numbers of mitochondria.

When planning a training programme, a number of principles should be borne in mind. These include the principles of overload, specificity, frequency, duration and intensity.

KEY TRAINING PRINCIPLES

Overload
The principle of progressive overload is the foundation of any exercise-training programme. Overload can be achieved by increasing the frequency with which you train, by increasing the duration of your training sessions, by increasing the intensity of your training sessions (i.e. how hard you ride), and/or by manipulating the amount of recovery time between your training sessions.

Specificity
The principle of specificity states simply that you get what you train for. Run training may improve your general health and fitness but it won't make you a better bike rider. The same is true of the different types of cycle training: short sprint training will make you better at short sprints, while 20-minute intervals will make you better at 20-minute intervals! But, these sessions will also have more general effects on specific aspects of your physiology; notably, with these examples, neuromuscular power and threshold power. While not giving you the biggest 'bang for your buck', these sessions will still have a positive impact on your ultra-distance performance. And they keep training interesting!

Frequency
Most elite cyclists train once a day, with one, or sometimes two, rest days per week. For professional cyclists each session will likely be a long ride, comprising a number of components from long hill intervals to repeated sprints. Compared to sports such as swimming and running, it is less common for cyclists to complete more than one session per day; however, this need not be the case. Indeed, for ultra-distance cyclists, juggling work and family commitments, completing morning and evening sessions is one of the best ways to bag the training kilometres needed to excel in ultra-distance cycling – think specificity! This also allows each session to target specific aspects of your physiology, or focus on specific areas of weakness.

Duration
No matter the discipline, all cyclists will benefit from sessions of long duration because cycling is, at its core, an endurance sport. Of course, this is particularly true for ultra-distance cyclists, the purist endurance cyclists of them all. Long-duration cycling stimulates important adaptations in your body's ability to use fat as a fuel, allowing you to spare what are always limited stores of carbohydrate for when you really need them.

>>Life gets in the way of even the best training programmes.>>

Intensity

You can and should manipulate all of the key principles described here to get the most out of your training; however, the most obvious effect will be seen when manipulating your training intensity. High-intensity cycling (i.e. high power intervals) recruits large, fast twitch muscle fibres. These fibres respond quickly to overload, meaning that your 'top end' power can be developed quickly. Low- and moderate-intensity cycling relies on slow-twitch muscle fibres, which respond, comparatively, more slowly. Many ultra-distance cyclists do little or no high-intensity training – which is understandable, given the specificity comments above! There is, however, a time and a place for all training intensities, even for ultra-distance cyclists. While being largely dependent on endurance prowess, successful ultra-distance cycling performance will still require periods of high power output. Increasing your top-end power 'ceiling' will also mean that your endurance riding is completed at a lower percentage of your maximum. The relative strain on your body is, therefore, reduced, meaning that you will recover more quickly and have more in reserve when you really need it.

Flexibility

This is not a textbook training principle, but the authors believe it to be just as important as those above. Flexibility does not refer to whether or not you can touch your toes (although that can be helpful!). This key principle encourages you to keep your training flexible, by giving yourself enough room for things to vary. Life gets in the way of even the best training programmes. If you are comfortable with some flexibility, both within individual training sessions and across a series of sessions, you will be able to respond to that late meeting, or an unexpected traffic jam, in a way that keeps your overall training objectives on track.

Flexibility is also related to another important training principle: keep it interesting. Sometimes, enjoying a session is more important than hitting the target mileage or power output. Learning to push through a tough session in which you find no enjoyment is a vital stage in the development of any successful ultra-distance cyclist. However, if you have to do this for every session, after a few days your desire to train will disappear.

It is important that you and your coach appreciate these key training principles. The way in which these principles are systematically applied will determine the success of your training programme. So, how do you corral these varied and sometimes competing principles into a workable training programme? As we all respond to training in our own unique ways, there will always be a need for trial and error. There are, however, some approaches to overall training structure that can help you frame your training journey to ultra-distance cycling success.

HONESTY IS THE BEST POLICY

There is an element of competition in many aspects of our lives, certainly in the work environment and often in our extracurricular activities. Nowhere is this more obvious than in a sports setting, where the aim is usually to win by outperforming other athletes. It is unsurprising therefore that this competitive spirit often leaks into our training. The goal of training is to improve performance and so it is easy to feel that you should be improving in every training ride.

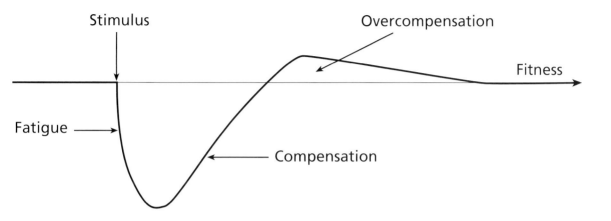

The law of overload

Figure 6: The principle of overload

'Joe the cyclist' starts preparing for a two x 20-minute threshold interval session. When he last completed the same session, two weeks ago, he was able to average 300 watts for both intervals. His training has gone well since then and so he feels that he should be able to average 305 watts today. After a quality warm-up that included three 20-second efforts at threshold intensity, Joe is now five minutes into the first 305W interval:

'This is feeling quite tough. No problem, I will ease into it in a minute or two.'

Joe is now 15 minutes into the first interval and he's hanging on for all he's worth:

'Something's not right today. Two 300W intervals were easy two weeks ago and I'm not sure that I can even complete one at 305W today. I'll just get to the end of this one and see if my legs come good.'

In the 10-minute Level 1 recovery spin between intervals, Joe is wondering what the problem is:

'Perhaps I haven't eaten enough today? Maybe it was that dodgy curry at the weekend? Is there something wrong with the power meter?

No worries, I'm sure I'll be fine in the second interval.'

Five minutes into the second interval, Joe's legs are screaming and he's given up on the session and looking for the quickest way home.

What was the problem? It is possible that poor nutrition caused the problem and it is also possible that the power meter was under-reading (a good reason to always zero your power meter pre-ride and to perform regular calibration checks). More likely, however, is that Joe's body was doing exactly what we would expect, given the overload training principle.

In Figure 6 you can see that after a training stimulus (e.g. a single session and/or a series of sessions) fatigue sets in and fitness – here synonymous with performance – nosedives. Over time the body 'compensates' for this overload and performance starts to rebound, eventually rising above the pre-stimulus fitness level. Without a new training stimulus, this overcompensation response eventually dissipates, such that fitness returns to baseline levels. However, if you time subsequent training stimuli just right, you can build on successive overcompensations to take performance higher and higher (see Figure 7).

Given his recent quality training, Joe was probably well into the fatigue stage of the overload curve. It was, therefore, inevitable that his performance would not have improved since his last 'two x 20'. Had he been honest with himself – 'Yes, my power is likely to be down today. I don't need to improve in every session' – and backed off to 300W, or even 295W, he would have completed the session and added another quality stimulus to his current overload cycle.

Another element of being honest with yourself relates to recognition of the need to work on your cycling weaknesses. The laboratory and/or field tests described above may have shown that particular areas of your physiology (e.g. $\dot{V}O_2$max, threshold, efficiency) are letting you down. Alternatively, riding with others might have highlighted that your weak descending skills are responsible for the loss of vital time. If you are always competing with yourself and others, you will be too often tempted to ride to your strengths. If you do this, your weaknesses will just become bigger and bigger drags. Be honest: if you have a weakness, work on it. You should still do plenty of the cycling that you enjoy, but the biggest performance gains will come from spending more time working on your weaknesses.

As Dominic's story at the start of the chapter so graphically demonstrated, his focus on long, steady, slow rides had made him good at riding slowly for long periods of time. In fact, he'd got very good at this, but this was inadequate preparation for breaking a cycling record. Similarly, Dominic's tandem riding partner was very fast over short distances, but Land's End to John o'Groats was a *non-stop* 1,365km ride. It would be no good if they got 150km in with Charlie spent and Dominic simply unable to go fast enough.

Figure 7: Optimal recovery time

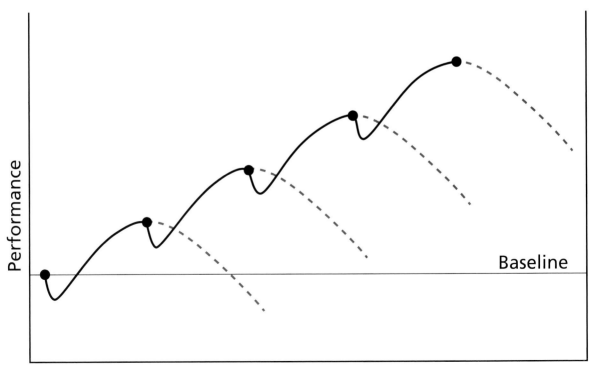

>> Training is a crucial ingredient for cycling success, but it is just one ingredient of a complex, multifaceted recipe. >>

APPROACHES TO TRAINING

Testing will give you a good idea of where you are now and where you need to be for success in your chosen event – the gap between these two is what your training plan aims to bridge. So what should your training consist of? Should you complete the same 20-mile loop every day? Should you always be 'on the rivet'? Or do you need to develop advanced mathematical skills in order to deal with the complexities of planning a 'periodised' programme?

When Fausto Coppi was asked what it takes to be a great champion, he replied, 'Ride your bike, ride your bike, ride your bike.' Similarly, as we saw earlier, when Eddy Merckx was asked what advice he would give to aspiring riders, he said, 'Ride lots.' While simplistic, there is more than a grain of truth here. However, while time in the saddle will make you a very competent bike rider, it is not enough to allow you to excel. You need to be a little more deliberate.

Research conducted by Anders Ericsson suggests that the number of years spent utilising a skill is only loosely related to performance. Similarly, the amount of time spent in competition is only loosely related to overall performance success. Instead, Ericsson has argued that virtually all differences in performance can be accounted for by the amount of deliberate practice a person engages in. In other words, what matters is not how many hours or kilometres you ride, but how deliberate your training is. If you want to be really good, you need to practise; and that's not the same as simply riding lots. Ericsson's thesis suggests that any individual can become an elite athlete if they engage in 10,000 hours of deliberate practice. Even if your ultra-distance cycling aspirations do not include multiple Grand Tours wins, the critical point here is that while 'ride lots' is good advice, it only tells part of the story.

So, by following a scientific (i.e. deliberate) approach to your training, with a 20-hour-a-week programme, will you be an 'expert' in just 10 short years? The answer, of course, is 'maybe; maybe not!' Training is a crucial ingredient for cycling success, but it is just one ingredient of a complex, multifaceted recipe.

PERIODISED PROGRAMMES

Cyclist X wins the Tour de France/Race Across America/Ultracycling Dolomitica. How did he do it? Perhaps he had the best bike and the best support team. Perhaps he chose the best parents. He must certainly have had the best training plan, right?

For many cyclists, the construction of a new training and racing programme is based on what they've done before and what they believe other people to have done. Of course, someone might have won a race in spite of their training programme. A race win does not mean that we should all buy Cyclist X's *Eight-week Performance Programme*. Instead, a training programme should be planned with knowledge of key training principles, experience of what has and has not worked for you in the past, and what your goals are. When constructing your training programme, you should first consider the macro level – the overall structure of the programme – before becoming more focused on training types (strength training, sprint training, etc.) and, eventually, the details of specific training sessions.

PLANNING AT THE MACRO LEVEL

Periodisation is the name given to systematic planning of a training programme by varying the training intensity of sessions, their duration, how often sessions are performed, and how much rest and recovery is required between sessions. Despite having an academic underpinning, periodisation is more art than science. However, science is beginning to catch up, as researchers study the effectiveness of different approaches to macro-level training planning.

The two most commonly used models of periodisation are traditional periodisation and block periodisation. In both approaches, training is considered at different levels of time and detail. At the top level is the macrocycle. For an Olympic athlete, the macrocycle might last for four years, but for most cyclists the macrocycle lasts for one year. The macrocycle is divided into relatively long *mesocycles* (see Figure 9). Traditional periodisation begins with a preparatory phase, a long mesocycle of aerobic base training made up of long duration, low- to moderate-intensity sessions. Next comes a period of high volume and high-intensity riding

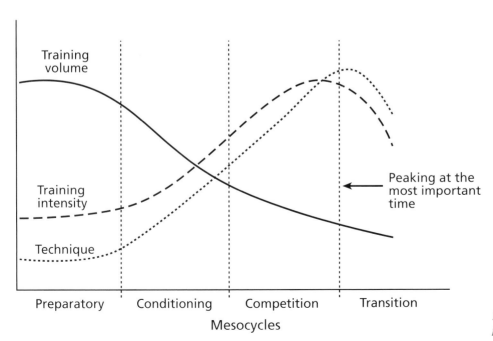

Figure 8: Traditional periodisation approach

known as the conditioning mesocycle, which is then followed by the competition mesocycle. During this competition phase training intensity remains high but training volume is reduced to allow adequate recovery that ensures race freshness. The competition phase might also include one or more taper periods that lead into high priority events. The final mesocycle is the recovery phase, essential for a physical and, often more important, mental break from training and racing. A classic recovery phase consists of two weeks of no training followed by two weeks of non-cycling training (such as swimming). There are, however, no hard and fast rules here; some cyclists need a six-week recovery phase, while others need just two.

One problem with the traditional periodisation model is that it is built around a single 'A' priority event. From a training perspective, this is ideal as you never have to compromise your training goals. Of course, having only a single priority event is risky, as any number of bad luck scenarios can play out once a year. Furthermore, as time goes by there is an ever-increasing expectation that athletes be able to perform at a high level throughout the competition phase. A road race cyclist might be competing two to three times per week from April to October. Peaking seven months after the start of the season is not all that helpful!

Such demands have led to the development of the block periodisation approach. While using the same training philosophies as the classic periodisation approach, block periodisation shortens each phase so that peak (or we might say 'fresh') performances can occur more often. Block periodisation consists of aerobic base phases of four to six weeks, condensed specific conditioning phases of two weeks, and short taper periods (around a week) during the competition phase (see Figure 10). This cycle is repeated for successive priority events, allowing a good level of performance to be achieved throughout the season. Note, however, that true peak performance is still only achieved at one point in the year.

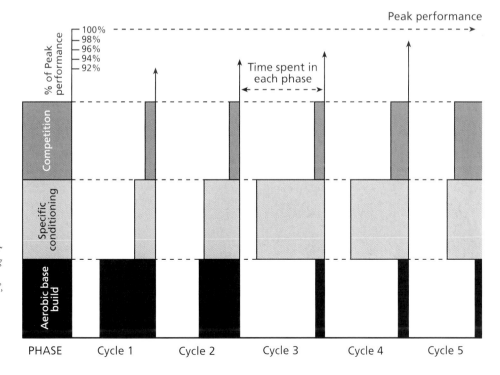

Figure 9: Block periodisation approach (adapted from Mujika & Larrsen (2012) 'Training methodology and periodisation for cycling', in Hopker and Jobson (Eds.) Performance Cycling: The Science of Success. London: Bloomsbury)

>> The overload principle makes clear that improvements will only be seen if you allow adequate time for your body to adapt and recover. >>

WHY DO PEOPLE TRAIN THE WAY THEY DO?

As suggested above, training programme design contains elements of both science and art. Periodisation continues to be taught in universities, but some athletes and coaches have been studiously ignoring this advice for years.

One reason for this is that research studies have, at different times, shown particular types of training to be highly effective in boosting performance. Prior to the mid-1990s it was generally accepted that long, steady distance riding was necessary to improve $\dot{V}O_2$max. Because $\dot{V}O_2$max was known to be an important determinant of cycling performance, if you wanted to improve your $\dot{V}O_2$max you had to do long, steady (Level 2) endurance rides. Then things began to change as a number of research studies were published that showed that high-intensity interval training had a big impact on physiological development and cycling performance. So, $\dot{V}O_2$max can be improved by doing a one-hour 5x5 session (5-minute intervals at Level 5 with five-minute recovery periods) – which has been proven effective – or by doing a five-hour Level 2 endurance ride that most people think is effective but for which there is little definitive evidence. We'll take the one-hour session, thank you very much!

So began a shift away from reliance on long, endurance training towards more 'scientific' and more time efficient interval training; a shift that has only become more exaggerated as evidence about high-intensity interval training has started to capture the public imagination.

HIGH-INTENSITY INTERVAL TRAINING (HIIT)

HIIT involves a number of very short duration (typically 30 seconds to one minute) intervals at maximal or near-maximal intensity. The headlines suggest that as little as three minutes per week of (albeit vomit-inducing intensity) exercise can produce significant fitness improvements (journalists usually ignore the time required for warm-up, recovery and warm-down).

In contrast to this high-intensity shift, evidence has begun to emerge in favour of the long, steady distance approach. In 2002, Schumacher and Mueller described the seven-month training programme completed by the German cyclists that set the 4,000m team pursuit world record at the Sydney 2000 Olympic Games. At a time when many thought that threshold and above (i.e. Level 4–7) training intensities were the way to success, the German pursuit team was clocking up 35,000km of riding per year. These kilometres comprised mostly long, steady distance riding interspersed with some stage racing (that would necessarily include some high-intensity riding) and just one track-specific period of high-intensity training in the eight days leading up to the Games. While the German team's success might have been in spite of the predominance of low-intensity training, we cannot ignore the fact that the same approach has been used to similar effect by successive Australian and Great Britain pursuit teams.

>>Recognise that performance = fitness + freshness as you approach a key event.>>

As both low- and high-intensity approaches appear to 'work', we might then ask, can we combine them? As the evidence in favour of a polarised training approach begins to mount, the answer appears to be yes.

POLARISED TRAINING

While investigating world-class Norwegian rowers, Stephen Seiler and colleagues reported that the $\dot{V}O_2$max of the rowers increased by 12 per cent, and that six-minute all-out rowing performance improved by 10 per cent, in the period from 1970 to 2001. Without further evidence, many would have said that this was due, in part, to an increasingly 'scientific' approach to training, as athletes adopted threshold and high-intensity interval approaches to training. However, over the same period, there was actually an increase in the volume of low-intensity training and a decrease in the volume of high-intensity training for these athletes.

The benefits of high-intensity training are not in doubt. There is, however, a limit to how much such training can be completed before one starts to overreach. Elite international endurance athletes organise their training on an approximate 80:20 basis: about 80 per cent at low-intensity and about 20 per cent at high-intensity.

It would be easy to dismiss the 80:20 polarised approach on the basis that it's only relevant for professional athletes with the time to complete 30+ hours of training per week; however, a 2013 study by Neal and colleagues suggests otherwise. In this study, a group of 12 cyclists completed two six-week training programmes: a polarised approach, comprising an average of 6.4 hours' training per week; and a 'threshold' approach, comprising an average of 7.5 hours' training per week. While improvements were seen with both approaches, a higher level of beneficial training adaptation was seen in the polarised group, suggesting that a polarised training intensity distribution is as likely to be beneficial for the time-poor amateur cyclist as it is for the time-rich professional.

IF YOU'RE NOT TRAINING, ARE YOU DETRAINING?

With so much focus on training, it is easy to slip into a mindset of 'If I'm not training, I must be losing fitness'. However, the overload principle makes clear that improvements will only be seen if you allow adequate time for your body to adapt and recover. Recognising that *performance = fitness + freshness*, as you approach a key event you need to allow time for your freshness to catch up with your fitness. This is usually achieved through a reduction in training volume, a process known as tapering.

Research findings suggest that a taper works when training intensity is maintained and training volume is decreased by 20–60 per cent. You should, therefore, reduce the frequency and/ or duration of your training sessions in the days and weeks before your priority races. A typical recommendation is for a taper that lasts between eight and 14 days; however, the precise time requirement is specific to the individual rider. Some riders need a full two-week taper, and some need no more than two days. As with so many things discussed in this book, it's recommended that you experiment with different taper designs during training. Don't forget to reduce your energy intake as you reduce training volume; there is no point being fresher if you combine this with being fatter.

Many riders struggle with the idea of tapering because they are aware of the principle of training reversibility, or detraining. This is where insufficient or no training results in loss of fitness. Research findings suggest that $\dot{V}O_2$max, muscle structures and blood volume begin to decline after 10–15 days of no training. This is why your taper should not be too long. Other systems, such as lactate metabolism and carbohydrate storage, decline more rapidly, i.e. after approximately five days. It's important to recognise, however, that this is five to 15 days of no training. Even during a taper, you will still be training.

You should not, therefore, worry about detraining during your taper. But what if you miss a couple of sessions through illness, or because there was a crisis at work? The key thing to remember is that detraining does not kick in immediately, and so you do not need to chase the odd missed session. If you are forced to miss your planned Monday and Tuesday sessions, just pick up the programme on Wednesday with the session that was planned for Wednesday.

YOUR TIME IS PRECIOUS: MEASURE YOUR EFFORT

Peak performance can only result from an appropriate balance of training and recovery. For those with limited time – anyone who is not a professional athlete – an efficient balance is critical. It is important to avoid 'filler' kilometres, instead aiming to maximise the benefit of every minute spent on the bike in order to achieve one's performance goals. Do you need to ride for five hours, or will you get just as much benefit from two?

In order to answer this question accurately, you need to consider further some of the principles of training described above, in particular, duration, frequency and intensity. Combined, these elements describe your training 'dose'. If you can accurately quantify your training dose, you will then be able to implement the key principles of training progression, specificity and overload.

Many cyclists have successfully used training volume (kilometres/week and/or hours/week) as an index of training dose, often in combination with the concept of pace (slow versus fast). However, changes in variables such as riding terrain, weather conditions (especially wind) and equipment make the link between riding speed and intensity a tenuous one, such that these basic indices fail to account for the important influence of training intensity. Fortunately, a number of alternatives are available.

Many cyclists have been successful when using training plans based on descriptive phrases of effort such as 'easy', 'steady', 'hard' and 'maximal'. Indeed, this approach has been formalised into a quantified rating of perceived exertion (RPE) scale. The RPE is defined by the intensity of discomfort or fatigue felt at a particular moment,

>> When compared to heart rate-based metrics, session RPE has been shown to be a reliable and valid method of quantifying intensity during both aerobic and resistance exercise. >>

and has been shown to correlate well with training intensity. Session RPE, a modification of the standard RPE scale, provides an objective rating for a session as a whole, rather than for a specific aspect (e.g. interval/set) of a session. When compared to heart rate-based metrics, session RPE has been shown to be a reliable and valid method of quantifying intensity during both aerobic and resistance exercise.

Nevertheless, you should be aware of some limitations. RPE is a subjective measure; the

judgement of how an effort feels is unique to the individual. One person's 'steady' may be another person's 'hard'. Session RPE is based on perception and so is affected just as much by mood and level of motivation as it is by training intensity. For these reasons, using RPE to rate training intensity allows little scope for comparison, either between separate athletes, or perhaps even between multiple training sessions performed by the same individual.

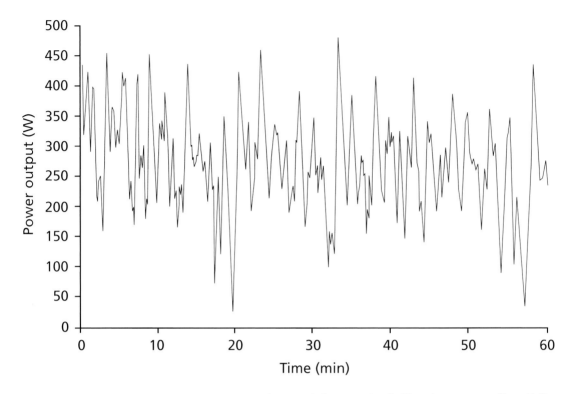

TRAINING WITH HEART RATE

In a laboratory setting, sports scientists measure oxygen consumption to determine the energy requirements of exercise or the amount of stress the body's systems are under. Oxygen is transported from the lungs to the muscles in the bloodstream, bound to haemoglobin. The greater the intensity of exercise, the more work has to be produced by the active muscles. This extra work means a higher oxygen demand in the muscle, which results in the heart beating more frequently to pump an increased volume of blood to the muscle. Thus, by measuring heart rate you are indirectly estimating oxygen consumption.

For heart rate measurement to be useful, it needs to be anchored to your physiology. For some riders, an average heart rate of 130 beats·min-1 indicates time-trial intensity, while for others it indicates a light recovery ride. The two main heart rate anchor points that you can use are your maximum heart rate (measured during a $\dot{V}O_2$max test) and threshold heart rate

(measured during a threshold test). Using a threshold-anchored heart rate, Table 4 (page 135) illustrates how your heart rate can be used to target specific aspects of your physiology. Your maximum heart rate can be estimated using simple equations such as 220 minus your age; however, such estimates can dramatically under- or over-estimate your true maximum heart rate and so should really only be used as a stopgap until you can complete a laboratory- or field-based test.

Heart rate data is useful as a pacing tool and for summarising your sessions; however, the lag in the heart rate response can make the pacing aspect quite challenging. Let's say that you are targeting a Level 4 heart rate of 170 beats·min-1 because you are carrying out a four x 10-minute threshold interval training session. Because it may take as long as two minutes for your heart rate to accurately reflect the true physiological demand of the interval, if you push really hard to achieve a heart rate of 170 beats·min-1 in this time you will probably be riding well above Level 4 intensity. The first two minutes of your

Figure 10: Power output from a typical road-based training session (adapted from Jobson and Passfield (2012) 'How to use cycling training data', in Hopker and Jobson (Eds), Performance Cycling: The Science of Success, London: Bloomsbury)

>> Irrespective of exercise intensity, heart rate may vary due to factors such as cardiovascular drift. >>

interval will have been wasted as far as your threshold focus goes, and you will probably have seriously reduced the probability of completing the full interval. You should, therefore, pace the early stages of mid- to high-intensity efforts using RPE, adjusting when your heart rate starts to settle. The more that you ride with heart rate, the more used to this phenomenon you will become, and the more accurate your heart rate-directed pacing will be.

Irrespective of exercise intensity, heart rate may vary due to factors such as cardiovascular drift (where heart rate increases over time, despite no change in your power output), changes in temperature, hydration status and body position on the bike. More subtle use of heart rate data in the form of heart rate variability and/or heart rate recovery may, therefore, be preferable to the use of 'raw' heart rate readings.

Monitoring heart rate is undoubtedly a more objective means of guiding and tracking training than 'Rate of Perceived Exertion' (RPE). However, in addition to the limitations mentioned above, it is important to remember that it is a measure of the body's response to a given exercise intensity. In contrast, recording power output provides a direct mechanical measure of how hard you are working.

TRAINING WITH POWER

In recent years, a plethora of mobile power meters have become available that allow the continuous measurement of work rate (i.e. power output) when riding your own bicycle during training and competition. The ability to quantify accurately the mechanical work of training, as well as the detail and extent of these data, makes cycling unique in allowing such insight into the demands of sporting preparation and competition. However, the inherent variability in power output during training poses a number of challenges when attempting to evaluate the exact nature of any training session.

Consider Figure 11 (page 156), an example of a power output file from a typical road-based training session. The first thing you will notice is how variable power output is. Nevertheless, it is possible to identify key features, such as the number of above-threshold efforts completed or the point where the highest power output was achieved, simply through visual inspection. Beyond this, a number of methods exist to summarise sessions (or sections of sessions).

>> Cycling is a rich tapestry influenced by many things, not least enjoyment. It is vital you keep the numbers in perspective. >>

CALCULATION OF AVERAGE POWER

Average power provides a useful method of comparing sessions. If you complete a steady endurance ride with an average power output of 240W today, that a month ago could only be completed at 220W, you have taken a significant step forward in your training. Average power is, however, limited when it comes to the evaluation of high-intensity or variable-intensity sessions.

Calculation of Normalized Power® accounts for the disproportionate psychological and physiological strain experienced when effort is not constant. Commercial software packages that automate the calculation of Normalized Power® are available (e.g. TrainingPeaks' WKO+), although the calculation is relatively simple if you are familiar with standard spreadsheet software. With average power, it is not possible to differentiate between a session completed at a constant endurance pace and a session that includes short bouts of very high-intensity effort (e.g. sprints) interspersed with very low-intensity recovery riding. Calculation of Normalized Power® would demonstrate that the physiological demand of these sessions is in fact very different.

IS IT ALL ABOUT THE NUMBERS?

Much of this chapter focuses on the scientific approach to your training and racing. Numbers are necessarily a big part of this picture as you plan the number of mesocycles in your macrocycle; as you generate results in your laboratory testing; and as you record the heart rate and power output from every turn of the pedal. However, cycling is a rich tapestry influenced by many things, not least enjoyment. It is, therefore, vital that you keep the numbers in perspective. As you initially adopt a more scientific approach, the numbers may take on a disproportionate importance. However, over time, you will develop a strong understanding of how the numbers relate to everything else (e.g. your mood, the weather, your race pace) such that they become just another aspect of your cycling success. At some point, you and your coach will have such a good understanding of how your numbers relate to your lifestyle and your training response that testing, for example, can become less frequent. Indeed, you will reach a point where your testing simply confirms what you already know!

≫More power combined with no change in body mass means more speed.≫

IS IT ALL ABOUT THE BIKE?

STRENGTH TRAINING

Specificity is essential in any form of training. If you want to become a better runner, run training will have a far bigger beneficial impact on your performance than swim training. Similarly, if you want to become a better ultra-distance cyclist, cycle training will usually be more effective than a weights programme. Nevertheless, recent research does show that strength training may have a place in your training arsenal.

It would appear that, at least for some riders, heavy strength training has a positive impact on endurance cycling performance, and on traditional indicators of cycling performance such as cycling economy and lactate threshold. So why are we sometimes wary of engaging in such training? Setting aside personal preferences, the main reason is usually a desire to avoid weight gain.

Strength training undoubtedly causes an increase in muscle and total body mass; however, it is possible to induce strength gain without an increase in body mass. Research has shown that 8–14-week programmes of combined strength and endurance training result in increased muscle mass and reduced fat mass. The combination of these effects is no change in total body mass. More muscle means the potential to produce more power. More power combined with no change in body mass means more speed. While endurance exercise appears to reduce the strength gains from a strength-training programme, the avoidance of total body mass gain allowed by the addition of endurance training could be invaluable for you.

STRENGTH TRAINING AND CYCLING PHYSIOLOGY

As explained above, cycling performance is influenced by three essential physiological attributes: $\dot{V}O_2$max, threshold and economy. There is no evidence to suggest that strength training improves $\dot{V}O_2$max, but there is evidence to show that $\dot{V}O_2$max development is not hindered when strength training is combined with endurance training.

Maximal aerobic power (MAP) is a close correlate of $\dot{V}O_2$max. It is, in essence, the power output recorded at the point of maximal oxygen uptake (i.e. $\dot{V}O_2$max). Despite being so closely related to $\dot{V}O_2$max, MAP is actually the better predictor of cycling performance – suggesting that your cycling performance is more likely to be improved if you increase your MAP than if you increase your $\dot{V}O_2$max. Heavy (but not explosive) strength training appears to result in an improvement in MAP. The differing responses of $\dot{V}O_2$max and MAP are likely the result of MAP being affected by multiple underlying physiological factors, such as aerobic capacity, anaerobic capacity and efficiency, whereas $\dot{V}O_2$max is a 'pure' measure of aerobic capacity.

There is evidence to suggest that strength training improves lactate threshold, but only when multiple strength training exercises are performed. Making a single muscle stronger does not result in a threshold increase. Instead, training multiple muscles allows the load to be spread across more muscles. Each muscle fibre has to work less hard for the production of any given amount of total work (e.g. weight lifted). In a cycling context, the body is therefore able to produce more power before each muscle fibre reaches threshold. In order to improve

≫As muscles contract during a pedal stroke, they cause momentary blood flow restrictions.≫

your lactate threshold, your strength-training programme should, therefore, consist of lower body exercises that target the main muscle groups involved in pedalling.

Strength training has also been shown to improve cycling economy (a variant of cycling efficiency), particularly during prolonged cycling. There is no difference in cycling economy during the first two hours of riding when comparing 'normal' training groups with those that supplement with heavy strength training; however, this starts to change during the third hour of riding, as strength-trained cyclists begin to demonstrate higher economy. Further research is required to determine whether or not this effect persists over ultra-distances, where small differences could result in big performance gains. Further research is also required to establish the reason for economy improvements. By increasing maximal strength, the percentage of maximal effort required in each ultra-distance pedal stroke would decrease, and so it is likely that the improvement is linked to higher use of type I muscle fibres, which are more economical than type II fibres, and to reduced ratings of perceived exertion.

The improvement in all of these physiological factors may also be due to a strength training-induced improvement in blood flow to the working muscles. As muscles contract during a pedal stroke, they cause momentary blood flow restrictions. The reduction of relative pedal force described above will likely reduce the frequency and duration of these restrictions, allowing more oxygen and fuel nutrients to be delivered to the muscle and more waste products to be removed.

STRENGTH TRAINING AND CYCLING PERFORMANCE

Because of the physiological improvements seen following strength training programmes, we would expect to see improvements in cycling performance. Indeed, research studies have demonstrated improvements in time trial performance following heavy (but not explosive) strength training. There is less evidence relating to ultra-distance cycling performance, simply because of the practical challenges of studying such performance. It is likely that the benefits will be just as significant as in time trials lasting 30–60 minutes; however, you will have to experiment to find out if this is the case for you. A 12-week combined endurance and strength training programme, leading up to a lesser priority event, will tell you whether strength training should become a regular part of your ultra-distance cycling training regimen.

YOUR FIRST STRENGTH–TRAINING PROGRAMME

Strength training will usually take place during the preparatory and pre-competition phases of training through the inclusion of two dedicated sessions per week. Combined with a programme of endurance training, this will lead to marked strength increases within approximately 12 weeks. Before embarking on such a programme, it is important that you establish a correct, safe lifting technique. As in all other aspects of your training, specificity should be an important consideration of your strength-training programme. You should seek to use strength-training exercises that are, at least in part, similar to pedalling movement. There is also some suggestion that single-leg exercises are more

APPLES HAVE CORES, CYCLISTS DON'T

For a number of years, you won't have been able to read a fitness magazine without coming across articles promoting the importance of core strength and core stability. Even in cycling publications, stability ball work and other core-focused exercises have been publicised as universally beneficial for preventing back pain on the bike and improving cycling performance.

WHERE IT ALL CAME FROM

In the 1990s, research in Australia suggested that weakness in one small muscle of the body's trunk, the *transverse abdominus* (TrA), was responsible for the majority of lower back pain. With back pain such a prevalent complaint in modern society, the physiotherapy world adopted this universal cure for all and was, in turn, followed by the fitness industry: the core stability trend was born! Small, precise and isolated movements that targeted the TrA were not only prescribed for people suffering from back injuries, but also for fitness enthusiasts and athletes searching for performance gains and injury prevention.

THE PROBLEM

One of the biggest issues with isolating the TrA is that it doesn't work in isolation. It works with every other muscle that makes up the abdominal wall in its multiple roles, of which spinal stabilisation is only one. Research has failed to show any conclusive link between back pain and weakness of the TrA in isolation. A good analogy is that your trunk is like a tent, with all the guy ropes and pegs representing the muscles and other soft tissue structures. You need to make sure that all the guy ropes and pegs are right, rather than focusing on one individual peg; the TrA. Even when patients have recovered from bad backs after performing TrA-focused rehabilitation, it is not clear whether the exercises were responsible. They might have improved anyway due to the rest, not performing the activities that could have been aggravating their backs. And, of course, the recovery may have been a simple placebo effect.

The benefits of these narrowly-focused exercises – that are often conducted in a lying-down prone position – to sports performance are even less clear.

They have their place in a rehabilitation scenario but, in other sporting contexts, they have been mis-sold. Knowing how to prescribe and progress these exercises requires in-depth knowledge and an extremely intensive approach. For the vast majority of time-stretched cyclists, who already have reasonable functional fitness for cycling and life in general, time spent on these types of exercises, without detailed instruction, is often time wasted.

Within British Cycling, the expression 'core stability' is no longer used; instead, functional trunk strength and robustness are the watchwords. Functional trunk strength and coordination are what are needed to be able to pedal strongly, perform on-the-bike tasks such as putting on a rain cape and, in the case of track sprinters, lift heavy weights in the gym. Robustness is the capacity to absorb training and avoid injury, both on and off the bike.

If you imagine performance as a pyramid, cycling-specific fitness is the point at the very top. Relevant strength work might not directly benefit your performance on the bike, but it will indirectly build a wider base of robustness and conditioning to your pyramid. This in turn will allow your point to rise higher through an improved ability to cope with consistent training, and it will avoid lay-offs due to injury.

WHAT DOES THIS MEAN FOR ME?

You are probably already able to ride your bike for multiple hours and to perform the day-to-day tasks and movements that your non-cycling life involves. If this is the case, the exercises that are typically prescribed for 'core strength' will have little relevance or benefit to you. Even if you do sometimes suffer from a sore back on the bike, this can be the inevitable result of a poor bike set-up or simply the result of a tough day in the saddle. Indeed, the pain could be due to factors completely unrelated to cycling. If back pain is limiting you, either on or off the bike, consult with an appropriately qualified professional. Devoting your valuable time to exercises that are unproven to help with either back problems or cycling performance is pointless.

Phil Burt, lead physiotherapist
with the Great Britain Cycling Team
and consultant physiotherapist to Team Sky

beneficial than double-leg exercises, as the force developed during double-leg exercises is less than the sum of maximal single-leg exercises. During maximal double-leg exercise, each leg may not be working at its maximal level and, therefore, each leg may not be receiving a maximal training stimulus.

Specificity is further achieved by training the correct type of muscle contraction (concentric, i.e. shortening) at the correct leg angle. Peak pedal force is achieved with the knee at approximately 100 degrees (crank arm at 90 degrees), and so strength-training exercises with the knee between 90 degrees and full extension will be most effective. The velocity of strength-training movements will usually be lower than is achieved during actual cycling. Therefore, it is important to perform lifts as quickly as possible. (This puts extra emphasis on your ability to use good technique!) In particular, the concentric phase of the lift should be rapid, while the eccentric (think pedal upstroke) phase should

be quite slow to avoid the risk of injury.

A cycling-specific strength-training programme might comprise half-squat, single-leg half-squat, step-up, single-leg leg-press, single-leg hip-flexion and toe-raise exercises. In a 45-minute session, a 10-minute warm-up should normally be followed by the exercise that involves the largest muscle mass. Progressing through a total of no more than four exercise types, the session will end with the exercise that requires the least amount of coordination.

The benefits of strength training dissipate quickly, returning to pre-training levels in as little as eight weeks. For this reason, a strength maintenance programme should be followed during the competition phase of the season. While the exercise details (type, angle, velocity) should continue as detailed above, strength can be maintained with a 50 per cent reduction in strength-training volume (e.g. one session per week with approximately half the number of sets).

>>When riding in wet or muddy conditions, use a water bottle with a cap that covers the nipple.>>

DON'T FORGET TO WASH YOUR HANDS

It's not something that many riders give much thought to, but personal hygiene is an important aspect of ultra-distance cycling. With so much time needed for training, being ill can have a significant impact on your preparations and racing. The three main causes of infection are via the air, physical contact and common source exposure (e.g. food poisoning). You are at greater risk in places where people are gathered together, such as airports, cinemas, train carriages, buses, changing rooms, home, sports labs, shops, workplaces and restaurants. Avoiding such places in your daily life may simply not be possible; hand hygiene therefore becomes critical in minimising the risk of infection.

Sleep loss (discussed in Chapter 6: Approach) can also contribute to a weakened immune system. All this might sound like paranoia, but if you've been training for a year for an event and you have a family holiday booked around the trip, taking a few precautions when travelling to the event is a small price to pay to remain healthy for the race. There are a number of things you can do in training and when racing that will help.

On a long ride, little time has to pass before you become covered in road grime, be that dust, mud or grime sprayed up from wet roads. The notion of hygiene in these circumstances can be seen as something of a joke, but it is still worth making the effort.

- When riding in wet or muddy conditions, use a water bottle with a cap that covers the nipple. This keeps water, mud and other debris, sprayed from tyres and other road users, from coating the water bottle. After every use, wash and dry your bottles thoroughly to avoid any build-up of bacteria. Most bottles can go in the dishwasher.
- If your journey to work involves a commute and the use of communal washing facilities, avoid sharing towels, razors, soaps and equipment. Also avoid the use of shared whirlpools and Jacuzzis, which will help avoid the risk of skin infections. If you have any open wounds, make sure they are thoroughly cleaned and that any dressing is replaced regularly.
- If you have a bike set up on a turbo trainer, wash the bar tape regularly and replace it from time to time. Any sweat you generate will be absorbed by the bar tape; every time you train, the tape is warmed up, providing perfect conditions to breed bacteria.
- Avoid Athlete's Foot by washing your feet thoroughly after each ride and making sure your shoes dry out fully. Wash your kit after each ride to avoid the build-up of bacteria. If you are training once or twice a day this can mean getting through a lot of kit. But better that you are inconvenienced by washing than by ill health.
- On long rides, you may find yourself caught short, kilometres from anywhere. When you need to go to the toilet, a small travel pack of wet wipes is useful to both clean yourself and your hands afterwards. Relying on hand-cleaning products in public toilets is the triumph of hope over experience. Wet wipes are also useful for freshening up on long rides.

>> Training with a power means understanding the purpose of every training session and staying within prescribed training zones. >>

Despite your best efforts, sometimes you will get ill. Give yourself time to recover properly. A good rule of thumb is that if the symptoms are from the neck up, such as a sore throat or cold, you can still train; just go gently. If symptoms are below the neck, involving the chest and flu-like symptoms, rest. Returning to training too early after suffering ill health due to a virus can lead to myocarditis, a disease in which the heart muscle becomes inflamed and damaged.

The evidence suggests that moderate aerobic training in trained athletes helps your immune system. Overtraining, on the other hand, has the opposite effect. Early indicators of overtraining are as likely to be psychological factors as physical. Being very tired as a result of training is not something to overcome, but something to respect. As has been discussed above, rest is as important as training, and this applies equally to staying fit and well.

SUMMARY

Much of this chapter is predicated on training with a power meter. By doing so, you can determine your training zones, accurately measure performance improvement, and use it to pace yourself through an ultra-distance event. If you choose not to train with a power meter (or at least a heart rate monitor), it is unlikely that you will have the tools to implement much of the scientific theory described here. Simply going out and cycling a lot, while providing some benefits, will not do justice to your potential. Training with power means understanding the purpose of every training session and staying within prescribed training zones. It requires both discipline and effort, but the results are worth it.

One of the most effective approaches to ultra-distance training relies on a polarised structure: lots of Level 2 riding and some much shorter, harder, higher intensity efforts, from Level 3 through to Level 7. Repetitions of 15 seconds might seem irrelevant to a priority event that could last days, but they make a significant difference to your fitness. If it is your intention to become a fitter cyclist, you will most benefit from working with a cycling coach. The time taken to develop training plans and monitor training impact is considerable. As an athlete it is very useful to understand why you are doing what you are doing, but don't worry if you decide that your time is better spent doing the training rather than the planning; this is where a strong athlete–coach relationship can lead to record-breaking results.

CHAPTER 6:
APPROACH: DEVELOPING AN ULTRA-DISTANCE MINDEST

Ultra-cycling is predictably unpredictable. At some point, things will go wrong. Being mentally resilient will enable you to overcome the seemingly impossible again, and again, and again.

DIGGING DEEP

We were about 1,330km into our record-breaking tandem ride. It was dark, raining and a strong wind was hammering into the bike from the side. In our minds we knew the record was ours; we just had to complete the final few kilometres. The UHF radio we used to communicate with the support car crackled into life.

'Do you realise that if you can maintain this average speed, you will complete the ride in under 45 hours?'

Instantly our cadence picked up and our effort increased. Without even discussing it, we were both highly motivated by this thought. Even though the wind shifted to the north, becoming a savage headwind, our determination was such that our work rate remained higher than it had been in the previous hours. To put this into context, we had already been riding continuously for 44 hours. It seems that, whatever the distance, somehow, we can all find that extra 10 per cent that allows us to forge towards the finishing line, be that the end of a 10-mile time trial or the end of an ultra-distance record-breaking ride.

Charlie and Dominic

Ultra-distance cycling is as much about mental toughness as it is about fitness. This chapter explores what mental toughness is and the things that can be done to improve your ability to cope with – and even thrive on – the stresses of riding a long way, fast.

MENTAL TOUGHNESS

What is mental toughness? What does it take to become mentally tougher? There are those unbelievably hard sessions that require digging deep into the depths of self-motivation to complete, as they are so physically and mentally demanding. Many is the time we have sat and stared at our bikes for 10 minutes, plucking up the reserves to get started on a particularly demanding session. Do these sessions generate mental toughness? Can they be completed only by those who are mentally tough enough? And if so, how do you become tough enough? There are those other moments on long training rides when the weather is miserable and a mechanical failure brings the ride to a halt. The overwhelming desire is to abandon the session and ring for a pick up, and yet it seems somehow important to sort things out for yourself, carry on, and prove 'you can cope'. Is this mental toughness?

Then there is the issue of arrogance. Some of the best athletes in the world come across as arrogant. When asked if he was the best sprinter, the British cyclist, Mark Cavendish – renowned for his prodigious ability to sprint to stage victories in the world's biggest races – replied 'yes'. He describes his response as honest rather than arrogant. James Cracknell, the Olympic rower-turned-cyclist who made two attempts on the tandem UK End-to-End record, was reported (unfairly, in the authors' opinion) as being arrogant. In fact, a great many elite athletes are perceived as arrogant. Is arrogance an important element in having the mental toughness to be the best

»Taking on an ultra-distance goal often involves the 'suspension of disbelief'. »

at what you do? Specifically, is mental toughness something that is innate? Or can it be trained and developed, and if so, how? What does it take to be strong enough mentally to succeed? If ever there was a sport that required mental toughness it is ultra-distance cycling – the ability to cover seemingly impossible distances at one sitting, and the associated pain and fatigue from asking so much of your body for a sustained period.

There is some doubt as to what exactly mental toughness is and how to measure it. It covers a number of different facets, including personality, experience and the impact of context. A useful starting point is to suggest that mental toughness is the psychological wherewithal to cope well with the demands of training and competition. It is also about having the confidence and ability to stay focused and in control when under pressure, and in the face of adversity. In other words, if you are mentally tough, you have what it takes to thrive under pressure.

Like almost every other personality trait, it seems that your degree of mental toughness is influenced by your parents and by the environment in which you grew up. However, while some people are predisposed to be mentally tougher than others, it does seem that there is a lot you can do to become mentally tougher.

Mental toughness exists within a context. The principles behind the steps you can take to become mentally tough may be transferrable, but toughness is in part derived from doing the activity in which you wish to be mentally tougher. In other words, just because you are mentally tough as a cyclist does not mean you would be mentally tough as a rugby player.

BELIEVE

Taking on an ultra-distance goal often involves the 'suspension of disbelief' – you have to suspend all logic that states that there is no way you are going to be able to complete what can seem like a ridiculous challenge. Yet, there is no point in training if you do not think you are going to be able to do it. With enough training, possibility becomes probability. During the race, probability becomes certainty as you cross the finish line. Without the certainty of having already done it, mental toughness requires a belief in yourself that you can achieve your goal, and a confidence that you are going to be able to overcome the hurdles that will arise. The shift from possibility to probability arises from experience. As training hours are logged and sessions completed, confidence grows. Mental toughness is built on this confidence. The thing to note here is that it is not blind faith in your ability but an evidence-based belief. For example, surviving the experience of a 12-hour training ride in appalling weather conditions can be the basis for the confidence of knowing that you can cope in similar race situations. In contrast, to claim confidence in your ability to survive bad weather based on a two-hour gentle ride in the sun is less than honest.

Belief is not based on wishful thinking. It is not the simplistic 'anyone can do anything' mantra. Instead, it is the evidence of experience driving an inner confidence that reinforces the belief in your ability to take on and deal with significant challenges. The more experience gained, the greater the mental toughness that can be developed. Mental strength can be used to create a mental framework that increases confidence as conditions worsen, knowing you can cope

>>Hard work drives inner confidence.>>

because you've been there before. The element that underpins the confidence from experience is of course hard work. To have completed the training that provides the confidence means having done the necessary work to remove the element of doubt and provide the inner confidence. Just as the experienced driver does not have to think about the basics when manoeuvring a car – they just know they can – so too does the experienced well-trained cyclist have the inner confidence to just know they can do it.

This point explains the misinterpretation of confidence as arrogance in elite performers. Hard work drives inner confidence. You may well have found yourself riding with a group of less-trained cyclists who have upped the pace on a hill. You look down and see your power output is at Level 5 or even Level 6. You know from all your hard work that you can sustain a Level 5/Level 6 power output for a matter of a few minutes. You have the confidence that it is only going to be a few seconds before those around you have burned themselves out and descended into Level 1/Level 2 in a desperate attempt to recover. You hang in there, biding your time and, sure enough, the effort begins to drop off dramatically. You have the confidence in your ability to either take advantage or stay relaxed, knowing that you are more than capable of dealing with whatever happens. This is mental toughness derived from confidence. The same is true in a race.

You will be able to gauge how mentally tough you are when you are next due to complete a training session and it is cold, wet and miserable outside and you are tired. The lure of a beer or a glass of wine is overwhelming, and in order to train you're going to have to dig deep to get out there and get started. All ultra-distance cyclists face these moments; those that choose to train are tougher than those who do not. Training when you really do not want to is something of a paradox. It is precisely because you get yourself out to train, even when you do not want to, that is, in a way, motivating for those who are mentally tough. There is a reinforcing value in training in the face of adversity, or training when you know everyone else would have given up. There is, dare we say it, a smug satisfaction when coming back from a training session in appalling conditions to find that others opened the front door, took one look outside and went back to bed. Note, however, that this is different to starting a session and realising that you simply do not have the physical reserves to complete the

»Hard work drives inner confidence.»

session, choosing instead to abandon and rest. The latter comes from a deep understanding of your personal capabilities, whereas the former is an expression of your motivation. This is the difference between toughness and foolhardiness. Mental toughness is something accumulated over time. It is a self-reinforcing mindset, built on the solid foundations of hard work, self-reflection and realism.

OVERCOMING OBSTACLES

Another source of mental toughness comes from your ability to overcome obstacles. These can be things that get in the way of getting out and training when you want to. Whatever the obstacle, mental toughness is the difference between being unsure whether you can or cannot solve the problem, and certainty that you will solve the problem even if you are, as yet, unsure how to do it. Participating in ultra-distance rides requires unreasonable behaviour. It requires you to find solutions when most people would simply call it a day. It also requires you to put yourself into positions that will force you to have to manage and thereby learn the limits of your capability. This is resilience.

HAVE A PLAN

A characteristic of people who outperform others in any high performance activity is the ability to cope with distractions and problems. This is achieved in part by having a comprehensive plan of what to do and when. This includes a plan in the event of something going wrong or the inevitable distractions that accompany such an event. The advantage of such a plan is that it allows you to stay focused on what you need to do, as well as reducing the need to expend energy planning and preparing just before a major event. As will be shown below, such mental effort degrades performance. The plan might include all the things you will do when you arrive at the race location, for example, pre-driving the route; deciding the sequence in which kit will be prepared; arranging where items of food and clothing will be stashed on the bike. Your plan might also include what will happen in the hours and minutes before the race starts – what to eat and when, whom to talk to and whom to avoid, and where you will sit while waiting for your number to be called. The more detailed your plan, the better.

If you can think of something that might go wrong but you do not have a plan for it, you are missing a trick. For example, it is possible that your bike computer will fail. What's your navigation plan in the event that this happens? Is it possible you will have a puncture? What's your routine for dealing with this? You need to make sure you do things in the most efficient way, you do not leave kit behind, and you don't miss out an important step like checking the inside of your tyre for the object that caused the puncture. If the chain snaps, have you practised installing a split link beforehand, to know what to do?

Several members of the Land's End to John o'Groats tandem support team made the same point.

'We do not care if he's fit enough; what we want to know is, is he mentally tough enough?'

The power output data, as far as they were concerned, was a given. The numbers had to be right, but that was just a question of training. They had witnessed one riding partner mentally collapse during an attempt to break the tandem record, and the other mentally and physically collapse during a latter attempt. So we needed to discover a way of finding out if Charlie was the man for the third (and successful) attempt. One Friday after work, we started riding at 7 p.m. on a cold winter's evening. After just 80km we had to ask for some spare inner tubes to be delivered to us following a third puncture. With just under 485km to go, we could not afford to be without spares. We carried on through the night, arriving at one of the toughest points on the route we would be taking during our record-breaking ride, 24 hours after we had started the training ride, which was about the same time we would arrive at this point in the attempt.

But we were not finished. We turned the bike into the hills and we climbed over snow-strewn roads late into the evening. It was intimidating scenery; kilometres and kilometres of barren moorland and fell sides. We'd been riding for almost 30 hours when we arrived at the overnight accommodation. The next two days saw us take on hundreds of kilometres of small mountain roads, some with little more than the width of a car tyre. After two days of this, we set off on the more direct return leg – another 22-hour day in the saddle. By now, my riding partner was suffering with knee pain and a deep sense of fatigue. Halfway through the journey home I knew he had what it took; despite the pain and discomfort he was experiencing, he hunkered down into the time trial position and we set ourselves the challenge of going faster. When next asked if he was tough enough, I was able to recount the detail from this epic four days of training. My riding partner had found his limits, recognised them and used this knowledge as a way of finding greater strength and reserve to carry on. He was, and remains, as tough as old leather.

Dominic

The list can go on and on, but the more prepared you are, the less you have to worry about at the start of an event and the better able you will be to deal with problems when they arise. You should also give some thought to your initial response when something does go wrong. For example, a checklist could look like this:

- Stop! Think! This is a reminder to take the time to understand the problem before rushing in. More often than not, the solution is significantly better if you take a moment or two to think it through before acting.
- In sequence. This is a reminder to do things in the right order and to be meticulous in where you place things on the ground to make sure that whatever you have taken off or out of a bag ends up back in the right place, ready for the next time.
- Check. Go through everything to make sure it is all as intended (e.g. the tyre is properly seated following a puncture, or there are no tools left on the ground).
- Refocus. Get back into race-mode and focus on the race strategy. This is essential to avoid the mad panic of effort to try and recover lost time.
- Relax. Relax into the groove of the race and allow your mental state to get back to where it needs to be.

FOCUS

Another characteristic of mentally tough people is that they maintain an absolute focus on the goal and all the things they need to do to achieve this. The goal is always in the front of their minds, influencing every decision. The goal takes precedent over every other activity. It means that achieving the goal is, in effect, something of an obsession. It means thinking about everything in terms of the extent to which it contributes to achieving the goal, and avoiding or minimising those things that do not. This also requires a degree of preparation. For example, cycling to a meeting may require you to establish whether there are showers available. If they are not available at the meeting venue, does the local

»The very things that make it possible to do ultra-distance cycling, such as your family, cannot be taken for granted or abused.«

Table 5: Things you can anticipate creating issues

Factor	Why?
Weather	The reliability of weather forecasts depends on the type of weather. Being prepared for weather other than that forecast could be useful.
Food	Will the type of food you need be available? If not, what's your plan?
Kit failure	Where are the nearest cycle stores pre-race? Does the race route pass any cycle stores?
Influence of others	A race start may be filled with nervous, anxious people and this can be destructive. Where can you wait to avoid the hype?
Electronic failure	If you are using electronic devices, they will probably go wrong. What's your back-up plan?
Mechanical problem	Can you learn enough to keep the basic functions of the bike working?

leisure centre have facilities? This requires effort, but the reward is the ability to train – and this is what focus is all about. Focus helps you to make training a non-negotiable part of your life.

Mental toughness does also mean knowing when life is out of balance, and when there is a need to turn the dial down on the training while things return to a more even keel. In other words, it is not a blind focus on exercise; rather, it is a selfish prioritisation of sport over other activities, but not to the exclusion of everything else. Life is complex, and the very things that make it possible to do ultra-distance cycling, such as your family, cannot be taken for granted or abused. Training to do an ultra-distance event means that everyone around you will have to make sacrifices. Longer rides may mean that

you miss family events, or do not attend evening functions because of the impact on your ability to train the next day. Miss all family events or social nights out, and you may find the very support that enables you to do what you do has disappeared. Mental toughness is subtler than a blind, relentless drive towards the pursuit of a goal. Instead, it is more akin to surfing a wave. It is finding that sweet spot that allows you to do the very best you can towards the achievement of your goal, without wiping out. To be in the game, you have to get on the wave in the first place. At first, just like novice surfers, you learn in the smaller waves, falling off, getting back on again, and building your skill and understanding so you can surf ever bigger waves.

>>Mentally tough people control what they can control and do not worry about the rest."»

PERSONAL RESPONSIBILITY

Personal responsibility is summed up nicely by the phrase, 'You cannot excuse your way to success'. You can blame a lack of performance on the weather, work, family or your coach. You could well be right, but these are simply excuses. The bottom line is that you did not perform as well as you wished. There are some things beyond your control, the weather being one. However, you can control how you prepare and adapt to changing weather. Mentally tough people control what they can control and do not worry about the rest. Controlling the controllables means finding ways of taking control of as much of your performance as you can, and mitigating the risks where you cannot. For example, the weather plays a significant role in ultra-distance events, be it the heat of the desert or the likelihood of snow and ice in the high mountains. The amount of heat and cold are outside of your control, but the ability to look at weather forecasts and historical weather data is within your control. Knowing there is a high possibility of very cold weather means you can choose to take the appropriate clothing. Mitigating risk is very much within your control. The key point is working out how to bring things within your control such that you can take personal responsibility for getting the right outcome.

It also means taking responsibility for doing what's required. A coach can set a great training plan, but it is you that has to do it. Even without a great training plan, it does not mean you cannot train. People can provide you with a rich tapestry of advice, but it is you who must decide the best advice to follow and who must do the work. Owning that final responsibility is part of being mentally tough.

»You will suffer from sleep deprivation in ultra-distance events. Dealing with it is a core skill.»

IN TANDEM

Riding on a tandem is a significantly different experience to surviving on your own in an ultra-distance event or race. If you have established a good working relationship with your riding partner, they will understand your mood and the things they can do to help you come through a low patch. You will know them well enough to know what is required when they are struggling. This understanding doesn't happen on its own; it is something that requires work. At the outset, you may feel disinclined to share how you feel for fear of your riding partner thinking you haven't got what it takes. You need to overcome this apprehension. Some people may prefer to be left on their own when they are struggling to work it through themselves. Others may benefit from talking through what they are feeling to get it into context and to form a plan to get through it. Things like putting in earphones and listening to loud upbeat music can help, as can a telephone conversation with a loved one (easy to do if you are on the back of a tandem). You will only know by experience and by discussion. If you do not, you may find that your well-intentioned actions have the opposite effect, and serve to make the problem worse rather than better. If you feel uncomfortable with initiating these types of conversations, consider the use of a sports psychologist to help you.

SLEEP

THE BOTTOM LINE

You will suffer from sleep deprivation in ultra-distance events. Dealing with it is a core skill. The level of fitness required to compete in such events has many benefits. The sleep deprivation that also accompanies such events is unhealthy. There is some evidence that our ability to cope with sleep deprivation is in part genetically determined, and while this means that some people are better than others, the difference is not whether you will be affected, but how badly and how quickly.

Sleep deprivation does not necessarily refer to days spent staying awake. It's often the impact of something as simple as a long day. If you were to get up at 6 a.m., by the time midnight comes around on the same day, your reaction speed will have slowed and both short- and long-term memory will be affected. You will be poorer at making decisions, worse at thinking things through, and will have more difficulty staying focused. Add to this mix the continuous exercise of riding a bike for hours or days at a time, and the problem gets worse. The evidence suggests that if you stay sleep-deprived for long enough in your daily life, you will probably end up fatter, with higher blood pressure.

SLEEP DEPRIVATION IS DANGEROUS

If you are sleep-deprived, you're more likely to have a car crash. Someone who has slept just six to seven hours is twice as likely to be involved in a motoring accident as someone who has had eight hours' sleep. If your sleep drops to fewer than five hours, you are five times more likely to be involved in an accident.

The organisers of the Swedish endurance cycle event, 'The Vätternrundan', a 300km circumnavigation of Lake Vättern, warn participants not to drive within six hours of having finished the ride. To do so would be in violation of Swedish traffic legislation, which states 'Vehicles may not be driven by anyone who, because of illness, exhaustion, alcohol or drugs is unable to drive safely.' The Swedish Traffic Police enforce this law after the Vätternrundan event. Some states in the US define driving having not slept for 24 hours as reckless. You can expect a very long custodial sentence should you end up injuring or killing someone as a result of an accident attributable to sleep deprivation. Being sleep-deprived carries with it the same level of risk as being intoxicated. Going without sleep for 24 hours, or having very limited sleep of just three or four hours per night for four or five days, is the equivalent of being drunk.

MY EXPERIENCE OF SLEEP DEPRIVATION

You might delude yourself that 'I can cope', but if you get sufficiently tired your brain will take over and you will fall asleep. That is what happened to me in a race at three in the morning, having just crested a col. Despite my best efforts, I fell asleep, waking to find myself rolling at speed into a stone wall that bounded the road. It was a close call, but I managed to avoid hitting it. A similar thing happened when taking part in the London–Edinburgh–London Audax, a 1,350km ride. In the early hours of one morning, I awoke to find myself riding along the verge, having veered off the main carriageway. In both situations I was lucky, but the next time I may not be quite so fortunate.

Dominic

THE IMPACTS

While your ability to uptake oxygen is not affected by sleep deprivation, your perception of effort when sleep-deprived will be. You may think you are working harder than you are. This is where a power meter can help. Power is absolute. You might feel like you are working at 300W, but if the screen shows 220W then that is what you are doing. During the 'witching hours' (2–4 a.m.), despite one's best efforts, power output often drops, sometimes to pitiful levels. It seems to require a disproportionate effort to hit the required numbers. Interestingly, it picks up as daylight returns and you've 'survived the night' – a function of your circadian rhythms.

If you're tired, you're more likely to choose the easy way out. Rather than prepare proper meals, you're likely to go for fast food options or to eat out. This in turn can impact your health and ability to perform optimally. During a race, rather than stopping to sort out an issue with your bike or to put on the right kit, you keep going. Short-term, it may be the easy thing to do, but you could end up paying the price later in the race. Sleep-deprived people are not very good at taking on new information, or responding to environmental demands. The evidence is unequivocal – mental fatigue impairs physical performance. Your ability to perform physically is ultimately limited by your perception of the effort involved and is not, as you otherwise might have believed, due to cardiorespiratory factors or muscle response. With increased sleep deprivation your insulin response slows, which means you will not be as effective in getting energy from what you have eaten. Ghrelin (a hormone that stimulates appetite) increases and Leptin (a hormone that inhibits appetite) is decreased. You end up wanting to eat more, and are less effective at storing energy. The net effect is that sleep-deprived people eat more than they need and as a result are more likely to be overweight. You also use more energy when you are sleep-deprived. One effect of this is that it leads to an antioxidant imbalance as a result of the

>>Sleep deprivation is profoundly unhealthy and dangerous.>>

increase and duration of cell activity. Short-term, this helps you stay focused and perform, but, over time, without the restorative benefit of sleep when the body reverses these antioxidant imbalances, they build up, impacting on brain and liver function.

If you are sleep-deprived, you will experience a drop in core body temperature, which is why, when you are tired, you often feel cold. The body is less effective at thermoregulation.

FOXED BY LACK OF SLEEP – MY EXPERIENCE OF HALLUCINATIONS

The first time I hallucinated due to lack of sleep was on a non-stop ride from London to Paris and back. I was convinced the signposts on the side of the road were turning into people who were running alongside me. The arrows painted on the centre of the road, indicating two lanes merging into one, became white foxes that wouldn't suddenly get up and run away. On another ride, I was convinced there was a group of cyclists waiting ahead. Instead, it was the branches of a tree moving in the breeze in front of a set of traffic lights that created the effect of the flashing red light of a cyclist. On another ride, the hedgerow appeared to be whirring cogs and wheels of the most amazing machine. When I stopped, they became a hedge, only to return once I started riding again. At first, the hallucinations were scary. I was struggling to separate perception from reality. However, as I have experienced the phenomena more, I am aware of what's happening and it becomes another vital signal that I need to do something about my physical and mental state – time to stop and sleep.

Dominic

PERFECT STORM

A solo unsupported race is the perfect storm of duration and effort to allow sleep deprivation to wreak havoc. Lasting at least 24 hours, the mental reasoning of riders becomes equivalent to that of a drunk. Given the navigation requirements of ultra-distance races, you may end up taking a wrong turn that could cost you hours of effort. Just at the point when you need to be making some sensible and life-saving decisions, you will be more likely to choose a poorly thought through, easy option, which could be storing up trouble for later. This could be due to changes in weather, a mechanical problem with the bike, or as a result of human error. You will feel hungry but will probably only be able to eat what's easily accessible. Your ability to stay warm will be hampered. The perception of effort expended means true performance will fall away. This in turn will impact your mental state, creating the feeling of going nowhere fast. As fatigue builds and begins to overwhelm you, you could find yourself crashing kilometres from anywhere, on your own, without the wherewithal to get help.

MEASURES TO MITIGATE THE RISKS OF SLEEP DEPRIVATION

Sleep deprivation is profoundly unhealthy and dangerous. There are so many negatives it is difficult to find anything to recommend it. However, if you still insist on participating in events that involve extended periods without sleep, there are some things you can do. If measures such as these are put in place, they can help mitigate the risks.

Coffee

Caffeine works by blocking temporarily the receptors in the brain that make us want to go to sleep. Adenosine, a neurotransmitter, promotes sleep by binding with receptors in the brain, slowing cell activity and increasing blood flow. Caffeine binds to the adenosine receptors and, instead of a reduction in cell activity, it speeds it up which, in turn, impacts on the pituitary gland, releasing fight or flight hormones. This results in dilated pupils, and an increase in heart rate and blood pressure. Sugar is released from the liver into the bloodstream, blood flow to the stomach is reduced, and muscles are readied for action. In short, you're all fired up and ready for action. The effect is temporary, lasting for a few hours. If you consume a lot of coffee, you develop a tolerance for its impact. The side effect is insomnia, and it also creates feelings of restlessness, nervousness, irritability and dizziness. Before an ultra-distance race, you would be wise to abstain from caffeine for a sustained period so you become re-sensitised to its effects. Even caffeine cannot overcome extreme fatigue and, given enough sleep deprivation, your desire to sleep will take over. But it can help.

Light

We are extraordinarily sensitive to light; particularly blue light. Light can help trick the brain into staying more alert. On a bike in the middle of the night, turning the screen on your bike computer to full brightness may provide some benefit. In addition to a front light on the bike, add a head torch to your helmet to ensure there is light wherever you turn your head. If you have to stop to do something, do it under a street light. You will be able to see what you're doing, and the light will give you a useful boost and help you stay awake.

Stop

If you recognise you are starting to get very tired and struggling to concentrate, and caffeine has not worked, then it is time to stop. You will either stop because you choose to, or because you have crashed; one or the other. Assuming you are on your own and kilometres from anywhere, you

>> It can take anything between five and 20 minutes for your brain to become alert after a nap. >>

will need to be prepared. If it is likely to be cold (bearing in mind you will feel colder anyway), carry a warm layer. There are some superb ultra-light insulated pullover-style jackets that compress into a very small bundle, work when wet and weigh next to nothing (see Chapter 4: Equipment, page 101). Consider carrying a thermal blanket – useful in emergencies too.

Next, you need to find somewhere to stop. We're talking about having to take extreme measures here. But be under no illusion, it is better to stop and have 30–45 minutes' sleep than to continue on and endanger yourself by crashing. Lying on the ground can be deeply unpleasant if it is cold, although a snooze on a grassy bank in summer can be delightful. If it is the middle of the night, bus shelters make a great place for a sleep. With a roof over your head and sides that keep the wind off you, many have some form of bench seating that separates you from the cold ground. Church porches can offer a useful place of shelter. *In extremis*, farmers' barns are a good place to stop. Straw and hay are particularly fine insulators and make for a comfortable place to take a nap. Lying on discarded cardboard at the back of a shop is just about as bad and low as it gets – but it works! Wherever you decide to stop, obey two simple rules:

- Do not damage anything.
- Do not leave anything of yours behind. Leave only footprints and tyre tracks.

If you have a support vehicle, ramp the heating up, turn off all the lights inside, recline a seat or, if in a van, erect a camp bed. Get changed into the kit you wish to wear having left the pit-stop, lie down and take a nap. Get the team to throw a duvet or sleeping bag over you. Ask them to wake you up in 30-45 minutes. Meantime, have them prepare a hot drink and some food, ready for you when you wake up.

Coming to
It can take anything between five and 20 minutes for your brain to become alert after a nap. During that period, it is easy to make some silly decisions or to forget something. Although you will be in a rush and want to get going, give yourself sufficient time to become alert enough to make sure you have everything with you, have changed clothes, eaten, and so on.

Games
If you're on your own, there are some things you can do to help you stay awake. One trick is to do some mental exercises. For example, you could do your 'times tables', or recite poetry, or sing at the top of your voice. This is a lot easier to do on your own than if you have a support vehicle tailing you!

Get wet!
Sometimes, pouring cold water over your head can help. The shock of the water stimulates the nerves and the body responds with a fight or flight reaction, i.e. 'What the hell was that!?' This sudden alertness is the impact you're seeking. Similarly, a really good wash and freshen up can help you feel a lot better, as can sucking on a slice of lemon.

Talk to someone
Having a conversation forces your brain to be more active. It also helps the person you are talking to get a sense of how tired you really are. If you're having a conversation and realise it is complete gibberish, you are in the danger zone and it is time to stop.

»Any hallucination is a clear sign that it is time to stop.»

TRIGGERS

If you're working with a support team, agree before you turn the first pedal who can take what decision. Trying to work out what to do when you are extremely tired lends itself to trouble. Better to agree who has authority to make what decision from the comfort of home. For example, in the Land's End to John o'Groats record-breaking tandem ride, the team agreed that if, in the view of the doctor supporting the attempt, we were at significant risk of becoming unwell or sustaining a serious injury, he had the authority to call the attempt to a halt. In a previous attempt, one of the riders had collapsed with exhaustion. While this was a clear end to the attempt, it may not always be this obvious.

If it is clear that the aim of the ride is no longer going to be achieved (i.e. the record broken, or the finish made before the cut-off point), the team leader should be authorised to call it a day, bringing the ride to a halt. As the rider, in the heat of the moment you may violently disagree, but you will not be thinking straight due to fatigue. The support team will have had more opportunity to weigh up the evidence and make an informed and considered response based on the criteria you agreed at the outset.

WARNING SIGNS

Let's assume you're doing an ultra-distance ride, solo and unsupported. Sleep deprivation and fatigue are insidious and it is often far too late that you realise you're in trouble. Either you will have fallen asleep and had a lucky escape, or you will have made a bad decision that has forced you to retire. It is helpful to learn to spot three or four signs that tell you it is time to stop and rest.

A question of maths

One of the things to do when tired is your 'times tables'. Struggling to get past 4x4 for example (yes really, mental functioning is *that* impaired) means it is time to stop. One athlete recounted that for over an hour he tried to work out why 4x4=20. He simply could not figure out the correct answer. Fortunately, he did realise this was not a good sign, and that a short nap was necessary.

Power down

Throughout this book, the use of a power meter has been advocated. In addition to the many training-related benefits, a power meter can help you spot signs of excessive fatigue. When your power output drops below where you would expect it to be, and you're unable to generate enough power to get it back on target, or it seems like a huge effort to do so, it is a sign of sleep deprivation and/or fatigue. Take a short break and see what happens. If it is no better after this, consider abandoning. If it has picked up again, keep going.

Gibberish

You meet someone else on the road and try to have a conversation, but what comes out is nonsense. It is time to stop!

Wandering

Normally you can hold your bike within the width of a white line on the road for as long as you wish without any difficulty. Struggling to keep on your side of the road, let alone the white line, is a good indication that all is not well.

Hallucinations

Any hallucination is a clear sign that it is time to stop.

Cold

If you start to get very cold and have run out of layers, it is time to stop, not only because of fatigue but because of the deadly effect of cold and sleep deprivation.

You have crashed

Accidents do happen. There is no such thing as 'risk-free' cycling. Because it is predictable that you are more likely to have an accident while participating in an ultra-distance race, you can therefore plan what to do in the event this happens. If you have a support crew, it is their job to manage the situation and secure whatever emergency support is needed. If you are on your own, the use of a GPS tracker helps those who may be hundreds of kilometres away to monitor your progress. If the tracker stops, they can either call you to check you are OK, or call in help. The tracker provides a GPS location that can be used to identify where you are. Some trackers have an SOS button that allows you to call for help to predetermined numbers.

Trackers vary. Some are able to do all this via GPS alone. Others rely on a combination of GPS and mobile phone signal. Which you choose depends on budget and attitude to risk. The advantage of trackers over mobile phones is battery life. Most will last for a couple of months between charges. A mobile phone used in the same way may struggle to make it through the day. If you do not wish to use a tracker, calling or having a pre-written text ready to send someone every few hours will narrow down the search area in the event you fail to check in. Be aware that if for any reason your tracker stops working, this can cause worry back home as they try to establish whether there is a problem. A back-up plan is useful in these circumstances. For example, if a designated person sees the tracker has stopped, he/she will, in the first instance, try and call you. If there is no response and the tracker continues to stay stationary, that person should try calling again and then, if still no response, call for help. You need a clear protocol.

THE IMPORTANCE OF SLEEP

Sleep is a serious business. It is an essential part of recovery and enables you to function at your best. Going without it potentially has very serious consequences that should not be underestimated. There is nothing macho or clever about being sleep-deprived. It undoubtedly makes ultra-distance events the challenges that they are, and, with careful management, you can make it through to the end unscathed, but you should do so with your eyes wide open as to the risks, as well as the road in front of you.

HABITS

'What we do, is mostly what we do.'

Just in case you think you have very few habits, examine your daily routine from the moment you get up through to going to bed. Do you follow the same sequence when you use the bathroom, eat your breakfast, have a shower, do your teeth, get dressed, travel to work, park your car, arrive at your desk, place your coat? It is only when you stand back and look at what you do that you realise so much of your day is habit. In fact, because it is habit, it does not even register any more. If you're still not convinced, ask your partner to tell you what you always do and in what sequence – you will be surprised.

If you drive a car where the indicators and wiper controls are on the opposite side to your usual car, you will probably turn the indicators on when you wish to clear your windscreen, and vice versa. This is a good example of a habit dominating normal behaviour. After a while, this stops and you become adjusted. In fact, you replace one habit with another.

Habits are both a friend and an enemy of high performance. If you have got into the habit of waking at 4.30 a.m., often before the alarm clock goes, creeping downstairs, switching the coffee machine on, getting into your kit, drinking a coffee, grabbing your bike computer and the details of the training session to be completed and, by 5 a.m., you have started your warm-up, then you probably go through this whole sequence without even thinking. In fact, such

»As habits form there are changes in the parts of the brain that are involved.»

is the habit that on rest days, you will probably still get up, put the coffee machine on and then realise you don't have to train. Given that so much of our lives is simply the repetition of habits, having the right habits will make us more likely to achieve the performance we seek. Conversely, the wrong habits will lead to poor or unhelpful performance.

WHAT IS A HABIT?

In essence, a habit is automatic behaviour triggered by a specific cue in the environment (the context in which you are in) that is independent of the goals or intentions you may have. In other words, you fall into a pattern of behaviour triggered by a specific circumstance, such as putting on your seat belt (behaviour) when you get into a car (context). You do not even think about it; the act of getting into the car is enough for you to reach for the belt. In fact, the habit is so powerful that even if you did not want to put on the seat belt, the chances are you would have done so before you even realised it. Habits form when you do the same thing again and again in the same context, such that you form direct associations in your memory between the contextual cues and your response. Putting your seat belt on each and every time is an example of repeating a behaviour in response to a specific contextual cue: getting into a car. There are many other simple examples.

- The ping of a text message on your phone (cue); reaching for the phone (response)
- Your phone ringing (cue); reaching for the phone (response)

- The act of sitting in front of your computer (cue); opening your email (response)
- Sitting in front of a plate of food (cue); adding seasoning (response)
- Turning out of a junction (cue); moving into the correct side of the road (response) (not always the case when abroad!).

A habit is more than just a word for repeating the same actions. Research has shown that as something becomes a habit (for example, parking on the driveway at home), the part of the brain involved is different to that involved when you are doing something consciously to achieve a specific goal (such as working out where to park in an unfamiliar location).

As habits form, there are changes in the parts of the brain that are involved. When we are working towards a goal and our behaviour is not yet habitual, the active areas of the brain are those associated with goals, such as the pre-frontal cortex. As the habits form, the activity shifts to the part of the brain associated with stimulus control, such as the *Basal Ganglia*. As behaviours become more automatic or habitual, they do not need as much conscious effort. Our response is more efficient and immediate; we do not need to think about it. This efficiency and immediacy makes it much more difficult for us to control them by consciously thinking about them. By the time we have thought it through, it is too late, we have already repeated the habit.

≫Habits take a while to form, but are difficult to change – so you better have the habits you want.≫

STAGES IN A HABIT

There are three stages in a habit: the cue, the routine and the reward (see Figure 11).

Example 1

The cue:

Attaching your bike computer to your bike.

The routine:

Switching it on, checking the power meter has registered, setting the device to calibrate and loading up the route to be followed.

The reward:

The satisfaction that everything is working and ready to go, and the opportunity to start your ride.

Example 2

The cue:

A beep every 30 minutes on your device.

The routine:

Eating some food.

The reward:

Positive impact on performance.

Example 3

The cue:

The bike computer on your desk.

The routine:

Uploading data, completing the feedback section in the training log.

The reward:

Job done, activity completed.

Research shows that brain activity during the routine phase of a habit drops significantly when compared to doing something that isn't a habit. In other words, we simply aren't thinking much about what we are doing. This is important because often most of our efforts to change habitual behaviour are misguidedly focused

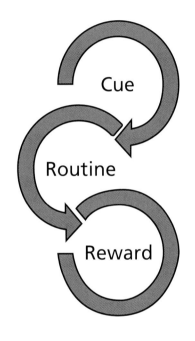

Figure 11: The three stages in a habit

on getting people to change their routine – the precise point when the person is not really thinking about it. In the above examples, it is going into auto-pilot and doing what has to be done. You will probably recognise the sensation of driving home and not really being able to remember much about the journey, or starting a training ride and having to think twice about whether you calibrated the power meter (because you just do it without thinking about it).

Habits take a while to form, but once formed are difficult to change – so you better have the habits you want! The benefit of habits is that, once you have the right ones in place, because they are relatively stable, you do not have to think about them as much and can concentrate your efforts on other things.

»Make as much as possible a habit and practise this in training, when you have more time and space to get it right.»

UNDER PRESSURE

Research into habits has shown that when we put people under pressure (in this case, students studying for exams), they tend to default to their habits, both good and bad. It is as if we simply do not have the bandwidth to cope with the effort required to be vigilant to changing our habit, and do everything else as well. The demands of ultra-distance cycling are such that, as we become more tired, we have less capacity to pay attention to everything we need to be doing. If we can make sure that as much as possible has become habitual, we can maximise our mental reserves to cope with issues as they arise (which they invariably will) as well as other factors such as navigation and other road users. Examples include:

- Make eating on the bike a habitual exercise.
- Make drinking on the bike a habitual exercise.
- Make riding a continuous pace a habitual exercise.
- Make choice of line on the road a habitual exercise.

There are many more, but the point is clear. Make as much as possible a habit and practise this in training, when you have more time and space to get it right.

CHANGING HABITS

There is no quick and easy way to change a habit. Change requires hard work. It can be difficult to work out what cues your habitual response. You therefore need to be attentive and vigilant. If you analyse your patterns of behaviour, you can work out when you do what and, therefore, determine how to change the context and thereby break the cue. Context drives behaviour.

You also have to decide what it is you are going to do when cued to do so. You have to premeditate your action. For example, when reaching the base of a hill you will stay seated until one-third of the way up, at the very least. The evidence suggests that, if you reward yourself for doing the right thing, you will be more likely to do it again. This might be as simple as allowing yourself a cube of chocolate at the end of a ride to reinforce the value of the exercise.

FRICTION-FREE

If your context is such that, when you want to go out and train, your kit is all over the house and it takes an age to find what you need, it becomes easy to give up. If, when you get up in the morning, your kit is all in one place and ready to go, it is far easier to go training. Make the process as friction-free as you can. If you know you have a turbo session scheduled first thing in the morning, make sure your bike is ready to go the night before. If you have to swap wheels or tyres, by the time you have done this your motivation may have diminished and your available time decreased. If, however, your bike is on its stand, ready to go, and your kit is all in one place, ready for you to climb into it in the morning, and the coffee machine is topped up with water, then you have created a context where you are far more likely to be successful.

HUNGRY FOR SUCCESS

A different strategy is required to overcome temptation than is required to overcome habits. For example, if, like many of us, you find it hard to keep on top of your weight, being attentive and vigilant – the actions required to change a habit – is likely to increase your awareness of the food around you rather than help you avoid it, which is not helpful. What's required is to avoid coming into contact with the food in the first place, i.e. stay away from the places where you are likely to be sorely tempted. If you do find yourself confronted with delectable delights, distraction can work. Find something else to do, or engage someone in a conversation. In short, do anything that takes your mind off the food.

DREAMING

Once you have the habits of high performance in place, you can afford to let your mind wander. This is a dimension of sport not often discussed. Just because you are training does not mean you're not working. Dr John Wilson, one of the most knowledgeable individuals on the subject of people development, has spent considerable time examining this aspect of performance. His thoughts are on page 195.

> **It appears that we spend approximately six to eight hours of each waking day letting our minds drift when they are not focused on immediate tasks.** >>

DREAM ON: FIRST YOU NEED A SCARY GOAL

HEY, YOU! YES, IT'S YOU I'M SPEAKING TO! Are you really paying attention to what you're reading right now? OK! That's better. Now that I have your attention, we can look a little more closely into why we daydream and let our minds wander into all sorts of wonderful escapades, *liaisons dangereuses*, plans, dreams and even mundane things such as what to eat for dinner this evening. We spend a significant amount of working time on 'auto-pilot'.

The facts are that our minds often tend to wander when we are reading, and although our eyes may be following the words, our mind is far away, thinking about other things. It isn't just when we are reading, of course; our minds frequently wander, and mostly we aren't caught out except by ourselves. However, we can probably remember when a teacher told us to pay attention in class, or perhaps in a meeting we were suddenly asked a question by the boss, and rapidly had to gather our thoughts and pretend we were closely following the proceedings.

Recent developments in brain imaging, such as CT scans and functional magnetic resonance imaging (fMRI), have resulted in a number of discoveries into how the brain operates. One particular experiment involved a study of people's brains as they undertook a demanding and absorbing mental task and were then given a recovery period. What surprised the researchers was that during these periods of rest, the subjects' brains became more active than when they were concentrating on the given tasks.

We all feel the need to give our brains a rest following periods of heavy study or concentration, and the assumption has been that our brains were relaxing. In fact, contrary to previous belief, our brains are never dormant but fire more widely when they are apparently having time out. The area of the brain that is most active when we are not focused on external activities is called the 'default mode network', and some of its functions involve personal memories, our sense of self and planning and predicting the future.

Building upon this surprising discovery of brain activity even when we appear to be mentally resting, other researchers began to investigate the extent to which we 'mind-wander', uncovering a quite remarkable fact. It appears that we spend approximately six to eight hours of each waking day letting our minds drift when they are not focused on immediate tasks. Assuming that we sleep eight hours a night, this means that half of the time we are not consciously in the present moment. Rather than being a negative habit that demonstrates an inadequate intellect, it appears that daydreaming and mind-wandering are natural functions of the brain, highly beneficial for our thought processes.

Given that daydreaming and mind-wandering are in-built functions of the brain, shouldn't we capitalise on this ability, rather than trying to repress it? Sportspeople increasingly practise using their imaginations to envision events and enhance their performance. This visioning involves mentally rehearsing each specific physical movement, which builds strength in the neural connections – the more we do this, the easier it is to get into the groove and perform better and more consistently.

Visioning is a conscious activity, but mind wandering and daydreaming are less focused and more spontaneous. They often guide us to important things in our lives and help us find solutions to problems in a natural way. Untether your mind and let it be free to wander and drift wherever it chooses, and you might be surprised what great scary goals it presents to you and how it will help you find a way to achieve them. Dream on!

Dr John Wilson

> >> Being able to develop the right mental approach is also helped by getting enough sleep and eating properly. >>

SUMMARY

If there is one word that underpins this chapter it is control. Much of the first part of the chapter is about how to put yourself back in control when things go wrong or get tough. There are things you can do in preparation, like exposing yourself to extreme environments in a controlled way, which will help you in an event or race environment. You can also learn the simple steps to take when something has gone wrong; steps that help you to plan what to do and then to start doing it. These experiences drive confidence. They also require the capacity to think and process what's happening. This capacity can be increased by making much of what you do a habit. That way you won't need to consciously think about doing the right thing – it will just happen. Being able to develop the right mental approach is also helped by getting enough sleep and eating properly. However, ultra-distance cycling demands that you be able to cope with some sleep deprivation. Recognising when sleeping is the right thing to do is just as important. Ultra-distance cycling places a great physical and mental strain on you. Being mentally fit is as important as being physically fit.

CHAPTER 7:
SPONSORSHIP AND PR

It's an expensive sport – so share the costs. Learn how to generate value others will pay for in the form of sponsorship.

Long-distance riding is expensive, so it is good to find a way of defraying the costs. To do that, you need some sponsorship. To get sponsorship you need to be clear what your personal brand is. What is it that someone might want to sponsor? In effect, you are the product. Companies provide sponsorship because of the benefits it brings. You need to be clear about how you can deliver value. One of the most common ways of delivering value is through supporting a company's PR (public relations) effort. Therefore, what is PR, why do companies use it, and how can you contribute to their PR effort?

Even accepting that the income of a cyclist is on average higher than the national average, if you do enough riding the chances are you will start to look longingly at sponsorship contracts, wondering whether you too could negotiate a deal. This is because the more you ride, the more kit you will wear out. As you get more skilled as a rider, you are likely to be using equipment that is more expensive. The costs can start to mount up. So what does it take to get sponsorship?

The more favorable the cost:benefit ratio, the more likely you are to get the support you want. »

SOMETHING FOR NOTHING

There are people out there who will be inspired by what you are doing and on the strength of this alone offer you some form of support. Almost everyone else will only provide you with sponsorship because what you are doing is, in some way, seen as helpful to what they are hoping to achieve with their business. This means the focus is not your cycling as such, but what your cycling will enable them to achieve. For the sponsor, it is a question of the cost of supporting you versus the benefit that support brings. The more favourable the cost:benefit ratio, the more likely you are to get the support you want. Your success as a cyclist from the perspective of a sponsor is not so much the results you achieve but the way in which you generate value around the sponsor's goals.

For example, if your target company for sponsorship has an aim of selling more bikes, and you have the same demographic profile as one of their potential customers, and you are doing something likely to provide a compelling reason to buy their bikes, then you have a good starting point for a discussion. In contrast, if you are a middle-aged, male cyclist and your potential sponsor's target market is clothes for teenage girls, finding a compelling story could be something of a challenge!

The point is, to get support we need to offer something a sponsoring company deems valuable, and in return they will provide us with support that we deem valuable. Jonathan Turner, former head of digital at Team Sky, described how they used to sit down with sponsors to work out what their objectives were and how best Sky could help them achieve them. Some companies wanted articles about their products on the team website, while others wanted to run competitions. Sometimes it wasn't possible to meet sponsors' needs. For example, a mapping app provider wanted the team riders to capture their rides on their mobile phone app. Unfortunately, at the time, mobile phone batteries were not up to the challenge, due to the duration of the rides that Team Sky athletes undertook.

> **»Your brand creates an expectation about the value you bring.»**

YOUR BRAND

Whether you like it or not, you have a personal brand. This is the asset that people pay you for when they sponsor you. To paraphrase Tom Peters, the management guru, your brand creates an expectation about the value you bring. Brands exist in the mind. They are attributes someone ascribes to you. It is the way someone thinks and feels about you. Your brand is the unique combination of specific elements that separates you from others. Thus, it is not the logo you have or the way you present yourself that is your brand, it is the experience this delivers and the thoughts these things generate. People choose to buy one brand over another in part because of how it makes them feel and the associations they have with that brand. The way your brand influences how someone feels will determine whether they want to be involved in your projects. Remember, you're not just competing with other cyclists, but all the other activities a company could choose as a vehicle for promoting their products and services.

You're competing for space on someone's phone or tablet, or whatever device they are using to consume content. As well as competing against other cyclists, you are also competing against things on Facebook, Twitter, in the news, in emails and on blogs and articles.

Your brand has to make it through the internal company processes. Think about what being involved in your projects from a sponsorship perspective might mean for those involved. Imagine the scene: a manager is sitting in a meeting and is going to bring up the idea of supporting your project. They have to tell the story in a compelling way and inspire people who've probably never met you or know very little about you. They will be listening to the story, devoid of any emotional involvement in the first instance. The person putting your case has to feel confident enough, and be sufficiently inspired, to want to take your case forward. A strong and clear brand makes this job a whole lot easier. It is about knowing what your brand 'is not' as much as it is knowing what 'it is'.

»Your strategy, despite whatever you might claim it to be, is what you do.»

THE BRUTAL FACTS: ARE YOU THE PERSONIFICATION OF YOUR INTENDED BRAND?

It is an interesting exercise to write down what it is you would like people to feel about you and what you do. How would you like them to describe you to others? What's the experience you would like to provide when others interact with you? Now face reality; compare this with what you really do. What's the difference? For this, you will need to be self-aware and honest with yourself.

YOUR STRATEGY IS WHAT YOU DO

Your strategy, despite whatever you might claim it to be, is what you do. By this I mean your intention might be to get up every day at 5 a.m. and train, but if on average you get up at 5.30 a.m. for four days of the week then your real strategy is to train four days a week at 5.30 a.m. You might intend to write a blog every month, but if you only manage one every few months, then your strategy is to write blogs three or four times a year. The point is, we have to be able to face the brutal facts. By examining the evidence of what you actually do, compared to what you would like to do, you can begin to really understand the brand you have, rather than the brand you would like. It's then up to you to decide: 'Do I redefine my brand based on what I do?' or 'Do I change what I do to create a stronger brand?'

A strong personal brand is about being clear what you stand for and being authentic in what you do. It is not about pretending to be something you are not.

BRAND TOUCH-POINTS

From the emails you send, to the content you post on social media, down to the kit you choose to wear when you are on the bike and the state of your bike, all of these things are what communicate a message about you to someone else. These are your brand touch points. These touch points are what deliver an experience for others that tells them what your brand is. Are they congruent with what you would like your personal brand to be?

You can either do things that enhance your personal brand or things that detract from it. For example, at its simplest, if you purport to be about fitness and health, but when you meet with your sponsor in a cafe and you order a hot chocolate with cream and marshmallows and a side order of chocolate fudge cake, irrespective of whether you can justify such refreshments, the association with such foodstuffs cannot be considered healthy. This creates dissonance with your stated brand and the lived experience of your brand. What's clear is that there is no downtime for your personal brand.

KEEP IT SIMPLE

In an insightful article called *The 22 Immutable Laws of Branding*, Al and Laura Ries open with the claim that 'The power of a brand is inversely proportional to its scope.' That is to say, the narrower your scope and the tighter your focus as a brand, the stronger it is. What this means is that you do not have to be hip and radical and at the same time earnest and serious. In fact, to do so would be to weaken your brand.

»Before approaching anyone for support, it is a good idea to work out what support you need.»

This can feel a bit counterintuitive. Surely if someone is offering you support, regardless of who they are, it is good news? However, it may be that accepting support from one sponsor precludes support from another. For example, you are unlikely to find both a low-cost supermarket and a high-end watch manufacturer sponsoring the same athlete. The core values of the two brands and their position in the market are likely to be very different. This was a lesson brought home to the authors when one sponsor asked them to desist the relationship they had with another. This was because one sponsor was targeting unfit but enthusiastic riders, while the other, main, sponsor was targeting middle-aged couples. What one brand represented was seen as incongruent with the other. If you are clear about what your personal brand is, such mistakes are easier to avoid.

THINGS YOU NEED TO THINK ABOUT TO GET SPONSORSHIP

There appear to be three skills that are essential to master to get sponsorship support.

- The ability to create a compelling pitch.
- The ability to generate great PR content.
- The ability to be good at managing relationships.

Before approaching anyone for support, it is a good idea to work out what support you need. If it costs money, consider its inclusion. There are obvious items like equipment, clothing and nutrition, and less obvious items like support crew costs, vehicle hire, massage, physiotherapy treatment, bike cleaning products, workshop tools, cameras and so on. Create a spreadsheet and list everything you need or will be likely to need to achieve your cycling ambitions. Divide the list into three columns: those things that are essential; those that would be nice to have; and those few remaining items that would be a luxury, but you could survive without. An example of the latter might be a coat that remains warm even when wet for pit-stops; the idea being to throw it on the moment you come into a pit-stop, do whatever you have to do and remove it at the last minute, in so doing maintaining your core temperature. Almost any coat would do, but if it's not on your list, the sponsor cannot help. This exercise will help you get a sense of the support you require. When you know what you want, you need to know what your potential sponsors want. That means doing some research.

ADDING VALUE

Whether it is a major multinational company with a clearly articulated strategy, or a 'Mom and Pop' outfit where the vision resides in the owners' heads, every business has a strategy, whether stated or not. Their strategy is simply a way of expressing what they are doing and what that is delivering by way of value.

Determining a large organisation's strategy is significantly easier than a smaller one. Reading about their business on their website, as well as commentary on other websites, is a great place to start. Ensure you look into related areas such as their corporate and social responsibility policy. Find out if they are sponsoring people already, and what that entails. Does your brand look and feel similar to those people and projects with whom they are already involved?

Smaller businesses with little published online are more difficult to analyse on a company-

>> You may need sponsorship to achieve your ultra-distance goals. >>

ADDING VALUE

For four years, Dominic was lucky enough to be supported by a manufacturer and retailer of tandem bicycles. While they represented a large proportion of UK tandem sales, they were a small business. The demographic profile of the majority of their customers was middle-aged couples. As a small company and a supplier of niche products, mainstream publicity is hard to achieve and advertising prohibitively expensive. Through working with them and their PR company, Dominic was able to generate a series of blogs and articles that were picked up by mainstream cycling magazines. Through the charitable work associated with the cycling challenge Dominic was undertaking, he was able to secure local and national radio coverage and a small amount of TV coverage. Added to this an active campaign on Facebook and Twitter, and he successfully achieved an audience reach of approximately 2.4 million people.

As a 40-something cyclist, Dominic also reflected the demographic profile of the company's target audience. The value of this coverage was seen, by the company, to be substantially greater than the cost of providing bikes and parts, as the relationship generated a much higher company profile than had hitherto been achieved. In return for this work, Dominic was provided with a training bike, a race bike, a substantial contribution to the overall costs of his cycling record attempts, and kit at a tiny fraction of the retail cost. The company also became a key part of the record-breaking support team.

specific basis. It is possible to understand a significant amount about their business by looking at industry-sector reports and market reviews.

The purpose of your research is to identify the links between what the business is trying to achieve and how your cycling efforts could support that. Most commonly, it is the story that drives the association between what you are doing and what the company is seeking to achieve.

BUILDING YOUR CREDIBILITY

If you are a bit anxious or worried about someone doing something, a question you will often ask is, 'Have you done this before?' For example, suppose you discover a crack on your beautiful custom-made steel bike. The solution is to remove and replace a section of tubing. Your local bike shop offers to do the work. The last thing you want is for them to create further damage, so you ask, 'Have you done this before?'

You may need sponsorship in order to achieve your ultra-distance cycling goals. Your potential sponsors will want to see that you have done something before they sponsor you. The guiding principle seems to be that sponsorship is provided once you can demonstrate you can do what you claim you can do. If you promise to write great blogs, you need to have written some great blogs. If you promise to win some races, you need to have won some races. Just as in a food shop you will often be offered a sample to taste before you buy, so too will you need to have a portfolio of evidence that supports any claim you may make about generating value for the sponsor. The challenge then is to build up a collection that illustrates your capabilities and how they can deliver value.

THE REALITY OF PR AND SPONSORSHIP

RUSSIAN AROUND – DOMINIC'S EXPERIENCE

It was 2 a.m. I sat on the edge of my bed in a Moscow hotel, waiting for the phone to ring. I was due to speak to the broadcaster, OJ Borg, on BBC Radio Five Live's 'Bespoke' programme about the second UK End-to-End record attempt. I was extremely tired. It had been a very early start, a hard day at work on top of a busy week of training. In under three minutes, the interview was over. The show had over-run and, as the final item, we had been squeezed into an ever-shorter slot. This was one of a dozen radio interviews I did relating to our record attempt. Some were really strange, such as the interview I did with a broadcaster whose sole area of interest was the application of anti-friction products before, during and after the ride. For many I realised that I was a convenient way of filling time.

Then there were the more intrepid journalists – those willing to jump on the back of the tandem and come for a spin. These were always great fun as the interview moved from being a somewhat transactional affair to something very different as they had their epiphany about what sitting on a tandem bike for 45 hours 'non-stop' would actually feel like. Added to this was the fun of trying to speak into a microphone as we rode, or descending at speed directly towards the brave camera-person looking for that artistic sequence.

On top of all of this were the monthly blogs in a cycling magazine, regular updates for the website of a sponsor and a variety of magazine interviews.

Our aim was simple; we wanted to gain coverage for the record attempt with a view to raising awareness for both our chosen charity and for the bike and kit sponsors. Success was defined by three criteria:
- Increasing the amount of charity donations.
- Reaching the target market for tandem bikes (active middle-aged people, likely to be professionals and/or employed in public services). For us that meant creating content that was accessible to those interested in, but not necessarily knowledgeable about, all things cycling, and using tandem cycling as a medium for telling stories.
- Raising awareness in the cycling community for the attempt, with the aim of securing association between the attempt and the kit sponsors.

When our earlier record attempts failed, I did not look forward to the review discussion with our main sponsors. These people had invested their hard-earned money into this venture. They too had bought into the dream. But we had failed. I left it a day or two before making the phone call. I hurt inside from the failure, and felt ashamed and embarrassed by it. I readied myself for a cold and critical discussion, which would have been very reasonable in the circumstances. I was shocked, stunned and not a little amazed at the warm and friendly response. They were disappointed we had not succeeded, but from their perspective it had been a great success. The amount of coverage for their products had been beyond their expectations. Their only question was 'When are you doing it again?'

It was my turn for an epiphany. I had unwittingly fallen into elements of successful PR without really realising what I was doing. Being a great athlete is just a small part of being sponsored. Being sponsored means developing a strong personal brand, having a strategic awareness of the business supporting you, and working in partnership with them to add value. It requires an active approach. In a small way, it requires you to think of yourself as a part-time employee whose remuneration happens to be in equipment or other support.

Dominic

THE PURPOSE OF PUBLIC RELATIONS

Public Relations (PR) is about managing people's perceptions about a business in the light of the context in which the business operates. It is managing the messages that influence its reputation. A reputation is something given to the business by others. Therefore, if you can influence the way they think, you can affect the reputation you have. A reputation can also be damaged in the same way. Lance Armstrong's infamous collapse from sport icon to cheat meant his sponsors had to change tack dramatically to distance themselves from him. PR is critical in managing crises such as this.

PR seeks to influence groups of people who in turn will influence the broader population. Thus, it is about providing information that has value. Influencing opinion can in turn influence behaviour. Unless the information is seen as having a value, PR has little benefit.

While PR is often used as a pejorative term, and those working in the industry labelled with an unfortunate stereotype, the reality is that it is crucial to the success of business, particularly given the mass of communication channels now available. Good PR is based on evidence, underpinned by integrity, and is honest in its message. It is not necessarily about being liked or likeable; it is about facilitating a change of opinion.

For the purposes of sponsorship, you need to understand what the PR objectives of a company are, and how what you create can help deliver those objectives. Success is defined by the outcomes the sponsoring company is seeking to achieve.

Figure 12: Ingredients necessary to get the best from PR

INSIGHTS FROM PRACTITIONERS

A number of experts in PR have provided their insights for this book, notably Stephen Waddington, chief engagement officer at Ketchum and former president of the Chartered Institute of Public Relations, and Sarah Townsend, one of the founders of McKenna Townsend, a PR company operating out of Ringwood in the UK. Both were asked about the attributes of someone who was easy to work with from a PR perspective (see Figure 12).

NO. 1: CONTENT, CONTENT, CONTENT

You need to generate content. Without content, there is very little a PR company can do. That content can take a variety of forms, such as blogs, video blogs (vlogs), articles, photos and videos. There needs to be a regular feed of material to enable the public relations activity to take place. You need to be able to tell a great story and you need to get it out there. When communicating, get the most important stuff out there first.

NO. 2: HAVE AN OPINION

The content should be insightful and express an opinion. At times, that may mean sticking your head above the parapet and going against the tide of opinion.

NO. 3: HUMAN INTEREST

Demonstrate your personality. Provide the human interest story. For example, when writing a blog about training, it may be better to talk about the emotional challenges and mental battles involved, than the amount of power you produced or what your heart rate was doing. Jonathan Turner from Team Sky described how one of the primary objectives for Digital at the outset was to 'bring the riders to life, to tell their stories'. In so doing, it would help fans connect with the team. Sky primarily used Facebook for this purpose. They would use pictures of things like preparing food for the riders, or other pictures from behind the scenes. They realised there were five or six dominant advocates on Facebook who in effect moderated the site, so they promoted their pictures, comments and posts.

NO. 4: BE HELPFUL

Give others insight into how to succeed. These might be top tips or handy hints. Make it easy for journalists too, by providing them with photographs and good copy they can use.

NO. 5: SHARE THE JOURNEY

If training for an event, write about the milestones and how the journey progresses. Talk about the challenges along the way (both good and bad).

NO. 6: BE RESPONSIVE

There will be times when something crops up in the news, or a journalist is seeking input into an article they are writing, when a quick response will generate good coverage. Be prepared to respond quickly to such opportunities.

NO. 7: HAVE A GREAT WEB PRESENCE

Get your stuff out on the various channels regularly.

NO. 8: BE AUTHENTIC

Be genuine. Have humility.

NO. 9: BE CLEAR ABOUT YOUR VISION AND PURPOSE

Know what you are seeking to achieve and why.

EVALUATING PR

Determining the effectiveness of PR depends on what you set out to achieve. Did you reach the people you set out to reach? Did they comprehend the message you were trying to deliver, and has this resulted in them doing something different? You can gain insight by using tools such as Google Analytics, which will tell you how many times a web page has been visited and indicates the profile of visitors. You can assess the readability of your work by using such formulas as created by Gunning and Flesch. One oft-used method is the quantification of media coverage expressed in terms of the equivalent cost, had you been required to pay for advertising to achieve the same. What this does not tell you is what people did with the information, and how they were affected. Understanding this requires more effort. As Jonathan Turner points out, in addition to creating content it is also important to optimise that content. There's not much point in writing something if no one reads it.

SUMMARY

People sponsor you for a reason. The more you understand that reason and the more value you deliver, the more likely you are to get sponsorship. It's an exchange of value. Writing articles, making appearances, and testing kit all take time that could otherwise be spent training. Make sure that any activity directed towards sponsorship is as effective as possible and gets you the maximum return for the effort made. This means taking time to understand how your sponsors define value, what their strategic ambitions may be, and how you can best support these endeavours. Be clear about what you stand for and what your personal brand represents. The best brands do not try to be all things to all people. Don't try to be something you are not.

Consider working with a PR agency. If you do, be prepared to be responsive and to generate usable content. The easier you make it for people to tell your story, the more likely they are to do so. Finally, remember, most people consume content on smart devices. You need to be able to attract attention away from everything else that is competing for space on that screen. Just being good at riding a bike is not enough.

Dealing with the press

CHAPTER 8: TEAMWORK

Getting to the finish line of any race depends on the support of a great many people. How to establish, develop and maintain your network of support is a core requirement for the ultra-cyclist. You can't do it alone.

SUPPORT TEAMS, TEAMWORK AND COMMUNICATION

At a glance, cycling looks like a sport for individuals, a view further exaggerated by the many solo hours in the saddle for the ultra-distance cyclist. However, it is near impossible to do ultra-distance, whether that be a self-supported ride or a fully-supported record attempt, without a strong support team around you. Whether it be friends, family or colleagues who help, you will find yourself dependent on others to make your ultra-distance dreams a reality. The focus of this chapter is the support team that makes success possible. Building such a team takes hard work.

Being a member of a support team is challenging. As Nigel Harrison, the person who has run all of Dominic's support teams over the last six years, explains:

Being part of a support team is not as hard as riding the bike, but it is not easy either. During our UK End-to-End tandem record attempts, the support team were on the go for just over 58 hours with little or no opportunity to sleep. When they did get a chance to rest, it was a question of slumping in the car seat for a few minutes' sleep, or a quick café stop for refreshments. Even this could get interrupted by demands from riders. Supported riding is a team effort. It is the team that wins or loses and not just the rider.

Sadly, though, only the riders' names make it into the record books.

Land's End to John o'Groats tandem
support team in the middle of the night

WHO IS IN A SUPPORT TEAM?

Below are some examples of the roles you may need a support team to fulfil. You do not need a separate person for each of the roles and you may not need all roles for every event. Do bear in mind, however, that if someone tries to fill too many roles, they will likely fail in all of them due to fatigue and stress. The nature of your ride will dictate the support you require and your ability to persuade people to join your team will dictate the choice you have.

The assumption is that you are the driving force behind the team and the decision to race. You may lead the preparation, but once you start riding the roles change. The objective for everyone is to get a bike from the start to the finish as quickly as possible within the rules of the race. Your role now is to ride the bike. It is someone else's job to manage the process of how this is achieved, based on the planning and preparation done beforehand. If you try to both ride and manage, you will compromise the overall outcome. As was shown in the sleep deprivation section of Chapter 6, you will be in no fit state to make decisions after just a few hours of riding. Thus, the level of involvement with members of the support team will vary depending on the stage you are at in your preparation and racing. For example, during training, working with your coach will be the dominant relationship, whereas during a race, your team captain, support crew and medic will be the most involved, with the coach behind the scenes and available if needed.

JOBS TO BE DONE, NOT ROLES

While people will have been allocated roles, the key point is that, whatever the jobs are, they need to get done; great teams are focused on the outcome, not the role. If anybody thinks 'It is not my job, so I'm not doing it,' then get yourself a new team member. The only reason for not doing something that needs to be done is because there is someone who can do it better and is going to do it.

CRITICAL DECISIONS

The middle of an event, when the whole team is tired, is not the time to be trying to fathom out the best decisions on issues of critical importance. It is far better to have worked out what the critical decisions are going to be in advance, and establish the criteria that underpin that decision. For example, a rider who is getting increasingly tired and ceasing to function effectively does not do so suddenly; it is something that creeps up insidiously. By the time the team realises that the rider is too tired, they may well have had an accident. It is therefore better that the rider delegates to the support team responsibility for whether to continue the ride. The support team can base their decision on whether the rider is able to speak coherently, is riding safely and is awake. Any one sign, such as wobbling across the road, is an indicator to stop the rider and check the other criteria, and on this basis make the decision.

The rider may object, may even be angry, but will probably be in no fit state to make sensible decisions. If the criteria for stopping are met, the ride must stop. It is a tall order to ask any one person to make this decision. It is helpful if two or three people in the support team can come together to agree the right decision. In this way, it is collective responsibility and not just one person's viewpoint. Unless there has been a catastrophe such as an accident or rider collapse, the decision to stop is a judgement. It needs to combine knowledge of ultra-distance riding and what the human body can do, as well as expedience and the health and safety of all, including other road users. A rider who strays into the path of oncoming traffic puts both themselves and others at risk, which is unfair and unethical.

Developing criteria in this way is useful for a range of decisions. For example, when attempting a feat dependent on the weather, defining what constitutes acceptable weather in advance will avoid a decision in haste at the critical time, and a missed opportunity.

Table 6: Team roles

Person	Role
Coach	Sets your training plan and reviews performance to enable you to make the most of your riding potential. As it is so critical, the athlete–coach relationship is covered further below.
Nutritionist	Helps you steer the fine line between having enough energy to perform optimally and staying as light as possible.
Physiotherapist	Helps you rehabilitate any injuries that may occur.
Psychologist	Helps you develop the right mindset as an individual and as a team to survive the challenges ahead.
Local bike shop	Stuff wears out and a broken bike is not much good for training. A good relationship with your local bike shop will help keep you on the road and they will often prioritise your repairs over others because they know the scale of what you are trying to achieve.
PR agency	To help promote your brand, your causes and to secure sponsorship.
Sponsors	The people that help make what you do possible. In return, you help promote what they do.
Team captain	While you are riding you cannot be thinking about anything else. Your team captain will execute your pre-agreed plan on your behalf.
Support team	These are the people that keep you fed and watered, while dealing with all of your in-ride kit requests. They are the people you will see most often during the ride and, while the role does not require high levels of technical skill, it needs a very positive, caring, can-do mentality.
Medic	While you hope nothing will ever go wrong, the chances of crashing increase significantly with fatigue and sleep deprivation. The medic's primary role is to prevent things necessitating the use of his/her skills. If things do go wrong, the difference between receiving medical attention immediately and having to wait for an ambulance can be the difference between life and death.
Bike mechanic	During the ride, things will go wrong with your bike. It could be as simple as a puncture or it might be more complex, such as a problem with the gears. A good mechanic will get you on your way quickly and while you are riding get the broken parts fixed before your next mechanical failure. During a pit-stop, while you are changing kit or eating they will be checking the bike over.
Riders	If you are riding as part of a team, your other riders are also part of the support network for you, as you are for them.
Route planner	Where there is a choice of route (such as in a place-to-place ride), route planning is crucial. Which route you take will depend on, for example, how much climbing is required, the quality of the roads and the number of towns that have to be passed through. While you will probably do this in advance of the ride, in the event of a road closure during a ride, someone in the team has to be able to identify an alternative, appropriate and fast route.
Meteorologist	Only really relevant to place-to-place record attempts where the weather can have a profound impact on performance.
Administration	Whether hiring cars, booking hotel rooms or organising transport, there are myriad admin tasks that need to be completed.
Family	Throughout everything you do you will need the close support of your partner/wife/husband. They are the ones who have to cope when you come home miserable because a session has not gone to plan, or help patch you up when you fall off the bike. More importantly, they can help you celebrate success because they know, more than anyone else, the effort involved, having witnessed how hard you worked to prepare yourself.

>>As leaders, we have to stop doing things that get in the way of that natural desire to be engaged.>>

BUILDING YOUR TEAM

UNDERSTAND WHAT ENGAGEMENT REALLY IS

An ideal support team has the right people (trait) in the right state of mind (state), doing the right things (behaviour) for the benefit of the riders (return on investment) and themselves. It starts by having people with the right traits – people who are self-motivated and self-driven and who demonstrate the characteristics you need in the team. Next is getting these people into the right state of mind, such that they want to do well and are prepared to go the extra mile in supporting you. Finally, and most importantly, they must follow through with actions commensurate with their intent.

As the team leader, you can do much to help or hinder engagement. The fundamental principle that underpins a great support team is that, at a deep and profound level, people wish to be engaged with the project. Think of engagement like water cascading down the mountainside – it wants to get to the valley floor. Engagement is all about channelling the water to maximise the force to generate power to achieve results. As leaders, we have to stop doing things that get in the way of that natural desire to be engaged. Understanding team engagement is about the study of actions or behaviours that may be inhibiting engagement as much as it is about actions or behaviours to promote engagement.

DELEGATION MEANS NEITHER ABDICATION NOR LOSING CONTROL

COME IN, NO. 1, YOUR TIME IS UP

The leader of a long-distance cycle ride group was dealing with information coming into his ear from the team radio about some riders who had taken a wrong turn. At the same time, his phone was ringing with information from the team in the support vehicle. He was also trying to check his GPS to ensure that the group was heading in the right direction (in addition to pedalling, changing gear and negotiating the traffic!). It was too much and he realised this. He passed on radio duties to another rider and eventually delegated the navigation role too. This left him considerably freer to focus on the overall management of the ride. It worked. The reduction in stress he felt was palpable.

This was a great reminder of the importance of the need to create space to think about the broader picture, while maintaining overall control. The lesson was about making sure you have the bandwidth to deal with the big picture by identifying things that can be done by others and letting them get on and do them. Having delegated responsibility to other riders, initially there was a lot of feedback as to what was happening but, over time, as confidence grew, less feedback was required. This raises some interesting observations about 'followership' as well as 'leadership'.

BE AN ENGAGING LEADER

The single, overwhelmingly most important driver of team engagement is you. Your ability to generate positive feelings and the right state of mind in the team will help generate great support. To engage people and keep them engaged, you should do the following:

- Demonstrate strong commitment to diversity – you need more than cyclists, or people who all think in the same way. This is the best way of challenging assumptions that may be constraining performance.
- Adapt to changing circumstances – particularly important during a race where things can and will go wrong.
- Clearly articulate the team goals – To win? To finish? To complete as a vegetarian?
- Accurately evaluate team member potential – what is it each person could do?
- Put the right people in the right roles at the right time – for example, the medic can do other tasks before a race, but during the race, make sure he/she has the space to be the medic.
- Demonstrate honesty and integrity – do what you say you will do when you said you would do it. Do not cheat. Who wants to support a cheat?
- Set realistic performance expectations – do not hope to win when you have not done the training. Be ambitious and temper this with realism.
- Encourage and manage innovation – success might come from finding better and alternative ways of doing things. Success in sport has a history of people pushing boundaries to find better ways of doing things. Just make sure that, whatever it is, it is legal, within both the rules and the spirit of the rules.
- Break down the project into manageable components – for example, training, nutrition and route planning.

- Help find solutions to problems – if someone is struggling to work out how to solve a problem you have identified, step in where necessary to bring some extra thinking to the challenge.
- Accept responsibility for successes and failures – do not blame others. You cannot excuse your way to success. It's your project, own it.
- Help team members understand how to complete team projects – especially if they are a non-cyclist.
- Explain the importance of a person's job to the success of the team – some tasks can seem almost inconsequential or pointless, such as being responsible for getting rid of rubbish. However, a clean working environment can make such a difference to how people feel when they are getting tired and still have lots to do. It can boost morale. Helping the person responsible for this task understand its significance gives a 'rubbish' job importance.
- Encourage team member development – assuming you intend to do more than one race, help members of your team learn more skills such that they and you benefit. Many aspects of being part of a support team are transferrable to other aspects of life.
- Give high-quality informal feedback – just as you give your coach feedback, so too it is important to let members of the team know how they are performing.
- Accurately evaluate team member performance – are they doing what you need them to do? There's not much point in them giving up their time to do the wrong thing.
- Make sacrifices for team members – they are giving up time (and probably holiday time) for you. Do what you can for them.
- Demonstrate a passion to succeed – people need to believe you are serious, especially if you expect them to work for a long period of time without sleep when they could be doing other things.

MAKE SURE YOUR PEOPLE KNOW WHY THEY ARE DOING WHAT THEY ARE DOING

A key element of being engaged is to know how what you do adds value. Inexperienced team members may not appreciate how some of the simplest things, seemingly so easy to do, can make such a difference to the rider – for example, making sure things are always done in the same sequence at pit-stops to ensure nothing is forgotten. A person's job needs to be understood in relation to others. For example, winning the race could be the primary goal. A beautifully-maintained bike is an important secondary goal but not at the cost of winning the race. Better to have an adequately-maintained bike and first place. If people better understand why they are doing what they are doing and how best it should be done, they can make informed decisions when faced with options. When they have this understanding, they are likely to be more engaged.

COMMUNICATION IS CRITICAL

This specifically relates to internal communication between you and the support team in the preparatory phase. In as much as you need to demonstrate the points listed earlier, communication needs to both reinforce and demonstrate the same principles. Communication is a key part of ensuring that people understand why they are doing what they are doing, for what purpose and how they should be doing it. The key here is authenticity and believability. People must be able to connect with the communication and see the messages as real and honest. Communication must have an integrity that echoes reality, which screams 'we get what you do and we value what you

do'. Communication has the opportunity to make people into team heroes, focusing on behaviour that the team values and in so doing helping build the culture of the team. This can be achieved in part by the style and composition of the imagery used. You might think this is a bit extreme for a cycling event, but remember you are trying to persuade people to give up holiday time to support you and it needs to both feel and be worthwhile.

Think about communication with the aim of achieving four goals:

- Purpose: Understanding why we do what we do and what we are aiming to achieve.
- Progress: How and what are we doing that is getting us there?
- People: Who is making the difference?
- Performance: Reward and recognition.

Use imagery that maximises the emotional connection, use messages that grab attention and that reinforce what you value. Use styles that fit with the mindset of the people that are in your support team.

YOU NEED THE RIGHT PEOPLE IN PLACE

It is incredibly difficult, if not impossible, to engage someone who does not want to be engaged. Recruit the right people into your team with the right traits to begin with. You have a duty of care to other members of the team to ensure you have the best possible chance of success. If there is a sense of someone being carried or causing unnecessary friction, then the message is that they are not as focused as they said they were on the objective.

>>The key is to 'control the controllables'.>>

CRACK THE CONTEXT AND YOU'RE 90 PER CENT OF THE WAY THERE

One of the most powerful drivers has been saved for last. Social psychologist Stanley Milgram wrote, 'It is not so much the kind of person a man is, as the kind of situation in which he finds himself that determines how he will act.' As much evidence has shown, it is context that drives behaviour more than anything else. For example, a speed camera, whether you like it or not, most of the time will slow you down. The fear of getting points on your licence (or whatever the motoring equivalent is in your country) drives your behaviour. In the same way, lowering the temperature in an office will change what people choose to wear – the context is driving their behaviour. In cycling terms, your refusal to pull over when you see the team parked somewhere dangerous creates the context whereby they know there is no point in stopping unless in a safe place. Only putting good food into your support vehicle creates the context where all you can eat is good food.

We can use the same principles to create an environment that drives team members to do things likely to help them become more engaged. The way you demonstrate your actions will help create a culture where 'It is simply the way we do things around here.' Culture is made up of customs and habits that drive behaviour. Make sure the customs and habits in your team are driving the behaviour you wish to see. Another way is to create a set of guiding principles that inform all decisions made by the team. These principles set a tone and a set of standards that create the context to drive up performance. They also set the limits. For example:

Will it make us go faster?	Whatever we are about to do, how will doing it help us go faster?
What's the evidence?	How do you know that what you are proposing will work?
Feedback	Discuss everything; nothing is sacrosanct in the interests of going faster.
Turn every stone	Question everything you do in order to understand why it is the best way or whether there is a better way.

FOCUS ON THE INPUTS

The Regional President for one of the world's biggest automotive manufacturers realised the importance of understanding inputs in cycling as well as in business. Too often, in his view, people focus on profit and cash as if they are the activity itself, rather than the outcome of well-executed strategies and activities, just like cyclists that focus only on average speed. This lesson was brought home to him on a cycle ride where much emphasis was placed by the ride leader on controlling effort, as measured by heart rate or power output, and in managing energy and fluid consumption in order to ensure a sustainable performance. By carefully managing these factors, the group achieved a good average speed. The focus was not on average speed itself. Average speed, like profit, is to an extent uncontrollable. Weather, terrain and wind direction can all impact on speed and there is little that can be done about these things; just as in business the economic climate and political decisions can impact profitability. The key is to 'control the controllables' – focusing on those inputs that will give you the best chance of

>> The best challenges are those that motivate people to overcome incredible odds. >>

delivering the outcome sought, whether that be profit or power, rather than on speed itself. This is what everyone in the support team needs to understand.

Success breeds success. By creating a successful experience, people will volunteer for considerable further hard work, inconvenience and the pressure of trying to juggle work, family and leisure. The positive experience is a powerful driver of engagement. That does not necessarily mean you have to win (although that helps) – simply that the experience for all was worthwhile. It provides evidence for others that being involved in your projects is a worthwhile experience. The Holy Grail in terms of team member engagement is discretionary effort. This is the work someone is prepared to put in over and above what might reasonably be expected. Get the way you manage your support team right and you will see this in bucket loads. It is one of the most humbling aspects of ultra-distance cycling – the effort others are willing to go to on your behalf.

IT BEGINS WITH A GREAT GOAL

The best challenges are those that motivate people to overcome incredible odds. Think about it: riding 10 kilometres is hardly a significant challenge for the fit individual. The best goals are demanding. Hatching the right goal is something that has to be carefully thought through, as it is the seed that sparks the performance. There are six key ingredients.

1. It has to be scary

As someone once said, 'I like to have a challenge that I say yes to and then think "My God, what have I agreed to?"' This captures the essence of the right sort of goal. At the outset it is just about possible to imagine doing it, but it is by no means certain. The right goal creates an emotional response; you can feel the excitement of the possibility of achieving it, but at the same time the fear associated with the scale of the challenge. You and the team are excited about the prospect of achieving the goal.

>> It's fine to have a crazy goal, but if there is no hope of achieving the goal then there is no point in starting. >>

2. It has to tell a story

A great goal will deliver great stories and lasting memories. The key questions are: Can you imagine yourself feeling a sense of pride and pleasure from achieving the goal? Can you imagine yourself telling others about the journey taken to achieve the goal? If the answer to both questions is 'yes', it is a great goal.

3. It has to be achievable

It's fine to have a crazy goal, but if there is no hope of doing what's required to achieve the goal then there is no point in starting. It has to be do-able. Given the context in which many riders have to train, 'do-able' does not mean realistic, it means, 'If I get really focused and make some tough decisions I will be able to carve out the time to do what I need to do, but it is not going to be easy.' This might mean training at 5 a.m., or hours riding the same section of road, or in the case of one committed rider, being followed by an armed security team the whole time! This last example was because, as a high-profile businessman working in South America, he was at high risk of being taken hostage for money.

4. It must have confidence in others

Understandably, given the effort required, it is essential that people have faith that the rest of the team are doing the necessary work to ensure that all logistics are covered and that robust contingency plans are in place. To go to huge effort, only to be let down by something that could have been sorted in advance, is simply unacceptable. The belief in the team is critical as it allows everyone to focus on what they have to do.

5. It must set high expectations

David Ogilvy, the advertising guru, said 'Set exorbitant standards, and give your people hell when they do not live up to them. There is nothing as demoralising as a boss who tolerates second-rate work.' As a team leader, you might not have the formal power to be able to 'give people hell', but it is the standards you set that others will take as the example. Make sure you set them high and that you deliver too! Demanding hard work is often, somewhat surprisingly, seen as a positive.

>> Find technologies that enable you to communicate as close to face-to-face communication as possible. >>

6. It must evoke a sense of community

Create and build a sense of community within your support team. Send out updates on training progress and any new developments as they occur. It is an important part of helping people to belong. The frequency and content is down to you. If people are working in isolation, it is good to hear how everyone else is getting on.

GET THE COMMUNICATION MECHANISM RIGHT

Wouldn't it be great if all your support team lived in the same town and were readily available to meet up and work on your next race project? If this is your world, congratulations! For the rest of us, our support teams are likely to be dotted all over the place with full-time jobs making face-to-face meetings, other than the race itself, impossible. This means you need to be a master of virtual communication to hold it all together. We humans prefer face-to-face communication. Evolution has led us to a place where face-to-face communication is what we are used to engaging in. Unsurprisingly then, things like email are very poor tools to enable people to work together – it is about as bad as it gets. You will have experienced an email exchange getting out of control as each party misinterprets the words and fires a challenging missive back that in turn generates more ill will in a vicious cycle of mutual self-destruction. The challenge is simple: find technologies that enable you to communicate as close to face-to-face communication as possible. Telephone calls are better than email; video calls better than telephone calls. If you have a choice, upgrade your communication medium to the best available to you.

THE CHALLENGES OF TECHNOLOGY

Technology has to both work and be very easy to use. Problems with technology can destroy the productivity of the most motivated group of people. With technology as it stands, it is not uncommon for the first 10-15 minutes of a video call to be spent messing around trying to get everyone connected due to problems with both hardware and software. When it works, making a video call has become the equivalent of sticking your head around someone's door and asking 'Have you got five minutes?' Video calls have made the greatest difference to the way we work with fellow support team members.

DISTRACTEDLY PRESENT

The lure of the flashing LED. The vibrating buzz that announces someone wants to tell you something. The furtive attempts to unlock your phone, casually open the right app and read the content, all the while nodding and pretending to listen, are both distracting and tedious. You can either concentrate on your device or your meeting, but not both.

Similar things can happen in virtual team sessions. If the medium is a telephone call, people can mute their microphone and make a tea or coffee, or respond to an email. Even when using video software, if everyone is looking at a document on screen, they cannot see when other people are no longer concentrating and are engaged in something else. A large screen can help here as it allows you to both view the document under discussion and to see the other people on the video call. You need people focused and present in the meeting. If your only option is a telephone conference call, something as simple as a register with everyone's name on it will allow you to check in with each participant after each discussion point to ensure their views are heard. While it feels a bit mechanical, it does ensure that everyone's voice is heard and all viewpoints are considered.

BE DISCIPLINED

It does not matter whether the meeting is face-to-face or virtual. Being clear about the purpose of the meeting and the outcomes sought helps ensure that the time together is efficient and effective. This is particularly important in the virtual environment, where digressions and tangents are not so easy to get back on track. It is also the right thing to do to avoid wasting people's time.

KEEP IT SIMPLE

With virtual communication it is even more important to ensure people are speaking a common language. A debate can become more heated and people more frustrated until the penny drops – people were talking at cross-purposes. It sounds tedious and a touch pedantic, but it is worth occasionally checking what people mean by a particular term and concept. For example, one rider reported his teammates were surprised by his lack of enthusiasm on a topic – it took a while for them to figure out he hadn't seen a significant email and for him to realise he was missing something. Once this misunderstanding was sorted, normal service resumed. However clear you think you are being, you should assume and be prepared for misinterpretation. It can seem somewhat forced, but when working virtually, communicate issues and decisions in painstaking detail. Consider having a lexicon of commonly used terms (such as the glossary at the end of this book) to ensure everyone understands what is meant when a given term is used. Do not be afraid to check what people mean by the words and concepts they are using. If you feel unsure, chances are others will too.

THE ESSENCE OF EFFECTIVE TEAMWORK

As a tutor on the Union Cycliste Internationale Sport Directors programme, I focus on the characteristics of effective teamwork and how these can be enhanced. The most productive workshop sessions are those that reflect on the positive experiences of individuals from their days in competition and professional teams.

Interestingly, the key themes that emerge from these sessions are as relevant to the committed amateur ultra-distance cyclist as they are to Tour de France riders and support teams. Recognising the value of empathy, the building and strengthening of relationships and the authenticity of behaviours will maximise the effectiveness of your support team just as much as it does with the pros.

EMPATHY

The ability of those around you to understand and empathise is a quality that provides a supportive environment and builds stronger relationships. Empathy is a quality that enhances trust, cooperation and problem solving and refers to a 'circle of safety' where those in teams and organisations feel they can operate more effectively.

RELATIONSHIPS

Professional riders can spend up to 200 days away from home and with their team in any one year. This is effectively a 'family' away from their real family. As Theodore Roosevelt stated, 'The most important single ingredient in the formula of success is to know how to get along with people.' Though you might not be away from home for such a long period, your work and ultra-distance cycling commitments will thrive on good relationships.

AUTHENTICITY

This is a reference to the real self. This self-knowledge will guide decisions that need to be made in a variety of contexts. For example, individuals in teams highly value the honesty and integrity of those around them. It creates trust and ensures that actions and behaviours in all situations are genuine and constant.

Richard Cheetham, Senior Fellow in Sports Coaching

The pace of change in technology is rapid, so keep in touch with developments. Be curious to experiment with new tools. The more tools you have at your disposal to ensure high-quality interaction between team members, the better. People are adaptable. Help them learn how to use what's available and they will be able to use it. Have faith in people's ability to embrace technology; millions now use smartphones without ever going on a course to learn how.

SUPPORT TEAMS IN ACTION

VEHICLE CHOICE

Given the length of time the support team will spend in the vehicle, it is important that it is comfortable for them. It also needs to be big and powerful enough to carry all the kit. It's also essential that a seat can be reclined to allow the rider to have a short nap. It is useful to have a flashing amber beacon for the roof to alert other road users that something is happening and they should take extra care (as long as this is legal in your country). Battery-powered magnetic amber beacons can be attached to the roof of any vehicle, as long as it is made of steel.

Automatic gearboxes make it much easier for a driver to follow a bike at slow speed. Plenty of charging points for phones, bike computers and the like is also essential. Be cautious about the load placed on the electrical system. If exceeded, it could bring the vehicle to a halt if a critical fuse goes. If this happens it can sometimes cause other problems, which may not be fixable on the roadside.

VEHICLE ORGANISATION

Searching for kit buried in a box in the middle of the night is difficult, frustrating and a waste of time. Whether storing items in bags or boxes, have a system and stick to it. Whenever you have to get kit out of a container, make sure the rest is returned to the right container and that the container is returned to the same place. If you know waterproofs are always stored in the left-hand top box in the boot, that is where you will find them. Have a hierarchy of accessibility. Put

MIDNIGHT ON THE MORTIROLO

The route of the Race Across the Alps includes the Mortirolo Pass. This epic climb of 12.4km steepens to 18 per cent in places. All was not going well. The support car had been upgraded by the car rental company and, while appreciably larger, was significantly underpowered. As a result, the support team were struggling to get the car moving on the steep sections due to the weight of the team and kit in the car. The decision was made to give the rider – Sanchez – enough food and water to get him to the top, where the support car and rider would re-group. About 10 minutes after the car left, it started to rain. It was light at first, but became a deluge. For over an hour Sanchez climbed into the night in a torrential downpour, with only the effort of the climb staving off hypothermia. While the support team was grateful for having a bigger vehicle, engine size had not been considered.

the equipment most likely to be needed at the top and the least likely at the bottom. Consider putting combinations of kit together, for example lights and reflective kit for night riding in one box; cordials, water bottles and electrolytes in another.

RUBBISH

It is quite staggering how much rubbish is generated during an ultra-distance ride, from empty water bottles, to food wrappers from the rider, and the food eaten by the support team. It's important to have plenty of bin bags to store it and get rid of it whenever a suitable opportunity presents itself.

WET KIT

Have good-quality bin bags for wet kit. Ideally, you will have multiple sets of kit likely to be used more than once, such as leg and arm warmers. In the event you do not, then the support team will need to get them as dry as possible before they are next used (assuming they are wet). The floor of the car with the heater blasting into the footwell is about as good as it gets. While it won't dry out wet kit, it will at least make it a bit warmer when it comes to putting it back on.

SAFETY

Be safe! It's not worth winning a race if you have put a member of your team in hospital. Before doing anything, be clear what it is you are about to do and why you are doing it. Some helpful things to think about are:

- When you park your vehicle, make sure you do not block the line of sight of members of the team and other road users.
- If you are tired, do not drive – swap with someone else.
- Keep a safe distance from the rider: bikes can out-brake a car easily, and running your own rider over is careless.
- Do not break traffic laws – in most races this will result in disqualification.
- If you have a spare bike on the roof, watch for overhead barriers in car parks. They can destroy a bike in one blow.
- Ideally, stop in a layby, and ideally a layby with a protective central reservation – these are much, much safer than laybys without such a feature.

- Wear a Hi-Viz (with reflective stripes) jacket so other drivers can see you clearly and can see that something out of the ordinary is going on.
- Agree the protocols of how you will look after the rider before the start of the race and practise them in a safe location.
- Do not try to do two things at once (such as drive and operate the phone or radio).

PIT-STOP CHECKLIST

Have a process for managing pit-stops. It saves time and makes sure the right things happen in the right sequence; for example, applying chamois cream before putting on fresh shorts. Imagine getting fully changed and on your way only to realise a few yards down the road that you forgot to apply more chamois cream! Do you carry on and run the risk of abrasions, or stop to re-apply? Either decision will have a negative impact on the ride.

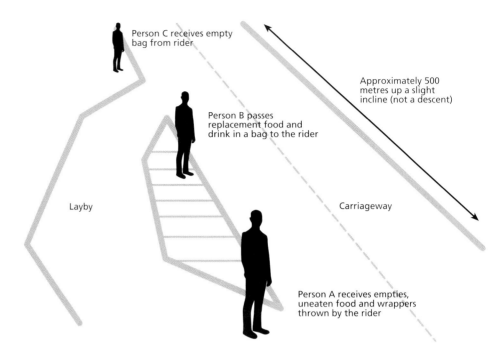

Person C receives empty bag from rider

Person B passes replacement food and drink in a bag to the rider

Approximately 500 metres up a slight incline (not a descent)

Layby

Carriageway

Person A receives empties, uneaten food and wrappers thrown by the rider

Figure 13: Passing food to the rider from a stationary position

FEEDING

In some races, passing food from a moving vehicle to the rider is permissible. In others, it is not. Different strategies are required for each.

Passing food/drink from a moving vehicle

This is something that requires practice. It is potentially very dangerous and should, in the authors' view, be avoided. If you do decide to employ this strategy, it should not be the driver who passes items to the rider! The driver's job is to concentrate on holding the car at a steady speed and an equal distance from the roadside at all times. They are also responsible for watching for traffic ahead and from behind and they may require the food manoeuvre to be abandoned. They should not look at the bike but at where they are going. The rider manages their position on the road in relation to the vehicle and calls when they are ready to either pass something to the support vehicle or to receive it. One item at a time is passed to the rider by a member of the support team, allowing the rider to stash the item before moving on to the next one.

Ideally, this is done on a slight incline on a straight where forward and backward visibility is optimal for the driver, as this neither sacrifices the opportunity to go fast down a hill nor creates an opportunity for a high-speed incident.

Passing food to the rider from a stationary position

Try to find a layby with a central reservation (see Figure 13). This allows the rider to use the layby itself if necessary and also provides much better safety for the support crew. The evidence is overwhelming about the significant reduction in road traffic accidents when laybys with central reservations are used, compared to laybys without.

Ideally, the layby will be on the side of a hill the rider is ascending, as this keeps everything at a sensible speed and also does not waste the opportunity of descending at speed.

Person A stands at the start of the layby (or just before) and receives the 'empties' from the rider (e.g. used water bottles and food wrappers).

Person B hands the rider a musette (food bag) containing whatever the rider has asked for,

>>There is a lot of kit required to support a rider during an ultra-distance race.>>

or the support team thinks they need. The bag should be held out at arm's-length, with the strap held open as a big loop into which the rider can either insert their arm or can grab the strap itself. The rider then stashes the content on the bike.

Person C receives the empty musette from the rider, ready for use at the next pit-stop. Person C needs to be positioned 500 metres further on from the layby to allow the rider time to stash the contents of the bag.

The manoeuvre needs to be practised to work out the right speed and location.

SUPPORT TEAM KIT

Each member of the support team needs to have a Hi-Viz jacket, a head torch (with spare batteries), a change of clothes, waterproofs and warm things to wear when working during the night or high up in the mountains.

VEHICLE KIT

There is a lot of kit required to support a rider during an ultra-distance race. Table 7 (page 237) shows a sample of some of the items that may be required, and their use.

COMMUNICATION

There are multiple ways of communicating with the rider, depending on the rules of the race. In some record attempts, the vehicle is not allowed to slow next to the rider to speak to them, in which case either they have to wait until the bike stops or use mobile phones or radios. Another option is to attach a megaphone to the roof of the vehicle and 'broadcast' to the rider, with the rider acknowledging the message by pre-agreed signs.

LAND'S END TO JOHN O'GROATS TANDEM PIT-STOP CHECKLIST

During the successful Land's End to John o'Groats tandem record attempt, the team had a pit-stop checklist to make sure things happened in the right sequence. This built upon lessons learned from the two previous failed attempts.

- Riders arrive at pit-stop.
- Take the bike from the riders.
- Hand the riders wet wipes if they need to take a toilet break.
- Have kit ready in the order in which it will be put on.
- Give riders a glove, and hold the pot of chamois cream open.
- Hand the riders a cloth/wet wipe to freshen their face.
- Hand the riders their warm coat if they are stopping to eat hot food.

While riders are changing or eating:
- Change bottles on the bike.
- Replenish food supply on the bike.
- Wipe and lube the chain.
- Check tyres for debris.
- Swap bike computers if necessary.
- Add lights if dusk.
- Remove lights if dawn.
- Make sure riders start from the place they stopped.
- Stand back and allow riders to start on their own.

">> Using a phone while riding is the equivalent of riding while sleep-deprived. >>"

Mobile phones

Pros:

- Everybody has one.
- Everybody's numbers can be programmed into the phone.
- Work over any distance where there is signal.
- Can be a back-up navigation tool and bike computer.

Cons:

- Can be fiddly to use.
- Not all are waterproof.
- Battery life when used as a bike computer is poor.
- Incomplete signal coverage.
- When in use is generally one-to-one rather than one-to-many.

A mobile phone is useful if the support car gets separated from the rider when going through a town in order to keep the support car informed of their location. A waterproof pouch is useful for protecting the phone and makes an excellent baffle to prevent wind noise (as discussed in Chapter 4: Equipment, page 101). If you have to make a call, it is strongly recommended that you stop to do so. Using a phone while riding is the equivalent of riding while sleep-deprived, such is the impact that using a phone has on your concentration.

Two-way radios

Pros:

- Simple to operate.
- Good battery life.
- Robust.
- Multiple channels so rider can talk to everyone (so everyone hears the message) and the support team can have their own channel.

Cons:

- Good ones need a radio licence and all have a limited range.
- Bulkier than a mobile.
- Restrictions on their use in some countries (e.g. India).
- Cost.

Two-way radios allow easy communication between the car and the bike, particularly if the rider is using a secrecy microphone, which is where the microphone is clipped to the collar of the rider's jersey and an earpiece inserted into the ear canal. As a result, they can hear clearly what's being said and the support car can also hear what the rider is saying. It is also much easier to use than a mobile phone as there is only one button to press to speak and listening requires the rider to do nothing if using an earpiece.

Megaphones

Pros:

- Easy to use.

Cons:

- Need to be mounted on the exterior of the vehicle.
- Limited two-way communication.
- Very limited range.

The megaphone is only really useful when the support vehicle is directly behind the rider.

The combination of all these devices is the ideal. Whatever solution you use needs to be practised in training by whoever will be involved in communication.

>>Whatever solution you use needs to be practised in training.>>

Table 7: Vehicle kit

Item	Reason
12V USB adaptor	To enable multiple devices to be charged at the same time
Amber beacon	For the car roof for safety
Bike spares	To repair the bike(s)
Bin bags	For the vast amount of rubbish you will generate
Cables	Charging cables to fit all devices being used
Choice of drink	Coffee, tea, water, electrolytes
Chopping board and knife	Useful for preparing food on the go in case different food is requested than that prepared
Duct tape	For temporary repairs of almost anything
Emergency contact details	Of all the team in case of emergency, and of the race organisers
First aid kit	In case of emergencies. Given the outside location, an emergency shelter and closed cell foam mat will help insulate the casualty and keep them warm until help arrives.
Flask	To keep hot water for preparing a hot drink quickly and easily for the rider or members of the support team
Food boxes and food	To organise the rider's food so that it is easily accessible
Gel hand cleaner	To maintain hand hygiene
Kit boxes and kit	To organise the rider's kit so that it is easily accessible
Kitchen roll	For mopping up mess
List of rider's requirements	Details of what the rider is likely to need and when
Mugs	To drink hot drinks
Musettes	For handing food to the rider from a stationary vantage
Notebook and pen	To jot down any key points, reminders, etc.
Rags	For cleaning the bike
Route map	Hard copy and soft copy to help navigate
Spare GPS	For the rider
Spare radio batteries	For the rider and the support vehicle(s)
Track pump	To inflate bike tyres
VHF/UHF radio	For communication
Wet wipes	Multi-purpose – for personal hygiene and freshening up
Zip ties	For temporary repairs

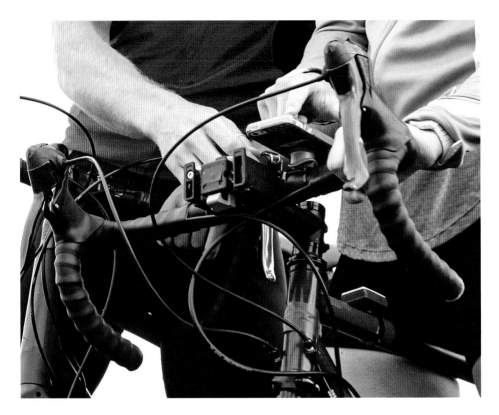

NAVIGATION

For the rider

These days, most ultra-distance events provide a race GPS Exchange format (gpx) file. These files can be uploaded to a suitable device and the route 'read' while riding. This is incredibly useful as it means less time has to be spent at junctions, working out which way the route goes. However, such devices do have limitations.

- Battery life – at the time of writing, the longest quoted battery life is around 18 hours. However, by the time the back light has been used and some of the other functionality, this time can significantly decrease. Therefore, on longer rides, back-up power from a dynamo or a battery pack will be required to keep the device working (as discussed in more detail in Chapter 4: Equipment, page 101).
- Road closures – in the event of a road being closed, the small screen on most of these devices makes finding a way around more of a challenge. Zooming out loses too much detail too quickly to make it an easy task. Re-routing, while a useful option, does not always work as sometimes it will simply try and take you back to where the road is closed rather than around it if no other reasonable alternative is available.
- Screen fixation – recent models provide spoken directions through headphones. Some models still rely on you to look at the screen for directions, which means at the very time you need to have your head up and looking around, i.e. at junctions, you're busy looking at the screen, trying to figure out which exit of the roundabout is required. This is dangerous.
- Capacity – some devices are incapable of holding the amount of ride data generated on an ultra-distance ride and crash once full, often deleting both the data stored and the original settings. The solution is to stop the ride and save the data more frequently, using appropriate software to stitch together each leg post-ride.

>>If you do not trust what your coach asks you to do, your motivation will be lower and you may even decide not to do the session.>>

These limitations mean it is useful to have a back-up navigation solution. Smartphones are the obvious choice, although the larger screen size can mean the battery drains within just a few hours. Keeping screen brightness down and turning off all non-essential apps and features can help significantly. A smartphone also allows use of online maps to check for alternative routes when a road is closed.

For the support team
The support vehicle can make use of a much wider range of technology to help the support team navigate. It is useful to have pre-driven the route and to have dropped markers onto the map of good places to stop for the bike and support team. As for the bike, having back-up technology is essential, as is the ability to charge devices. However good the tools are, they are only as good as the person using them. Time should be spent becoming familiar with all devices – this includes preparing the devices for the rider and knowing how to charge them.

Nigel Harrison, who has run the support team for Dominic on all of his ultra-distance supported rides, including his successful End-to-End record-breaking ride, details below what he believes are the requirements for a support team (pages 240–243).

WORKING WITH YOUR COACH

It is not essential to have a coach, but it helps. It is not necessarily the case that you won't know what to do, but rather the expedient solution of removing something else you have to think about from your life, enabling you to focus on what's important. A coach can spend the time thinking about what you should be doing in order to achieve your goals, and you can use this time doing the training. A coach can be a useful sounding board to test out ideas you might have to improve what you are doing. Their knowledge, combined with yours, is likely to be a greater resource than either of you alone. If you are new to working with a coach and to ultra-distance, you need to do what the coach advises. As experience grows, it becomes more of a dialogue. There are four elements that underpin a great coach–athlete relationship – trust, honest feedback, evidence and execution.

TRUST

If you do not trust what your coach asks you to do, your motivation to do it will be lower and you may even decide not to do the session. If your coach doesn't trust your feedback – perhaps because they feel they have to interpret your comments because you understate or overstate the difficulty of a session – then the sessions they set may not be appropriate to your circumstance. They may also lose motivation in coaching you. If you have selected the right coach in the first place, you need to trust what they ask you to do and be confident in how they respond to your feedback, and how that translates into the work set. Trust is something that you give to someone else. The confidence to trust develops over time.

>> It's normal for the crew to be tired, hungry and uncomfortable for long periods. >>

THE VIEW FROM THE SUPPORT TEAM

Q. What is the job of a support team?

There are lots of tasks that have to be done by the crew before, during and after the ride, many in conjunction with the rider(s), but the fundamental purpose of the support crew can be boiled down to two things:

1. Keep the rider(s) safe.
2. Keep the bike(s) moving.

In order to achieve this, there is a huge amount of stuff to attend to, but anything that doesn't point towards one of these fundamentals is a distraction. All the planning, preparation and organisation is essentially answering the question: how can we keep the rider(s) safe and keep the bike(s) moving?

Q. What's it like in the support vehicle?

On any endurance ride we always know (and appreciate) who is doing the really, really hard work (it's the rider(s), of course). However, sitting behind a bike for a long time can also be a real challenge; I have described it before as an endurance event of a different kind. First thing to note, it isn't boring! People tell me it must be tedious driving so slowly for so long ... wrong! Depending on the event type there is always (and I mean always) something to do or something to prepare for, and that's without the unforeseen things like mechanicals, navigation errors, road closures, sickness, etc. Usually it's a bit cramped and uncomfortable because there's invariably a huge amount of kit that has to be carried, so you have bags or boxes tucked under your legs and next to you on the seat. There are things that you need to have close to hand the whole time

(two-way radios, mobile phones, maps/iPads, GPS device, etc.); these also clutter your space. Many of these things need to be on constant charge because their batteries won't last as long as the ride and you can't live without them, so charging leads criss-cross the vehicle. There are boxes of food and fluids for the rider(s), which need to be easily accessible; the rider(s)' changes of clothing, which need to be organised so that they can be quickly accessed when requested; the tool kit and spares; the first aid kit; day bags; overnight bags ... you get the idea; it's crowded! But it has to be organised, and stay organised for the duration.

And it's generally busy: fluids to prepare (with the correct mix of electrolytes), food to prepare (with the right mix of carbs, protein, etc.), clothing changes to manage, wet clothes to dry, navigation to keep an eye on, weather patterns to follow, bike devices to charge, communication with the rider(s), communication within the support team, communication with family/friends of the rider(s) and support team, other calls to answer, navigation (especially through towns), progress checks against the plan, planned stops to prepare for, food/kit hand-ups, and so on. It really is non-stop. Among all this you have to keep your eyes on the bike in case anything happens or it stops. And all of that is without yet paying any attention to the needs of the crew themselves; they need to eat, drink and go to the toilet from time to time, and at some point will need to rest or sleep. They have to share driving responsibilities to ensure safety. To be honest, there is little time for these things, so we fit them around whatever else we have to do.

It's normal for the crew to be tired, hungry and uncomfortable for long periods. If it is cold

> **>>Most roles in the team are not technical in nature so can be filled by anybody(ish), but two or three roles have specific requirements.>>**

outside then they get cold; if it is raining they get wet. Come what may, they have to be standing in the right place at the right time, ready to hand to the rider(s) whatever they need or fix whatever problem has arisen. If the rider(s) are struggling then they may be hanging around in the cold/wet for longer than anticipated. If the rider(s) are going faster than anticipated, they have less time than planned to get everything ready. Then there's the rubbish to deal with … endless amounts of rubbish. I don't know how we create such quantities of stuff to throw away, but a roll of bin liners has to be one of the first things to go on the kit-list. Of course, we also have to find somewhere to dispose of it.

Q. What kind of people do you need?

Most roles on the team are not technical in nature so can be filled by anybody(ish), but two or three roles have specific requirements. The first two critical roles are ones that you hope and pray you don't need, but you have to have them there anyway (depending on the nature of the ride). First is the mechanic/bike technician. This is someone who is almost solely responsible for the performance of the machine, who knows it intimately and who can see problems arising that others (including the rider) might miss and who can fix them quickly. They will anticipate problems and mitigate the risk of these arising. For example, our mechanic on the End-to-End was John Hargreaves who, every time the bike stopped at a pit-stop, ran his hand around the tyres to identify and remove any sharp debris that may have lodged itself in there, thus reducing the risk of punctures. John spotted a broken spoke from 30 yards when eight other people had missed it. He swapped the wheel and while we were travelling along, replaced the spoke and trued the wheel.

The second critical role is the medic. Things can and will go wrong and you can never predict what or when, be it through an unforeseeable accident or through the rider's inevitable physical deterioration. This person has to be in a position to interpret the signs and not just rely on reported symptoms, because the rider's views get progressively less reliable. For example, when supporting a group of riders, one rider was struggling, so another dropped back to give him some assistance, in effect pushing him from almost the bottom to the top of the mountain. At the top, the tired rider who'd been pushed most of the way thought he was fine to carry on riding. We stopped him and insisted he got into the support vehicle. In a matter of minutes he was fast asleep and did not wake up for the next two hours.

You're going to be spending a long time together in cramped and uncomfortable conditions (see above). You're going to get tired, hungry and possibly cold/wet at some point, and yet you're still going to have to get on and do whatever needs doing. You therefore need to be reasonably comfortable in the company of the people in the car with you. Best case, you enjoy their company and are energised by having them around. Worst case, you need to be able to tolerate them for at least as long as the ride. When I asked someone to join the support team at short notice, his first question was 'What do you need from me?' Up to that point I don't think I had thought too deeply about it; we needed a pair of hands at fairly short notice. But as I began explaining the role, I found myself articulating some of the important qualities that go to make up the crew. I told him I needed someone who was resilient. This meant someone

>> There really is only one rule while driving: don't run over the bike! >>

who could last the course and not allow setbacks to distract them. Someone who was resourceful. A person who could just deal with what was thrown at them and get on with it. The person needed to be caring, i.e. they would put the riders first. Someone who was not needy and who didn't mind a bit of discomfort. They also needed to be willing to do whatever they were asked to do, however menial and seemingly boring. Above all, a sense of humour is vital! I stand by these qualities as highly desirable in crew-members. Finally, I think you need people that won't take it personally. In the 'End-to-End' final briefing I again made the point that:

We will get tired, we will be cold and hungry, things will go wrong. We will make some mistakes, we may get frustrated and we may start to take that frustration out on each other ... but accept that for what it is; it's in the heat of the moment when we're at a low ebb, it's not a personal attack, it's simply the frustration bubbling over. So when it's all over, don't hate somebody for something they said or did (or didn't do) on the ride, because they were in a very different place when they did that.

On really long events there is a need to share the driving for safety reasons; it just isn't safe to sit behind the wheel for 24 hours plus, even if you are going relatively slowly. When Katrina Harrison arrived in Edinburgh to take over the driving on the End-to-End she said to me, 'Right, what do I need to know?' I told her that there really is only one rule while driving: don't run over the bike! However, everyone already in the car started to tell her what to do. They were obviously trying to help and offer what advice and experience they had already gained over this and previous attempts, but it came across, in our tired state, as us telling

her how to drive. She can drive perfectly well, and was less tired than us (which was, after all, the whole reason for her being there). But it occurred to me that there are some things you do need to know as the driver, and some things that we do differently when following a bike. Tricks of the trade, if you will.

The rider doesn't want us to be too close, as it may be considered pacing, which isn't allowed, and the support car doesn't want to be too far back because that might allow vehicles to get in between us and the bike (we don't like that in the car if we can avoid it). There is therefore a skill or knack at staying the right distance back to offer sufficient protection to the bike from the traffic coming from behind. When vehicles overtake the support car, we hope they overtake the bike in the same manoeuvre. This isn't necessarily immediately obvious, but is something that you get used to, and we sometimes adjust our position relative to the bike depending on the speed and volume of the traffic coming from behind.

There are a couple of other instances when we take up a slightly different position on the road that you would never see from the bike. The first concerns roundabouts. As we approach a roundabout, we endeavour to be close enough to the bike to get round at the same time (although this is not always possible). What we would generally also do is take up a bit more of the road than normal in order to allow the bike to take the line it wants on the roundabout. We might pull out into the road a little in order to prevent other vehicles from using the space closest to the roundabout while the bike goes around it.

The second occasion would be on a busy road, usually a dual carriageway, where at times traffic

It's fun. In fact it's a huge amount of fun. It's incredibly rewarding and you have the chance to learn really powerful lessons along the way.

filters in from the left, from the slip road that joins the main carriageway. What we typically do here is again get a bit closer to the bike than normal and, as we pass the point on the road where the slip road arrives on the left side, we would veer left and straddle half of the slip road. At this point we slow down slightly in order to prevent any traffic that is joining from the slip road from a) cutting up the bike at high speed from the wrong side and b) getting between us on, what is by definition, a dangerous stretch of road.

These things are possibly not considered best driving practice, but we are not there to win driving awards, just to keep the bike safe and keep it moving! Remember, we do have an orange flashing light on the car as well as signs in the windows, explaining to other road users what's going on. Most other vehicles, when they appreciate what we are doing, are very accommodating.

Q. What else is there to know?

Keep it as simple as possible. We made some mistakes on the first two End-to-End attempts by over-complicating the support requirements. It's a complicated enough challenge already, so don't add complexity where it's not needed. When the ride is over, the support team aren't finished yet. Remember, the job is to keep the rider(s) safe, so depending on the event they may still need some help or support after they get off the bike for the final time and for some time thereafter.

Endurance events are by nature unpredictable, so you can't plan for every eventuality – accept this as a fact. Know before you set off that something (big or small) will go wrong to upset your well thought-out plan and, therefore, don't get frustrated when it happens. Accept the fact that

someone will have to do an unpleasant boring job; you can't keep all of the team happy all of the time. The primary focus is the rider. It's at this point that you will find out if you have the right people in the team. Little things can make a huge difference and there's no substitute for practising it beforehand (such as handing up a musette or timing how long it takes to boil a litre of water on the team's stove). The devil is always in the detail, so pay attention to the very smallest of details. Keep talking; constant communication helps. We all know it's important in high-performing teams, and it's all the more important when people are feeling tired, cold, hungry, and frustrated over a long period.

It's fun. In fact, it's a huge amount of fun. It's incredibly rewarding and you have the chance to learn really powerful lessons along the way. So enjoy it; take the maximum from it, it isn't a chore but it is a different way of enjoying yourself. If you want to capture all of this more succinctly in a 'Six key things the support team need' type approach, here they are:

- Have the right people on the team.
- Provide absolute clarity about what the objectives are.
- Ask a lot of the team.
- Keep it simple.
- Be thorough in your planning and preparation.
- Enjoy the ride!

Nigel Harrison

>> In your feedback to your coach, you need to be honest. There is no point in claiming a session was easier, or harder than it actually felt. >>

HONEST COMMUNICATION

In your feedback to your coach, you need to be honest. There is no point claiming a session was easier, or harder, than it actually felt. The feedback to your coach is not comment for public consumption but an honest, open set of insights into how you felt during the session, and what had happened before the session that may explain the result. For example, if you were up late the night before with a work issue, or had a late night with friends, it may help explain why the data from your session was lower than that which otherwise might have been expected. You are a human being, not a machine!

Feedback for each session should be supplied as close to finishing the session as possible in order to provide an accurate statement as to how it felt. Even a few hours later things can seem either more or less difficult than they felt at the time. You need to record how it felt 'in the heat of the moment'. It does not need to be an essay. It should contain as much information as required to accurately portray the session. As a rule of thumb, it's better to provide more than less.

Important as well is the quality of your relationship with your coach. If you would like more (or less) information, or need to change the frequency with which you speak or meet, you should have the conversation. The more aligned the coach and athlete, the better the quality of the relationship, which in turn results in much higher levels of satisfaction for everyone.

EVIDENCE

Subjective comments support the numbers. As explained in Chapter 5: Fitness, power meters (and, to a lesser extent, heart rate monitors) provide valuable data on what you actually did as opposed to how it felt or what you thought you did. By saving a record of the data from each session it can be accumulated in one place to provide evidence of your fitness and freshness.

Useful information can include:
- The details of the session.
- How hard it was to do (where -5 = extremely hard, +5 is really easy and 0 is commensurate with what you would expect).
- What the quality of the session was like (where -5 = unable to hit the numbers at any stage, +5 = exceeded all the numbers and 0 is exactly what was required).
- What was your mental state (where -5 = very pre-occupied and distracted, lots going on, +5 = in holiday mode, completely relaxed and almost switched off and 0 is in the zone and fully focused).
- How much sleep you had the night before and the quality of that sleep.
- How much stress you are under at work or at home.
- Weight and percentage body fat.
- Notes on what happened in the session, how you were feeling and any relevant information to help explain the evidence.

It is also useful to include your availability for training for the following week in order that your coach can design a plan that fits in with whatever else you have going on.

There is something immensely rewarding about looking at the accumulated evidence of lots of training sessions. Over the months and

>> There is no point in being coached if you do not do the work set. >>

years, the improvement becomes much more apparent than it does over a few days or weeks. It is very reassuring to see that what you are doing is working.

Evidence can be recorded using online tools or by a simple spreadsheet or table in a word processing programme. The key thing is to get into the habit of recording the information and sharing it with your coach (see Chapter 6: Approach, for more information about habits).

EXECUTION

There is no point in being coached if you do not do the work set. There will be times when fatigue catches up, or other activities, such as work or family duties, get in the way. If your plan is crafted properly, these should be exceptions rather than the rule. You might have lots of potential, but all that means is 'you haven't done it yet'. If you find yourself unable to do multiple sessions, it is time to reflect on why this is. Is it because you are not really committed to your goal? If it is, change your goal. Is it that you are being optimistic in the time you actually have available to train, when compared to the time you would like to train? Be realistic about what time you really have. Is it that the sessions are simply too hard? If it is, give the feedback to your coach so they can be adjusted to levels that are more appropriate.

It is salutary to know, through conversations with a number of coaches, that most athletes do not manage to complete the sessions set and most provide only limited feedback. As one coach said, 'Those that fail to engage are wasting their money and, if I could afford to, I would stop working with them as they are wasting my time.' It is a reminder of 'Your strategy is what you do.'

If you are going to invest in a coach, then get value from the relationship – both you and the coach will enjoy it much more.

IF IT WORKS WITH YOUR COACH ...

If it works with your coach, it will work with other members of the team too. A similar process can be used when working with a nutritionist. Instead of logging hours on the bike, it is about logging the food you eat. This helps you manage weight loss and, over time, you will learn about what you need and when in order to stay in form.

WORKING WITH YOUR PHYSIOTHERAPIST

At some point, you will get damaged; whether you have pulled a muscle, crashed or someone has crashed into you. It happens. When it does, it is helpful to have someone to help you mend more quickly. Physiotherapy is one such profession. It is a protected profession, which means it's regulated by law, and a physiotherapist may only call themselves such if they have completed state-approved training. Physiotherapists treat musculoskeletal, cardiovascular, respiratory and neuromuscular issues. They don't just fix things when they have gone wrong; they can also help you prevent them going wrong in the first place.

Unsurprisingly, most physiotherapists do not encounter many ultra-distance cyclists and the sort of training you do. While the body is the same whether you are a couch potato or a finely honed athlete, the perception of what you can and need to be able to do will be very different. It is important then that you invest time and effort in building the relationship with your physio

>> A physiotherapist is experienced in patterns of signs and symptoms, and relating these to cause and mechanism of injury. >>

GETTING THE BEST FROM YOUR PHYSIOTHERAPIST

First of all, get a recommendation for a therapist from a cycling friend or two; unless you really have to, don't just pick up someone who has a great website or is at a convenient address. In my experience, your friends are likely to recommend you to someone you will get on with. This really helps when you are standing in just your cycling shorts and the therapist is prodding painful parts.

Find out how long the first and subsequent visits last and how much they cost if you are paying for a private consultation. Be wary of paying upfront for 10 sessions because it is a good deal – you may need only one. It's also helpful to find out if the therapist's working hours suit your availability or whether, having seen you once, they have no slots free for the next three months!

Before your visit, spend some time thinking about what pain you are experiencing. Be prepared to describe:

• What happened?
• What makes it worse?
• What seems to make it better?
• Has it happened before?
• What medication are you taking?
• What does the problem prevent you from doing?
• Who else have you seen about the problem (Doctor? Chiropractor? Osteopath?)
• Be honest and open (even when you think it might be embarrassing).

Cycling injuries tend to be either related to a single incident – the source of the problem is easier to identify in this instance – or, more commonly, a slow insidious decline from discomfort to an inability to climb into the saddle.

In the event of an acute injury, take photos of bruises, broken kit and so on, as it helps to understand force, direction and potential cause for injury. If you are experiencing pain in a certain position when riding your bike, either get someone to take a photo of you from a variety of angles in that position or be prepared to take your bike in and a turbo trainer to demonstrate the problem.

A physiotherapist is experienced in patterns of signs and symptoms, and relating these to cause and mechanism of injury; but it is your body and you are experiencing the problem. They piece together the information and propose a hypothesis of the reason for your body malfunction. Searching the web for explanations for your own symptoms can be helpful but also sometimes a misleading distraction. Discuss what you have learned with your physio. It is helpful to be guided by what you can find on the internet, but it is more important to convey what you are really feeling, rather than apply any diagnostic interpretation in the first instance.

Often the wording that you use to describe a problem guides the therapist to the type of issue involved. The first consultation should be a dialogue with the therapist; be open with them and don't be afraid to say so if you think they have not adequately deduced the problem. If you are not convinced, ask how they came to decide on their working diagnosis. Sometimes it would be wonderful to have X-ray/MRI eyes and see what is going on inside, but often even these investigations are inconclusive and unhelpful; the therapist only has the evidence that you supply them with to make a diagnosis. Your treatment sessions will evolve. Occasionally the diagnosis will change on the basis of non-response to treatment, or progress and change because of improvement.

On the basis of the above, you will be asked many more questions. Some may seem a little unusual or

»Once you've been treated, do the work prescribed. If you're asked to do exercises twice a day, do them and keep a record.»

even irrelevant, but they will have a purpose, so answer them as truthfully as possible. When trying to find the root cause of an overuse injury it is often the smallest detail, or an old injury, which explains the problem.

Your physio needs to know what your training patterns are: how often, how far and how hard? Short-, mid- and long-term training goals? Is there an important event imminent or on the horizon? This helps the therapist to understand whether a patch-up job is required or whether modifications to technique are in order, which take longer to implement and may affect performance in the short term. Involving your coach, if you have one, at an early stage can be useful, especially if changes to training sessions need to be negotiated.

Understanding the motivation of an athlete, and what it means to them to have their wheels taken away, is a consideration. I try to make sure that training time (which is often 'me-time') can be replaced with a suitable alternative. I'm also aware that I'm asking someone to go 'cold turkey' from the endorphin high that exercise provides if I remove all training. This is important in long-term injury as the patient's mood reduces and the psychological effects of injury can be as shocking to the cyclist as the physical ones. If you are concerned about what you think the injury might be, explain these concerns. Your physiotherapist cannot allay your worst fears unless you explain what they are. There is no such thing as a silly question; ask whatever you need to understand fully what's happening and why.

If, on first meeting, the physiotherapist spends a cursory five or 10 minutes examining you and then hooks you up to a machine, you're in the wrong place. The best physios take time to examine you properly. In addition to understanding your injury, they will examine above and below and around the injury to see what else may be causing your issues, as well as getting a sense of your range of movement and flexibility. The best physios will also get a sense of your personality and how best to guide you to recovery.

Wear the right clothing. If you have a lower leg injury, wearing a pair of short shorts will help the physio see what they need to see. If they can't see properly, you will have to remove sufficient clothing until they can; so be helpful, wear the right things.

Once you've been treated, do the work prescribed. If you're asked to do exercises twice a day, do them and keep a record. Let's suppose that you haven't done the exercises. Is that because you weren't sure of what you were doing? Or because it hurt too much? Or because you lacked the necessary commitment? Whatever the reason, on your next appointment explain what you have actually done. Don't make it up, it's only yourself you're deceiving. You won't be the first person not to have done what you should, nor will you be the last, but denying it won't help you or the physio plan the next stage of the treatment.

Expect to have noticed some improvement after three sessions. If there isn't any, you need to discuss why this might be before reviewing the treatment or exercises. If no treatment change is suggested, find another physio, unless they have a jolly good explanation!

Lastly, don't expect miracles! The tissues take time to heal – weeks or sometimes months. The aim of treatment is to provide the best circumstances in which the body can mend itself. As I said before, this doesn't always mean a halt to all training; it means changes so that you can try to keep up your stamina and fitness while avoiding damage.

Dr Claire Ryall

❯❯Do not view what the physio does in isolation from the coach.❯❯

such that they can learn about what you do and your expectations of yourself, and you can build confidence in the solutions they propose. When you get this relationship right, the experience is superb. Do not view what the physio does in isolation from the coach. Ideally, introduce them to each other such that when you do become injured they can establish the right training programme to speed your recovery and minimise the impact on your training. When you are likely to be feeling low because of injury and an inability to train properly, knowing there are two people thinking hard about how they can best help you can really lift your spirits.

Working closely with your coach and physio really works, as Dominic had to discover following a quite severe and most unfortunate injury while training. The account of this experience follows.

UNDERSTANDING, TEAMWORK AND CONTEXT

Just 500 metres from the end of his ride, and chasing a great time for the route, Dominic was flying down the hill out of town. It was early evening and the warm late-spring sun was low in the sky. The motorist turning right did not see Dominic. Seconds before impact, in one of those rare moments of clarity, Dominic was able to adjust the angle of the bike to convert the head-on collision into a savage blow from the side. Lying on the side of the road in agony, tears of pain and frustration welled up. In just a month's time he was due to make a second attempt on the UK End-to-End record. His hopes, dreams and months of effort were dashed in the space of just a few seconds. The pain was intense. The impact of the collision had been sufficient to snap the bike frame. It seemed nothing was broken, but Dominic was unable to walk properly. A text exchange followed with Dr Claire Ryall, Dominic's physio, and within a couple of days he was undergoing assessment. Daily physiotherapy followed. In a demonstration of the teamwork discussed earlier,

Simon and Claire worked together to determine what training Dominic could do to retain fitness in order to keep his record attempt on track. Claire worked out how Dominic could carefully get himself into position on a turbo in order to complete the training sessions Simon planned. The recovery plan was appropriately extreme. It was demanding, uncomfortable and effective. Without the imminent challenge – an enormous physical one – a different plan of recovery would have been more appropriate. Knowing the size of the challenge, and the immense amount of hard work that had gone into getting everything prepared, as well as the very high levels of motivation to succeed, the recovery plan was very demanding and, as it turned out, incredibly effective. Without Claire's good knowledge of the athlete and willingness to work with other team members, Dominic would never have made it to the start line. Getting a support team organised, sponsorship in place and official observers lined up is challenging enough without having to rearrange it all at short notice!

>> Great teams don't just happen. They require an investment of effort no different to any other aspect of performance. >>

SUMMARY

For a sport that seems so solitary, the level of teamwork required is significant, more so if your events or races involve a support team. Great teams don't just happen. They require an investment of effort no different to any other aspect of performance. The only difference to many other situations is the requirement for people to operate in adverse conditions, freely and willingly, with no return other than the satisfaction of having helped you achieve your goal. With so many other competing pressures on your time, it is important to learn how to delegate responsibility to others. Let your coach devise the right plan and learn to trust and follow it. Recruit a good support team leader, and as your confidence grows in their ability, delegate more and more to them. Above all, keep people informed to help them feel part of the process. Being part of a successful ultra-distance team is one of the most rewarding and satisfying experiences to be had. Through the collective power of the team, ordinary people can do truly extraordinary things.

CHAPTER 9:
PUTTING IT ALL TOGETHER

Ultra-distance cycling is intensely rewarding, physically and mentally. Success is achieved through a series of carefully calculated moves that enable you to achieve your cycling ambitions.

IT'S HOLISTIC

This book has thus far focused on the inputs required to deliver a longer, faster ride. Sitting at home, the lessons may make a lot of sense. When riding, it's not always quite so clear. It requires you to examine what's happening; to be able to interpret the signs and symptoms before working out what to do in order to keep going. This is something of an art form, learnt through practice.

Let's imagine a typical ultra-distance cycling racing experience. You are riding along and starting to feel nauseous. The prospect of eating fills you with a sense of dread. You know you have to, but every time you put food into your mouth, you chew it and then spit it out. You simply cannot swallow it. You've been riding for the best part of a day and you're tired and cold. The wind is hammering into your face. The prospect of riding the same distance again has little appeal. You ache. You think you are on the right road, but a few errors riding through the last town have left you feeling like you are hours behind where you should be. In circumstances such as these, notions of $\dot{V}O_2$max, power output and race strategies seem irrelevant. In fact, you are beginning to wonder who you were kidding in trying to focus on those issues. Your world has shrunk to feeling sick and hurting. You feel a bit of a fraud. This is what it can feel like midway through an ultra-distance race. What then to do?

The first thing to understand is that this type of situation is common. There are plenty of variables at play, such as fitness, amount of sleep, weather, equipment, psychological state, personality and nutrition, to name just a few. The complex interplay between these variables means each cannot be treated in isolation. It requires a holistic approach. Perhaps the first thing to do is stop and take stock. It's very hard to come to harm when stopped. But don't just stop anywhere. Find somewhere suitable – a bus shelter or the porch of a building. Anywhere that gets you out of the wind. The next thing is to put on some layers. Having been working hard, the chances are you will be damp with sweat and will cool quickly. Your pre-ride choice of equipment will dictate what you can wear; whatever it is, put it on.

Next, it's time to address the nutrition issue. It may be that you are salt-depleted, in which case, pour a sachet of Dioralyte or spoon some electrolyte into the bottom of a water bottle with a couple hundred millilitres of water, swirl it around and drink it down. It will take a while, perhaps an hour or longer before the electrolytes start to have an effect – but the process of repair has started. While you may be unable to eat much solid food, pop a boiled sweet into your mouth and allow it to dissolve slowly. A sweet is not a huge source of energy, but it's better than nothing and it means you don't need to swallow anything – which, as you have discovered, you can't do at the moment. So far, you've managed the cold and the energy problems.

>> The ability to re-frame your circumstances is one of the greatest assets in ultra-distance cycling. >>

Having stopped for a few minutes, already you will begin to feel better, just by virtue of reducing the demands on your body. It's time to get your head around what's happening. Perhaps a short phone call home might help? A short conversation with a loved one may be just what you need. At this stage, thinking about the whole of the remainder of the ride may be too intimidating. Instead, set yourself some far smaller intermediary goals. This might be as little as riding to the next town or the top of the next hill. At first, you may abandon the idea of riding at your target power output and just concentrate instead on getting to the top of the hill. Later, you may set yourself a reduced target for an hour or two, 'cutting yourself some slack' in the process. The purpose of breaking the ride down to these tiny steps is to begin to experience success. Achieving the goal of making it to the top of the hill can lift your spirits, enabling you to tackle the next small goal. The combination of small wins, a call home, a bit of energy back into the system, feeling a little warmer, a few moments' rest and the restoration of your electrolyte balance will all contribute to getting back into the race.

As things begin to improve, you can introduce a little bit of solid food and see how that goes. If you are still unable to eat, keep sucking on the sweets until your stomach has settled. It will also help if you can draw upon your experience of difficult training rides; compare those rides to the current situation and remember that you've done it before! For example, battling the winter snow, bitterly cold, in the middle of the night and managing to make it through to dawn may enable you to re-frame your current circumstance as a minor setback, rather than a major concern. You could try putting on your favourite playlist on your music player to boost your spirits (assuming race rules allow this). In this way, by working through a series of practical steps, you will have managed all of the dimensions of performance discussed in this book.

What was a downward spiral of hunger, fatigue, mental stress and cold has been turned into an upward trend of warmth, energy, recovery and positive reinforcement. Things will keep improving as you get the basics right. This will allow you the mental space to remember those other things you have to do, like taking some photographs for the articles you will need to write in order to deliver on your sponsorship commitments.

The ability to re-frame your circumstances is one of the greatest assets in ultra-distance cycling. For example, when faced with strong headwinds, heavy rain or steep hills, it's useful to reflect back on the hours spent learning how to ride at a constant power. 'There is only 230 watts.' It doesn't matter what the weather or terrain has in store for you, control what you can control – your power output. It may be that this translates into a very slow forward speed, but as long as you are riding at your optimum power, that's all that matters. Thinking this way is liberating. While others may be worrying about speed, you are not. And this will translate into mental strength.

SPOT IT

The challenge is spotting that things may be going out of control as they happen. Many of the issues you will experience will creep up imperceptibly. You are unlikely to suddenly feel sick or tired or cold. The challenge is to spot the signs early enough to do something about it. This prevents the lows from being as deep and dark as they otherwise might be. If you have a support team, they can help with this, but you are in a far better position than others to spot what's happening. These low points will happen and it's useful to analyse – when you have worked through them – what led to the low in the first place, allowing you to make a habit of doing the thing that helps prevent the low.

For example, if you start to think about food, it's generally a sign that you need to start eating, although it's good sense to check this with what you have actually been eating. Similarly, starting to feel cold in your extremities is a good indication it might be time for another layer. Finding yourself blinking a lot and struggling to keep your eyes open is a clear indication that, either you have something in your eye, or you are tired and should find somewhere for a quick nap – fast. If you can identify half a dozen things to pay attention to and have in place a well-practised plan for when a symptom emerges, you will reduce your risk and increase your chances of success. Finding the right signs arises from paying attention to what happens when you ride your bike. All of this means developing the skills of being able to almost stand outside of yourself and observe what's happening.

Successfully riding a long way, fast, is mostly achieved long before getting to the start line of an event or race. Time is precious and perishable. Not everyone who rides ultra-distance is a professional rider – in fact, most aren't. Few have all day to train. Events have to be squeezed in around family holidays and work commitments. The key thing is to actively choose what to do and when. By making the decision a conscious choice, you can own it and manage it. The key thing to understand is that you cannot excuse your way to success. Ultra-distance cycling requires a lot of preparation. Things will, however, go wrong.

FAIL YOUR WAY TO SUCCESS

Ultra-distance cycling is a complex business. You need to get a lot of things right in order to be successful, and a significant number of things – such as the weather – are outside your control. To believe that you will get everything right, every time, is a triumph of hope over experience. Things are going to go wrong and sometimes these will be significant enough to bring your participation in a race or event to an end. Don't despair. Some of the best lessons come from having got things wrong. For example, having a fixable mechanical issue with your bike preventing you riding further, and then having to get a lift home for the want of carrying a particular tool is very frustrating; all the more so if you are just a few hours into a very long ride. The inconvenience caused to the person collecting you, your training and the discomfort of hanging around waiting for a lift should mean you never forget to take the right tools with you again. As you get more experienced, you will continue to fail, but the context changes. It may be that you 'failed' to hold an aerodynamic position for as long as you wanted, or you 'failed' to get your nutrition strategy right. Analysing and reflecting on these failures enables you to find opportunities for improvement.

In contrast, having successfully completed something, it's easy to ignore some of the things that could have made it better. There are many people who claim their success was a function of hard work, while quietly ignoring the elements of luck that contributed to their success, and the many mistakes they made along the way. Failure helps you make the tougher decisions you should have made in the first instance. Failing in training also allows you to test ideas and techniques to find out which work best. It's hard to find your limits unless you fail to achieve your training goals from time to time. But failure can be a lonely place. To paraphrase Count Galeazzo Ciano, success has many parents; failure is an orphan. While you might have failed to complete a specific race, take heart from the fact that just getting to the start line will have involved achieving a level of performance

few ever achieve. Your involvement in the sport should be because you want to do it; what others think doesn't really matter.

Finally, let's look at how all these things come together in preparing for, participating in, and just after an ultra-event.

AN ULTRA-DISTANCE EVENT: JUST BEFORE, DURING AND JUST AFTER

Having entered a race, you will spend months training. There comes a point prior to the race when you need to start thinking specifically about what's involved and what you plan to do. The following description of the preparation required for an ultra-distance cycling event makes the assumption that you will already have a very good idea of what's involved, that you will have read as many blogs, articles and descriptions as you can find, and that you will have used this information to develop a training plan designed to help you achieve your best in the race. A few weeks out is the time to start getting very detailed in your preparation.

THREE WEEKS OUT

By now you will have configured your bike exactly as it needs to be for the race. Ensuring the bike is serviced and mechanically sound will help remove a source of worry. This will involve new tyres and tubes, the selection of appropriate gearing combinations, and the replacement or servicing of all significantly worn parts. The rides over the next few weeks will ensure that all this maintenance work has been completed properly, while at the same time scrubbing the surface of new tyres, bedding in new brake blocks and allowing cables (if your bike has them) to stretch.

At this point you will be creating your final race checklist of everything you need to take with you. While you are unable to know the precise weather you will face, trend data from previous years will indicate the likely conditions and help inform your kit choice. Creating this list now will help you identify any items of kit you don't have or that need replacing. If you are racing supported, this checklist will include items for the support team and for the support vehicle.

You may well have spent considerable time examining the route, but if you haven't done so, upload the route to a suitable app or programme and examine some of the more technical sections to see what's in store. Google Street View is a great way of sampling sections of the route to see the type and quality of road surface. If necessary, add markers to the route of towns where you or your support team could potentially secure supplies. Check out the rules of the road. The right of way at junctions can vary from one country to another, as can the meanings of different signals. In the UK and the US, flashing your lights means 'after you'; in France it means 'I'm coming through'; and in Italy it signals 'don't do it'. Attitudes to traffic lights and pedestrian crossings also vary significantly from country to country. Be aware of cultural differences. They are not wrong – just different. Find out the number for emergency services in the event you are involved in an accident. Make sure you have the phone numbers of all your team/supporters stored on your phone.

Consider creating a crib sheet. This might include the route profile, the location of aid stations, towns where more supplies can be bought and/or any dangerous sections. Make sure it is pocket-sized and laminated for easy use during the race.

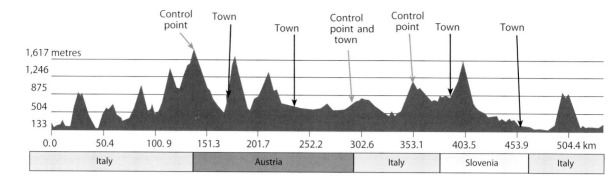

Control point   Town   Town   Control point and town   Control point   Town   Town

1,617 metres
1,246
875
504
133

0.0   50.4   100.9   151.3   201.7   252.2   302.6   353.1   403.5   453.9   504.4 km

| Italy | Austria | Italy | Slovenia | Italy |

Figure 14: An example of a crib sheet

Write out your race strategy in detail. The race strategy starts from the night before the race and includes the preparation steps you will take prior to departure. This will include the pace you intend to ride, the plan for food stops, the support team strategy (if relevant) and what you will do when things that could go wrong, do, such as a puncture, a gashed tyre, a chain snapping or getting lost. The more you can think of (and have a plan in place to deal with it), the more confident and comfortable you will feel. As a German Army Officer once said, 'No plan stands contact with the enemy.' Having written a detailed race strategy, hone it down to the essence of what you intend to do. For example:

- Keep any stop to the shortest time possible.
- Ride on the drops for anything less than a 2 per cent slope.
- Maintain 240 watts.
- Carry as little as possible and make sure it is as light as possible.
- Ride safely – it's not worth dying for.

These race principles are easy to remember when tired and will help you deliver the performance you seek. During the final few training rides, visualise riding in the race and operating to these principles.

Training in this period is classic tapering territory but, as with so many things, the taper required by one rider will be very different to that required by another. The aim of your taper should be to arrive at the start line with the best balance of fitness and freshness. Because the bulk of your training is towards the lower end of

the intensity spectrum – requiring less recovery time – a three-week taper is probably longer than necessary. Such a taper would allow you to start the race very fresh, but it could cause you to miss out on some fitness gains. Reducing training load 7–11 days before the race works well for most ultra-distance cyclists. If you track your training data using a product such as TrainingPeaks™, during the taper period you should see your Chronic Training Load (CTL) dropping a little as your Training Stress Balance (TSB) rises: you will be maximising your performance potential by trading a small amount of fitness for added freshness.

ONE WEEK OUT

Time to get all the kit together. You will probably still need to use some of it for training, but get as much as you can in one place. Inevitably, packing takes longer than you think – especially when flying with a bike. Check the weather forecast, which will help you refine the final choice of kit you take for the weather you will experience. For example, a prolonged period of wet weather will necessitate different clothing to a heatwave. The closer you get to the date of your event, the more reliable the forecast will become.

When packing your kit, remember you will have to pack it again after the race when you will probably be very tired and the quality of your thinking impaired. A small bag packed very tightly may not be easy to replicate when tired; better to use a slightly larger bag with a bit more space in it. Don't overfill your bike box. If you struggle to lift it, so too will the baggage handlers.

»Once all your kit is checked and prepared, relax. Get the weight of your feet.»

Assume the airlines will manhandle your bike, placing heavy luggage on top and probably dropping the bike bag/box at some point. If you pack it to withstand this abuse, it should survive the journey. There are very few cyclists who do not have a story of something getting damaged at some point while flying. Mark your bag really clearly. In the event it doesn't make it out on the same flight as you, this will help baggage handlers identify the bag as yours.

Take out appropriate insurance cover too. Some bicycle-specific plans will offer cover such that in the event that the bike is lost they will provide a replacement locally for you to use for the duration of your event. Note, some travel insurance policies specifically exclude cycle racing, so check you are covered before you depart. While you may be tempted to carry all sorts of extra last minute stuff, go back and visit your race strategy to check whether you are just having an irrational panic or have genuinely spotted an error in your planning.

Identify the bike shops (and their opening hours) nearest to where you are staying, in case you need any last-minute spares. Identify where the nearest supermarket is located for supplies.

TRAVELLING

If you're travelling on your own, you will likely have a bike box, kit bag and, possibly, a day bag. It's a lot of stuff. Give yourself plenty of time to get through the airport. Your bike will probably need to be checked into a separate oversized luggage check-in desk, which will mean a lot of walking around and modest levels of stress. Take your time. Make life easy on yourself by having a specific place in your bag for your travel documents. When you need them, get them out

and, when finished, make sure they go back into the right place.

At the destination airport, your bike may well come through a different place to your luggage. This is not always the case, so be prepared to check both the luggage belt dedicated to your flight and the oversized luggage belt. Do not be surprised if your bike doesn't make it on the same flight.

ON ARRIVAL

Get your bike built up first to check that it has survived the journey without damage. Be cautious when taking your first ride, especially if the country you are riding in drives on the opposite side of the road. Get yourself oriented, find out where the race HQ is and how long it will take to get from where you are staying to the start on the morning of the race.

Once all your kit is checked and prepared, relax. Get the weight off your feet. You are going to be racing for a long time, so make sure you are as rested as possible. Have no shame in asking friends, family and members of your support team to do things for you. Your job is to race; theirs is to support. This can feel wrong and impolite, but you've spent hundreds of hours training for this moment. Everybody understands this. You are not doing justice to them or to yourself in getting unnecessarily tired.

>>Ultra-distance requires you to be driven, motivated, resilient and committed.>>

RACE DAY

Eat a sensible breakfast two to three hours before the start. Don't be tempted to overload your system with food; you will feel bloated and struggle to perform. You may also find yourself needing to go to the toilet as a result of so much food passing through your system. Apply the relevant lotions (sunscreen, chamois cream and anti-friction products). Get into your kit. Go through your checklist to make sure you have done everything you should. Once ready, find a quiet spot and go through your race strategy one final time, then head down to the start. Don't get sucked into all the noise and hype. It's easy to find your stress levels rising unnecessarily when surrounded by other athletes. The chances are you will look at them all and think they look better, fitter, stronger than you – just as they will be looking at you the same way. Be prepared to disappear and find some quiet space to get your mental approach sorted.

THE START

If your training has gone well, you will find it very easy to rush off. Remember the race plan. If the goals is to ride at 240 watts then, however slow this feels, stick to the plan: it was created for a purpose and the first 10km of the race is no place to suddenly revise it. You may well find yourself overtaken by lots of people at first. It's not that they are faster; it's simply that they either have a poor plan or have abandoned it. You will pass them later in the race – it may take an hour, or 24 hours, but you will pass them. During the race, focus on the goals and stick to the plan. When something happens (and it almost certainly will) follow your plan and resolve the issue. In such circumstances it is easy to lose sight of the time taken and the likely impact on the race. This can leave you feeling low and frustrated. It's at times like these that you need to remind yourself of the goals and keep the focus. You cannot change what has happened, you can only manage what you choose to do going forward. So don't waste energy thinking 'What if?'; instead think 'What now?'. Remember to enjoy it! There's not much point in racing if it becomes a form of punishment.

THE FINISH

Celebrate! Whatever you managed to achieve, it was more than not starting, so enjoy what you did. As soon as possible after the race, eat some food to begin to replenish lost energy. Drink plenty. Be very careful in everything you do as you will be very tired and will have mentally switched off; it is really easy to have an accident at this point.

THE AFTERMATH

You may well find that your ability to regulate your temperature is affected for a short while. When you go to bed after the race, be prepared to add or remove layers depending on how you feel. You may experience some numbness in your hands or feet. This should pass after a few weeks: if it does not, seek medical advice.

Very soon after the race, ideally within the first 24 hours, write yourself a race report noting what worked, what didn't, and any thoughts on what changes might be required for next time. Make a note of any unusual things you saw or did, as these will be useful in any race reports or articles. Find out if anyone took photographs of you and get copies for use in publications.

≫Celebrate! Whatever you managed to achieve, it was more than not starting.≫

CHESS

The inescapable conclusion to all of this is that it is like a game of chess. The decisions you make today in your training and preparation will have an impact many weeks or even months later. The chances are that whatever you plan to do will have to change in the light of unanticipated events. Managing this complexity is what makes ultra-distance cycling such a hugely enjoyable and rewarding sport. Whether it's juggling family, work and training time, or the riding position on your bike, or the kit you carry with you; if there is one word that sums up the challenges of ultra-distance cycling better than any other, it's compromise. You must continually make judgements as to what is the right thing to do. While there is a large team behind every ultra-distance cyclist, it's you who has to ride the bike. Ultra-distance requires you to be driven, motivated, resilient and committed. You need to have faith, fitness and tolerance. Ideally, you need to have all these things at once.

THE REWARD

We are reminded, time and time again, of the joy of ultra-distance cycling. Being able to ride long distances means you get to see so many places and things while out riding. The routes of many races take in the very best an area has to offer. While 'normal' riders will be hanging up their shoes after a 100km ride, you'll just be warmed up and looking forward to the rest of the day. The ability to ride a long way means that getting lost for a few kilometres and having to add an extra 20–30km to your ride really doesn't matter – it's well within your abilities. It can lead to some crazy but fun notions – such as riding from London to Paris for lunch. For most, this would be a two- to three-day trip, but for you, as an ultra-distance cyclist with an early start, this is entirely possible. As you sit beneath the Eiffel Tower eating your baguette, enjoy the deep sense of satisfaction of being able to ride a long way, fast.

It is our hope that, through sharing our knowledge and experience, you are able to take a step further on your ultra-distance journey. See you on the road.

GLOSSARY

Aerobic: Conditions or processes occurring in the presence of, or requiring, oxygen.

Amino acids: The basic building blocks of proteins.

Anaerobic: Conditions or processes that do not require oxygen, which take place in the absence of oxygen.

Antioxidants: Molecules capable of inhibiting the oxidation of other molecules. Oxidation is a chemical reaction that transfers electrons from a substance to an oxidising agent, which produces free radicals. These free radicals are capable of causing cell damage, or even cell death.

Audax: Non-competitive long-distance rides completed within a pre-defined time limit. Also known as *Brevet* or *Randonnée*.

Body composition: The ratio of body fat, bone and muscle tissue.

Cadence: The rate of crank revolution (revolutions per minute or rpm) at which the cyclist pedals.

Caffeine: An alkaloid that is found in tea and coffee and is a stimulant of the central nervous system.

Critical Power: The slope of the work–time relationship, representing a power output that can be sustained for a very long time without fatigue.

Detraining: The effects seen when a cyclist stops training, including a loss of training-induced adaptations.

Drag: The resistance of air to the forward movement of the cyclist and their bike.

Economy: The energy required to sustain a given power output or velocity.

Efficiency: The relationship between the amount of work done and the energy expended in doing the work. It is usually expressed as a percentage of work done to energy expended: efficiency = (work done/energy expended) x 100 per cent.

Ergogenic aid: Any factor that enhances physical or mental performance.

Fatigue: Exhaustion of muscle resulting from prolonged exhaustion or overstimulation.

Frequency: The regularity of training, e.g. how many times a rider trains per week.

Heart rate variability: A measure of the variation in time interval between heartbeats.

Intensity: The quantitative indication of total training work rate or training effort.

Lactate: A dissociation product of lactic acid that occurs in the blood. Resting levels are usually 1–2mmol·L-1, rising with increasing exercise intensity, especially when there is a high reliance on anaerobic metabolism.

Lactate threshold: The exercise intensity at which the release of lactate into the blood first begins to exceed its rate of removal, such that blood lactate levels begin to rise.

Lactic acid: A product of anaerobic glycolysis. Most lactic acid quickly dissociates into hydrogen ions and lactate.

Macrocycle: A term often used to describe an entire training programme. The term macrocycle is used to describe a training cycle that typically lasts for a year.

Macronutrient: An essential nutrient required in relatively large amounts, such as carbohydrates, fats, proteins or water.

Maximal Aerobic Power (MAP): The highest power held for 30 or 60 seconds in an incremental exercise test to exhaustion.

Maximal lactate steady state: The highest exercise intensity at which blood lactate levels remain essentially constant over time.

Mesocycle: A period of training generally two to six weeks' long.

Metabolic rate: The energy expended by a person, usually expressed in units of energy per unit body mass, per unit time.

Metabolism: The sum total of all chemical reactions that occur in the body that are necessary to sustain life.

Microcycle: A short period of training, e.g. one week.

Mitochondria: A structure within the cell responsible for most aerobic energy metabolism. Mitchondria are often referred to as the 'powerhouses' of the cell because they are the sites where the majority of the body's useable energy is generated.

Normalized Power®: An estimate of the power output that you could have maintained for the same 'physiological cost' if your power output had been constant (e.g. cycling on a turbo trainer) instead of variable.

Overtraining: Training at levels that are beyond the physical tolerance of the body, with the result that extreme mental and physical fatigue are incurred. Even with two weeks' recovery, the body fails to adapt and return to expected performance levels.

Peak power output: The highest one-second power output achieved during a sprint test. This often occurs within the first five seconds of a sprint test and is an indication of the maximal rate of anaerobic energy metabolism.

Peaking: The process of achieving an optimal performance on a specific occasion.

Periodisation: A planned training programme in which the year is divided into periods or cycles, often of different durations. Each period has a different purpose or focus; e.g. a preparation period, a conditioning period, a competition period and a transition period.

Polarised training: The practice of conducting low-intensity training and very high-intensity sessions within a week, often in an 80:20 ratio.

Power output: The rate of doing work, where work is equal to force times distance. Power describes the rate at which energy is used and is measured in watts. A watt (W) is equivalent to one joule per second.

Rating of perceived exertion (RPE): An individual's subjective evaluation of how intense or strenuous a particular exercise intensity feels. Typically, this is rated on the 20-point scale developed by Gunnar Borg.

Recovery: The physiological process that takes place following a bout of exercise. Within this period the body replenishes muscle glycogen and phosphate stores, replaces and repairs muscle protein, and removes lactic acid and other metabolic by-products.

Repetition maximum (RM): The maximum load that a muscle or muscle group can overcome for a given number of repetitions (e.g. 1RM or 10RM) before fatigue prevents further muscle action.

Specificity: The training principle that states that training should stress the muscles and energy systems that are related to the required performance.

Taper: A period of reduced training volume prior to an important competition. Often training intensity and frequency are maintained during this period.

Training zone: A training intensity based on an individual rider's exercise capacity. These are often prescribed in terms of a range of power outputs or heart rates.

Transition period: A mesocycle of a training programme, which allows a rider to recover both physically and mentally following training or competition. This period is often characterised by a much lower volume, intensity and structure of training.

Ventilatory threshold: During incremental exercise, this is the point at which the rate of ventilation increases in a non-linear fashion. This is specifically in relation to oxygen uptake and occurs at a similar point to the lactate threshold.

$\dot{V}O_2max$: Also known as maximal oxygen uptake, $\dot{V}O_2max$ is the maximal rate of whole-body oxygen uptake that can be achieved during exercise and is calculated over a one-minute period. $\dot{V}O_2max$ sets the upper ceiling of a rider's cardiovascular fitness and aerobic power production. It is often expressed as a value in either litres per minute (L·min-1) or relative to body mass in millilitres per kilogram per minute (ml·kg-1·min-1).

Volume of training: A quantitative measure of the amount of training undertaken by a rider. Volume is the product of training frequency and duration, often measured in hours and minutes, or kilometres of training.

AUTHOR BIOGRAPHIES

Simon Jobson is Professor of Sport and Exercise Physiology in the Department of Sport and Exercise at the University of Winchester. Building on a PhD awarded in the area of cycling performance physiology, Simon's research interests focus on the assessment of cycling performance and the mathematical modelling of cycle training. He has published much of his research work in academic sports science literature and has contributed to many articles in the cycling press. As a BASES Accredited Sport and Exercise Scientist, Simon provides sports science support for cyclists of all abilities, including coaching a multiple National Masters Champion and two World Record holders.

Dominic Irvine is the Founding member of Epiphanies LLP (www.epiphaniesllp.com), a UK-based learning and development consultancy that helps people think and act profitably through developing their knowledge and skills in innovation, management and leadership. He has worked with leaders in multinational businesses in over 30 countries and writes for a number of business publications on a range of management issues. In his spare time he is a record-breaking ultra-distance cyclist. On 7 May, 2015, along with his riding partner and support team, Dominic set a new record for Land's End to John o'Groats on a tandem, taking one day, 21 hours, 11 minutes to ride the 1,365km. He has also competed in a number of other on- and off-road ultra-distance events.

ACKNOWLEDGEMENTS

While a great many people have helped us along the way, we wish to mention specifically those who contributed to the content of the book. These include:

Renee McGregor, the nutritionist who transformed Dominic's ability in particular to stay energised in ultra-distance races, and who was a significant help in writing the chapter on diet and hydration.

Dr Claire Ryall is a physiotherapist with whom we have worked closely over the years, and who has helped Simon to mend Dominic after incidents on the bike.

Phil Burt, lead physiotherapist to Great Britain Cycling and consultant to Team Sky, provided a particularly insightful piece on the myth that is core body strength.

Dr John Wilson, long-time friend and a leading expert in learning and development, provided valuable guidance on goal-setting and the importance of dreaming.

Nigel Harrison has led the support teams on all Dominic's ultra-distance races, as well as coordinating support on a number of group rides. His experiences of doing this over the years is immense, and his insights incredibly practical.

Sarah Townsend, co-founder of McKenna-Townsend, a PR agency, Stephen Waddington, chief engagement officer at Ketchum and president of the Chartered Institute of Public Relations, and Jonathan Turner, head of content at timeoutdoors. com, guided us through the world of PR.

Thanks also to James Wright, doctoral researcher, and Richard Cheetham, Senior Fellow in Sports Coaching, for fantastic contributions.

Many coaches and athletes provided valuable insights, in particular Ian Mayhew and Andrew Steel. Thanks also to Dr John Irvine and Stephanie Mawdsley for their editing and proofreading, as well as to the excellent team at Bloomsbury, specifically Kirsty Schaper, Matthew Lowing and Sarah Connelly. Joolze Dymond is the brilliant photographer behind many of the images.

While there is no specific contribution from Charlie Mitchell (Dominic's tandem partner), the hours and hours spent training together and the many three-way meetings between Simon, Dominic and Charlie were the source of much inspiration and learning.

John and Ruth Hargreaves at Orbit Tandems provided much encouragement and support over many years.

Finally, in Chapter 2 on 'In Balance', we talk about ultra-distance being a way of life. None will testify to this more than our families, who have provided endless support over many years to enable us to pursue our sporting and professional dreams. Liz, Helene, John, Tom and Chlöe – we salute you.

Thanks to Marc Anley and Stuart Tudor-Owen of Deloitte for their help and support in connecting us to some amazing people and Douglas Ryder, Team Principal, Team Dimension Data for Qhubeka.

INDEX

A

active foot warmers 126
adenosine 187
administration 221
aerodynamics 42–4, 51, 119, 128
airports/air travel 256–7
alanine supplements 83
altitude, impact of 104–6
amino acids 78, 85, 95
ANT+ technology 102, 117
antioxidant imbalances 184–5
apples 88
apps, mobile phone 24, 95, 103
arm warmers 127
Armitstead, Lizzie 94
arrogance 171–2
athlete's foot 163
average power, measuring 158

B

B12 96
back pain 161
Badwater Ultramarathon 94
bags 107, 109
bananas 75, 88
bandanas 128
bar tape 51, 163
batteries/battery life 102, 116, 117, 238
beans 95
beetroot 85
bib tights 127
bike boxes 256–7
bike pads 127
bike shops 221, 257
bikes 119
    bike fit 44–6, 119
    fit for purpose 122
    gear choice 122
    performance 120
    price *versus* weight 119
    tyre choice 122–3
    winter setup 124
bin bags 232
block periodisation training 149
blogging 208
blood glucose levels 74
blood vessel density 134
body composition 91
body odour 129
boiled sweets 88, 251
braking on corners 40
branched chain amino acids
    (BCAA) 85

C

cadence 35–6, 52, 54
caffeine 84, 187
cake 75, 76, 88
captains, tandem 52, 54, 55, 89
carbohydrates 72–6, 79–80, 84, 87, 91,
    92, 97
Cavendish, Mark 171
chamois (bike pads) 127
chamois cream 130
charitable work 9, 208
chocolate covered brazils and dates 88
citrate 83, 84
cleat position 37, 50
clincher tyres 123
clothing 44, 55, 61, 64, 104–5, 106,
    109–10, 113–14, 116, 126–7, 129, 232
    see also helmets; shoes
coaches 221, 239, 244–5, 248
    see also training
Coca-Cola 82
cocktail sausages 88
coffee 187
cold feet 125–6
colostrum 86–7
communication 54–5, 224, 229–30,
    232, 235–6
Coppi, Fausto 147
core strength 161
corners, taking 40
crank length 52
crashing 190
creeds 64
critical power testing 141, 142
crystallised ginger 88
cycling/life balance 57–61, 64–5, 179

D

dairy 79, 91
deep section wheels 43
dehydration see hydration
detraining 152
diet 70–2
    avoiding temptations 194
    being practical 96
    carbohydrates 72–6, 79–80, 84, 87,
        91, 92, 97
    electrolytes 69, 75, 89, 97, 251
    energy bars and gels 75, 76, 77
    example of race diet 88
    glycaemic index (GI) 76
    in-ride 74–7, 87–9
    mouth rinsing 76
    post-ride 77–80
    pre-ride 72–3, 258
    protein 78–9, 85, 91, 92, 95
    sleep deprivation 184–5
    supplements 83–7, 96
    vegetarian/vegan 94–6
    see also hydration
downhill riding 40–1
dreaming 194–5
drop of handlebars 51

Durable Water Repellence (DWR) 110, 113
dynamo lights 116–17

E

eating and drinking in-ride 74–7
    carrying food 107
    passing food 234–5
    uphill riding 39, 40
    water bottles 107, 163
efficiency/economy, cycling 139–40, 160
eggs 78
electrolytes 69, 75, 81, 82, 89, 97, 251
emergency services 255
End-to-End tandem record 11
energy bars 76, 77, 89
energy gels 75, 77, 89
equipment
    bags 107, 109
    chamois cream 130
    importance of comfort 103
    questions to ask yourself 101–2
    spare kit 107, 108
    temperature and clothing 104
    weather stations 103
    see also bikes; clothing; shoes
Ericsson, Anders 147
essential fatty acids 86

F

failure, opportunities in 253
family 57–9, 221
    see also life/cycle balance
fasted training 92, 97
fig rolls 88
financial issues 65
    see also sponsorship
fitness 133, 134
    laboratory tests 136, 137, 138–40, 141

self-testing/field testing 139, 141, 142
    see also training
flat pedals 50–1
flaxseed oil 96
fluid retention 80
fluorescent clothing 116
focus, importance of 178–9
food see diet; eating and drinking in-ride
food diaries 95, 245
foot warmers 126
fore/aft cleat position 37
frame bags 107
fruit and vegetables 95
fruit cake 75, 88
functional threshold power (FTP) 142

G

gear changes, tandem 54
gear choice 122
genetics 134
ghrelin 184
gilets 126
ginger snaps 88
gloves 44
glucose 74
glycaemic index 76
glycogen 79–80, 92, 97
goal setting 227–9, 252
Google Street View 255
GPS technology 24, 102, 116, 190, 238–9
Greek yoghurt 79
gut microflora 86

H

habit forming 190–3
hairpin bends 39
hallucinations 185, 189

handlebars 40, 51, 163
health risks 47
heart rate, measuring 156–7
helmets 43–4, 128
herbs and spices 96
hero foods 73, 74, 78, 79, 83, 85, 94, 95, 96
hex keys 107
high-intensity training 83, 91, 92, 144, 150, 151
High Visibility (Hi-Viz) clothing 114, 116, 235
highway codes abroad 255
holidays 65
holistic approach to ultra-distance cycling 27, 30, 251–3, 259
hood position 51
hot foot 50, 118
hydration 80
    Coca-Cola 82
    electrolytes 75, 81, 82, 97, 251
    hyperhydration 80, 84
    hypertonic solutions 80
    hyponatraemia 82
    in-ride 81, 107
    pre-ride 80
    sports drinks 75, 76–7, 80, 81
hygiene 61, 64, 129, 130, 163
hyperhydration 80, 84
hypertonic solutions 80
hyponatraemia 82

I

illness 163, 165
immune system 86, 91, 163, 165
in-ride
    food 74–7, 87–9, 107
    hydration 81–2, 107
indicating in traffic 55

insulin 184

insurance cover 257

iron 95

isotonic sports drinks 80

J

jackets 126

Japanese Odyssey 15, 18–19

Jelly Babies 75, 88

jerseys 126

junctions 54, 255

Jurek, Scott 94

L

laboratory fitness tests 136, 137, 138–40, 141

lactate threshold 137–9, 159–60

layering clothes/footwear 125

lean tissue 91

leg warmers 127

legumes 95

lemon wedges 88

leptin 184

leucine 85

life/cycling balance 57–61, 64–5, 179

lights 45–6, 114, 116–17, 187

Liquorice Allsorts 75, 88

loading protocols, carbohydrate 72

London-Edinburgh-London (LEL) 15, 16

low-intensity training 91, 150, 151

M

marginal gains 25–6

material choice, bag 109

maximal aerobic power (MAP) 159

mechanics 221, 241

medics 221, 241

megaphones 236

membrane jackets 110, 113

mental toughness 171–3, 175, 178–80

Merckx, Eddy 134, 147

merino wool 129

metatarsal pads 50

meteorologists 221

milk 83

mindset 169

    avoiding temptations 194

    dreaming/visioning 194–5

    focus 178–9

    habit forming 190–3

    injuries 247

    life/cycle balance 179

    making plans/being prepared 175, 178–9

    mental toughness 171–3, 175, 178–80

    opportunities in failure 253–4

    overcoming obstacles 175

    personal responsibility 180

    sleep deprivation 181, 184–5, 187–8, 189–90

mitochondria 134

mobile phones 102, 109, 190, 236

Montane Smocks 114

mountain climates 105

mouth rinsing, carbohydrate 76

mudguards 122

muscles

    blood glucose levels 74

    growth 85

    muscle fibres 134, 144, 159, 160

    muscular work and cadence 35

    pedalling 35, 37

    protein 78

    standing position 42

    strength training 159–60, 162

    weight management 91

musettes 75

N

nappy rash cream 130

navigation 55, 238–9

nervous system 35, 84, 96

Normalized Power 158

nutritional supplements 83–7, 96

nutritionists 221

    see also diet

nuts and nut butter 94

O

oats 74

omega 3 86, 96

omega 6 86

overload principle 143, 145–6, 151

overshoes 116, 125

overtraining 165

oxygen 134, 137, 156

P

packing your kit 256–7

pannier bags 109, 122

Páramo waterproofing 113–14

Paris–Brest–Paris 16

pedal cadence 35–6

pedal foot interface 50–1

pedalling 36–8, 52

perineum 47, 130

periodised training programmes 148–50

phones 102, 109, 190, 236

physiotherapists 221, 245–8

pit-stop checklists 233, 235

pizza, homemade 88

pockets 45–6, 126

porridge 88

post-ride

    food 77–80

    hydration 82

potassium 81
potholes 40
power meters 24, 39, 139, 157, 165, 184, 189
power output 39–41, 139–40, 141–2, 157–8, 189
power profile 141–2
power supplies 116–17
power-to-weight ratio 91
pre-ride
food 72–3, 258
hydration 80
probiotics 86
protein 78–9, 85, 91, 92, 95
psychologists 221
see also mindset
public relations (PR) 201, 210–11, 213, 214, 221

Q
Qhubeka 9
quinoa 96

R
Race Across America (RAAM) 15, 18, 19
Race Across Europe (RACE) 15
Race Across the Alps (RATA) 15
race day diet and supplements 87–9, 258
racing lines 40
racing preparation
checklists 255
examining the route 255
finishing and the aftermath 258
packing your kit 256–7
on race day 258
rules of the road 255
sticking to your race plan 258
tapering training pre-race 256

writing your strategy 256
see also support teams; training
rack-top bags 107
rails, saddle 47
rate of perceived exertion (RPE) 154–5, 157
reach 51
recovery 77, 78, 91, 135, 149
reflective clothing 114, 116
riding technique
aerodynamics 42–4, 51
bike fit 44–7
cadence 35–6, 52, 54
crank length 52
downhill 40–1
handlebars 51
importance of 34
pedal foot interface 50–1
pedalling 36–8, 52
reach 51
saddles 46–8, 50
sit or stand? 41–2, 55
tandem 52, 54–5
uphill 39–40, 41–2, 55
varying position 46
roundabouts 54, 242
route planners 221
rucksacks 45–6

S
saddle bags 107
saddle sores 130
saddles
choice 46–7
height 33, 46
position 33, 48, 50
rails 47
safety 233, 242, 243
see also sleep/sleep deprivation
salad 95
salt 84

sandwiches 75, 76, 88
seat post angles 120
Seiler, Stephen 151
self-testing fitness 139, 141, 142
shallow section wheels 43
shoes 50, 116, 118, 125
shorts 127
sit bones 47, 130
sitting position 41–2
skull-caps 128
sleep/sleep deprivation 15, 18, 60, 163, 181, 184–5, 187–8, 189–90
smartphones 102, 109, 190, 236
Smith, Martin 33
social media 208, 211
sodium 81, 82
sodium supplements 84
South Downs Double 92
spacers 51
spares 102, 103, 107, 108
spectacles 102
sponsorship 27, 201–2, 209, 214
adding value 205, 208
building your credibility 208
consider what you need 205
public relations (PR) 201, 210–11, 213
your personal brand 203–5
sports drinks 75, 76–7, 80, 81
standing position 41–2, 55
stem angle 51
stokers 52, 54, 55, 90
Strasser, Christoph 18
strategy, writing your 256
strength training 159–60, 162
sunglasses 102
superfoods 71
supplements, nutritional 83–7, 96
support teams 15, 26, 130, 188, 217, 249
coaches 221, 239, 244–5, 248

communication 224, 229–30, 232, 235–6, 244
decision making 189, 220
delegation 222
driving 242–3
essence of effective teamwork 230
focus on the inputs 226–7
guiding principles/team culture 226
kit 235, 237
leadership skills 223
navigation 239
Nigel Harrison on 240–3
passing food 234
physiotherapists 221, 245–8
pit-stop checklists 233, 235
roles 220, 221, 241
safety 233, 242, 243
setting goals 227–9
team engagement 222–4, 226–7
vehicles 232, 234, 237, 240–1, 242
sweat 69, 80, 129
sweat tests 81
sweet potatoes 73
sweets 75, 76, 88, 251

T
tandem riding 133
    communication 181
    nutrition 90
    riding techniques 52, 54–5
tapering training 151–2, 256
Team Sky 202, 211
team work
    see support teams; tandem riding
Teklehaimanot, Daniel 9
temperature 104–6, 113, 190
thresholds, physiological 137–9, 159–60
toe/heel position 36–7
tofu 96

top tube bags 107
Tour de France 9, 94
TrA (*transverse abdominus*) 161
traffic 42–3, 242–3
traffic lights 255
training 19, 20, 25, 133, 134, 147
    carbohydrates 73, 74, 92
    cycling/life balance 57–61, 64–5
    early starts 60, 65
    fasted 92, 97
    high-intensity 83, 92, 144, 150
    on holiday 65
    honesty 144–6, 244
    key training principles 143–4
    low intensity 91, 150, 151
    macro-level planning 148
    measuring heart rate 156–7
    measuring power output 157–8
    measuring your effort 154–5
    overload principle 143, 145–6, 151
    periodised programmes 148–50
    polarised approach 151
    rate of perceived exertion (RPE) 154–5
    recording data 244–5
    recovery 77, 78, 92
    strength 159–60, 162
    tapering 151–2, 256
    training zones 135, 136
    week by week planning 59
travelling to a race 256–7
tri-bar extensions 43
tubular tyres, light weight 122–3
Turner, Jonathan 202, 211, 213
two-way radios 236
tyre choice 122–3

U
Ultracycling Dolomitica 15, 17
unclipping pedals 45

unsupported riders 15, 17, 18, 107, 109, 119, 122, 185, 189, 190
uphill riding 39–40, 41–2, 55
urine colour 80

V
Vätternrundan event 184
vegetarian/vegan diet 94–6
vehicles, support team 232, 235, 237, 240–1, 242
ventilatory thresholds 137–8
virtual communication 229–30
Vitamin B12 96
$\dot{V}O_2$max 137, 150, 159

W
water 39, 80, 81, 163
water bottles 107, 163
watermelon 88
waterproof clothing 109–10, 113–14, 125, 235
waterproof pouches 109
weather 16, 17, 19, 103, 104–6, 113, 180, 221, 256
weight, bike 119
weight management 91, 119
wet kit 232
wet wipes 163
wheels 43, 44
whey protein 79
wind 16, 55, 113
wind resistance 41, 42, 43
work life and training 60–1, 64–5

Y
yoghurt, Greek 79

Z
Zabriskie, David 94

PHOTO ACKNOWLEDGEMENTS

Pages 8, 10, 21, 22, 40, 41, 49, 60, 66, 8, 69, 70, 81, 87, 89, 98, 100, 103, 115, 118, 121, 128, 153, 154, 162, 168, 169, 170, 183, 186, 194, 200, 221, 216, 218, 231, 233, 250, 254, 260 © Joolze Dymond

Pages 11, 13, 17, 25, 26, 28, 42, 72, 79, 83, 131, 155, 164, 177, 196, 214, 225, 238 © Getty Images

Pages 21, 32, 37, 38, 56, 75, 111, 112, 117, 127, 133, 134, 167, 174, 199, 206, 265, 106 © Dominic Irvine

Pages 30, 59, 105, 140, 145, 146, 148, 149, 156, 192, 210, 234, 256 © Bloomsbury Publishing Drawn by Dave Saunders

Pages 12, 18, 62 © Sergio Ros de Mora

Page 33 © Stuart Field

Pages 53, 93 © iStock

Page 90 © Katrina Harrison

Page 132 © @swpix & Fat Lad at the Back

Page 124 © Paulus Quiros